The Circle Of Life

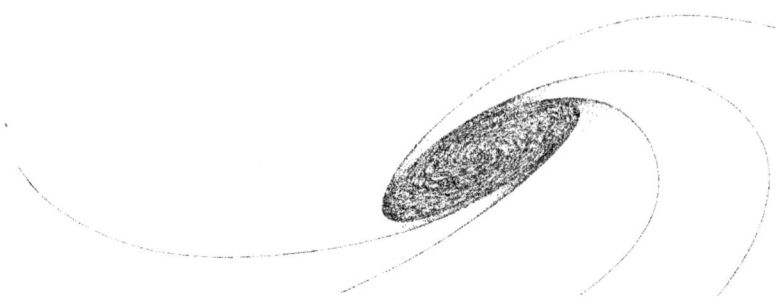

The cover art by Denver artist Steve Magyar—reminiscent of spiral galaxies, whirling fireworks, and the pattern traced by sparklers at night—suggests the energy, even vertigo we feel when our lives are "spun about" by spirit.

The Circle Of Life

Extraordinary Spirit Capacities in the Life of Service

Edited by Betty Pesek, Ellery Elizondo, and David Dunn

Chicago, Illinois USA

2000

The Institute of Cultural Affairs
4750 N. Sheridan Road
Chicago, Illinois 60640
Phone: 773-769-6363
Fax: 773-769-1144
Web: www.ica-usa.org

The Circle of Life
Copyright © 2000 by The Institute of Cultural Affairs

All rights reserved. No part of this book may be reproduced or transmitted in any form or by any means without prior written permission of the publisher, except in the case of brief quotations (not to exceed 1,000 words) and certain noncommercial uses permitted under copyright law. For permission requests, please contact The Institute of Cultural Affairs.

ISBN: 1-930913-00-1

Publication Notes
Publication supervised by Betty Pesek
Copyediting: David Dunn, Ellery Elizondo, Betty Pesek
Proofreading: Ellery Elizondo, Betty Pesek, Keith Packard
Book and typographic design, typesetting: David Dunn/Mirror Communication
Cover art: Steve Magyar
Printed in the United States of America by Johnson Printing, Boulder, Colorado

In grateful memory

Evelyn Johnston Mathews Edwards
1917–1998

Firm resolve
   gentle humor
      undivided listener
         contagious enthusiasm
   lively wisdom
      releasing hope
life-rootedness
   decisional flexibility
      ability to let go
   courage to create new response forms
      simultaneous concern and nonchalance
   sense of wonder
      presence that honors
life-giving exemplar.

Table of Contents

Foreword ix
Preface xi
Acknowledgments xiii
Introduction 1

Chapter One
Shocked and Surprised

Consensus 6
Both Sides 8
Growing Up 9
Absolutely Other 11
Visiting Mother Theresa 14
Precious Memory 15
"Those Who Wait On The Lord" 15
Metamorphosis 16
Smell The Jungle 19
Panic 20
An Egyptian Hello 21
I'll Bet You A Dollar 22
Unforgettable Characters ... 23
Drunk Shrimp 24
Mother's Advice 25
Shantumbu 25
The Falling Lizard 27
Pigs In The Bedroom 27
Baboons Direct the Buses ... 28
The Cyclone 29
Shocking 30
Considerations of the Whale . 32
Meant To Happen 34

Chapter Two
You're It!

Moth To A Flame 36
Lured By The Mystery 38
Being A Mother 39
"I'm The Greatest!" 39
Anger Transformed 40
Letter From Caño Negro 40
You've Got To Be Crazy 43
A New and Fearful Task 45
A Small Miracle in Salzburg .. 46
And Then It Hit Me 47
Miracle in Gunfoundry 48
The Altar Guild 49
The Company Store 50
A Meeting In Worcester 51
Bald-Headed Tom Sawyer ... 52
A New Day Dawning 53
Oklahoma 100 56

Chapter Three
Out Over The Edge

Who Would Have Guessed ... 60
A Rock Through The Window .. 61
The Flames Leapt Up 62
Learning To Read 62
Awesome Encounter 63
Terror At 36,000 Feet 69
Midnight Danger 70
You Stand On Your Head ... 71
My Life Took a Turn 72
The Unforgettable Egg 73
Encounter with *Desaparecidos* 74
Almost Caught 76
Will The Terrorists Return? ... 77
Eleven Flights of Stairs 77
Water Tank Miracle 78
Rupert's Vision 80

Chapter Four
Whatever It Takes

Ukrainian Meatloaf 84
1000 Single Beds 85
The City That Works 88
Right On His Derrière 89
Saving Face 90
Just Cry 91
A Taiwan Thanksgiving 92
Village Economics 94
The Earthen Dam 95
Finding The Center 96
Women of the World 97
Souvenirs 99
Raising The I-Beam 100
Where Is Our Luggage? 101
He Slowed Down A Train ... 104
The View From The Train .. 105
Casting Out Demons 106
Development Fighter 109
You Can't Do That 110
The Voyage of the *Tatami Maru* 112
Sir James 114
The Handkerchief 116

Chapter Five
Beyond Expectations

The Baking Sun 118
River Of Consciousness 119
Speaking Farmer 122
A Man I Can't Forget 124
East Meets West 125
The Chickens Are Coming . 126
A Certain Quality 127
Meeting Fr. Ilidio 128
They Started Grinning 129
What Am I Doing Here? 133
Wallboard For 4th Street 134
The Power Of Workdays 136
Life's Resale Shop 137
Midst Of A Revolution 138
"Then We Will Walk." 138
Growing A Larger World 139
The Wind That Made History 140
A Big Event 142
What Happened In Edgard? 143
A Word About Singing 145
All Need To Play 146
Seeing The World Transformed 147

The Sharbat Riot 148
You Can Do It! 149
Celebrating A Completed Life . 151
No Problem 152
The Preschool Miracle 154
Creating A Nation 157
The Blue Shirts 159
Yesterday And Today 160
The *Preschool Manual* 161
The Baptism 162
Lifeprints 164

Appendix/Indexes

The ICA: An Evolving Story ... 165
Indexes 166-171
 Titles and topics 166
 Authors 169
 Cities 169
 Communities 170
 Countries 170
 Photographs/credits 171

Foreword

Through multiple lenses of personal experience, this book offers readers a rich array of knowledge concerning social, political, economic and cultural transformation—the nitty gritty of human development. These brief episodes will amuse, amaze and challenge your assumptions about yourself and our world. They remind us that much of our growing comes through cross-cultural encounters. Anyone on a journey of awakening will take delight in these little stories.

The external events recalled here created interior responses. But exterior and interior are not to be separated: both are known interdependently. In these stories we hear the voices of people who, often as the outsiders, were deeply touched by external features of culture and physical surroundings. In the midst of the ordinary world, another world appeared, full of mystery, consciousness, care and tranquility. Many of these shared reflections convey this transparent connection between inner and outer reality.

These vignettes unleashed memories of the twenty-two year journey that my wife, Mary, and I enjoyed with the Institute of Cultural Affairs. They remind us of the glory of that time and the wonder of our lives on this mysterious planet. These stories would have provided Lyn Mathews Edwards—one of the Institute's founders and a principal player in or behind many of these stories—with many a chuckle, wry smile and surge of motherly pride. We were so young, naive and invincible, so full of hope—perhaps blinded by the brilliance of our own vision of human development. We survived and grew up, and in the process, had our eyes and minds opened wide to the ways of the world. It is humbling to recall how many villagers forgave us and supported us in our enthusiasm to serve and change their worlds.

Service is a slippery concept, however. Who is served and who does the serving? Sometimes the served are of greater service to those doing the serving. We try again and again to be of service in situations of suffering from poverty, violent conflict, environmental degradation, disease or ignorance. It is not a simple task. Sometimes the people we attempt to serve have their own agendas and our service is thwarted. Sometimes our service is inappropriate or ill conceived. Should we stop trying? Finally we do what we believe we must and leave the judgment of our deeds to history.

I recently visited a village in Nepal, a country I last visited thirty years ago on a global odyssey with the Institute. I was reminded that the UNDP began publishing its annual Human Development Report in 1990, whereas the Institute has been doing human development since the 1960s. Reading these wonderful stories connected past, present and future. For this I am grateful. The world is more than ever in need of the bold deeds of "those who care."

Robertson Work, Deputy Director
Management Development and Governance Division
United Nations Development Programme, New York
21 May 2000

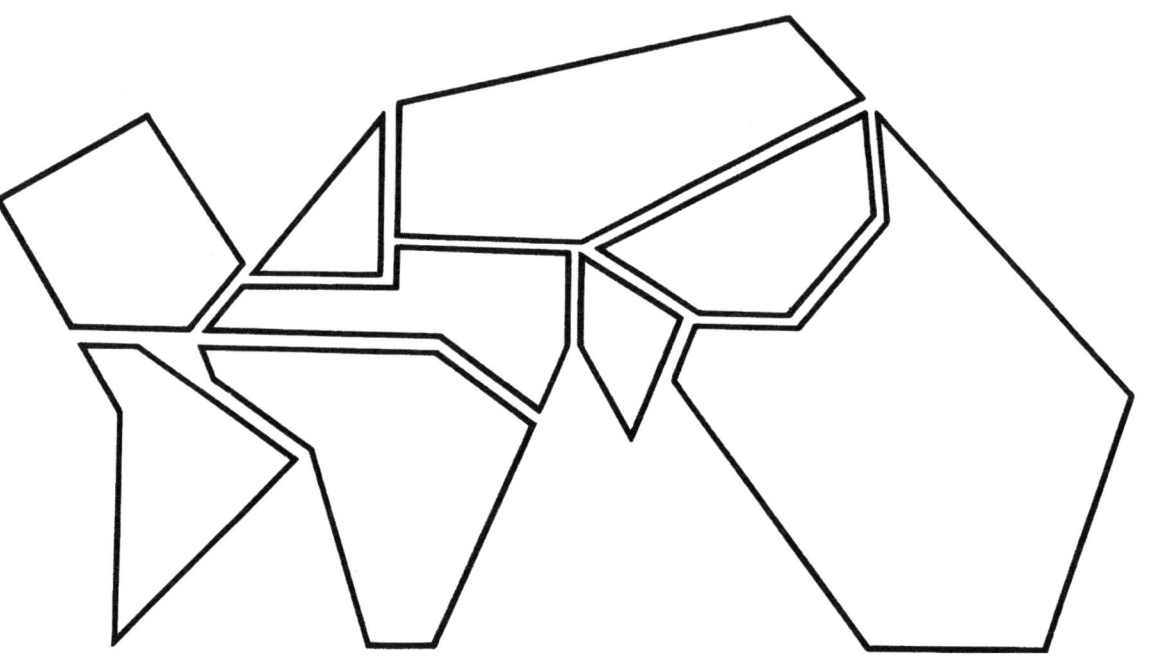

Preface

This is a collection of adventure stories—all real-life experiences of ordinary men and women. The stories are about the work of human development and the spirit capacities discovered and released in acts of service. Most take place in community settings, some in small, rural villages, some in city neighborhoods and a few in large organizations.

The unique focus of this book is the concrete manifestation of spirit—the energy and capacity to relate gratefully to newness, complexity and immensity. This energy and capacity seems to come from beyond us, but arises and operates within us and the teams in which we work. These are stories about the spirit arising within new and complex situations that helped to mobilize and support extraordinary accomplishments of service to neighbors and coworkers.

More than four hundred people affiliated with the Institute of Cultural Affairs (ICA) contributed twelve hundred stories from their life experiences to an effort called "The ICA Stories Project." You can read more about this project in the Acknowledgments which follow. The stories came from "storytelling circles" held in various parts of the world, and from individuals, who searched their journals and memories. The forms varied: some came on video, some on cassette tapes, some on paper, and some by telephone. Sadly, we could not include all of them here, though we hope that many will find their way to the world wide web, as an ongoing contribution to the storytelling movement emerging in the world today.

Why collect and publish stories about service and the spirit energy that sustains people in their work? In spite of booming economies in some parts of the world, millions of people are burdened with life-threatening difficulty. For them, the spirit capacity of neighbors or care-givers is of lifesaving importance. For all of us, the speed and complexity of change has forced us to learn new ways to work and get along in a dramatically smaller, more intimate world. For us, the spirit capacities recalled in these stories can mean the difference between anxious muddling and an exhilarating journey of continually learning how to live.

Choose an approach to this reading adventure which suits your interest. You may browse the table of contents for interesting titles, or turn to one of several indexes at the back to search for stories by title, topic, author, city, community, or country. You can learn more about the ICA in a short article called "The ICA: An Evolving Story," on page 165. Forty-one photographs accompany various stories throughout the book.

David Dunn

Acknowledgments

This book was born out of the late Lyn Mathews Edwards' wish to publish a sample of the stories which colleagues of the Institute of Cultural Affairs/Ecumenical Institute could tell. As she put it:

> "We have shared methods that we discovered and created for the sake of the civilizing process. We traveled all over the world, sharing these methods with individuals and groups, in order for them to live fuller, more meaningful lives. Now it is time to tell what happened to us, as we went about our work."

We acknowledge Lyn for inspiring us to gather and present these stories.

Many of the stories were collected in storytelling circles, the largest of which, with eighty people in attendance, took place on Lyn's 80th birthday, June 19, 1997, in Chicago. With a microphone in the middle of each table of eight to ten people, people talked about the funniest, the saddest, the most wonderful, the most frightening, the most fascinating, or the most satisfying events they could remember. The resulting tapes were transcribed by Lyn herself, and Betty Pesek, and filled three, three-ring notebooks.

Dozens of colleagues helped bring Lyn's dream of a book into reality. Initially, a group of colleagues from the ICA's Heartland Region spent two weekends in the spring of 1999 creating the foundation for a book. They described the book's intent, the audience to be reached, and the values to help select stories for inclusion. The five story themes identified by this group became the chapters of the present book.

Debra Drown helped with the early development of the book's concept and purpose. Larry Loepke helped refine the concept and design of the book from his publishing and marketing perspective.

Two professional writers have been mentors to the editorial team. In person, on the phone, and by email, Bruce Williams helped create the framework for the book and kept us focused on simplicity of design and language as we neared our publication deadline. John Burbidge regularly shared design and editorial guidance, and collaborated in the writing of the Introduction and The ICA: An Evolving Story.

Most of the authors shared information and insights in addition to their initial writing. Many helped us check the spelling of "far away places and strange sounding names," clarified dates and locations, identified pictures, and described unfamiliar customs and practices. In addition, many members of the "ica-dialogue" listserv network have contributed detailed information about events and stories in which they were involved or had some knowledge.

We acknowledge our colleagues at the Institute of Cultural Affairs, Chicago Office, for many forms of support. Special thanks to Keith Packard for sharing her expertise as an astute editorial guide and for proofreading with a cultural sensitivity borne of years of work in Imaginal Education. Thanks to Dennis Jennings and George Packard for helping us with financial management and good stewardship of the resources which made this book possible.

Two appeals were made for project underwriting. While she was alive, at the onset of the project, Lyn led the letter-writing campaign to raise funds. A second appeal was made soon after her funeral, inviting persons to make a memorial contribution. Eighty-five persons and groups contributed financially to the project, in amounts ranging from $20 to $2,500. These contributions enabled the project to continue smoothly and without interruption.

Special thanks to Denver artist Steve Magyar for helping the five dynamics of "the circle of life" take flight on the cover with his kinetic image of a spiral galaxy. The poetry on the chapter title pages is taken from poems written by David Dunn.

Finally, every project needs champions and guardians; those whose resolve, dedication and courage bring an idea to concrete form. The project began with Lyn Mathews Edward's idea: "I would like to honor and celebrate the possibility and pain of human life as experienced by members and friends [of the Institute]." It has come to fruition in the form of the book you now hold in your hands. On this three-year journey, it has been blessed by the graceful leadership of Betty Pesek, the seasoned judgment of Ellery Elizondo and the writing and design passion of David Dunn. This labor of love is a gift to those who have contributed so much.

Introduction
The Circle Of Life

Opening, closing,
hearing, ignoring,
risking, retreating,
expending, conserving,
delighting, despairing—
the universe creates
amazement in
every moment.

Introduction

The ability to see spirit at work in the ordinary events of life is the challenge of seeing people and circumstances full of mystery, possibility and promise. Such ability is a daily experience in the enchanted realms of fairy tales, but is it possible in real life?

In their musical, *Into The Woods*, Steven Lapine and Stephen Sondheim bridge these two worlds. *Into The Woods* is a dramatic metaphor for the journey in which we discover our dreams, tackle heroic chores, overcome monstrous obstacles and walk away filled with life. The drama draws us into the lives of characters who struggle, like we do, with despair, victory, defeat and fulfillment. They confront poverty, abuse, neglect, isolation or fear and in turn find courage, creative engagement, and some surprising turn of events.

It would be wonderful if we could all experience such gifts in our lives. The secret seems to be to find our "woods." But how do we do this? For the people whose experiences are retold in this book, the "woods" has been the life of service and the paths "into the woods" have been projects for the transformation of communities and organizations around the world. Their stories provide a unique glimpse into a life of openness, purpose, expansion, energy and fulfillment. They fall into five categories that have become the chapters of this book:

- experiencing striking events that figuratively "broke one's heart open" to care for the world
- taking an assignment or sensing a need that called one out of oneself
- living and working in unfamiliar circumstances without collapsing, going crazy or drowning
- expending extraordinary amounts of energy and emerging victorious against all odds
- receiving unexpected resources, colleagues, insights and blessings

Chapter One, "Shocked and Surprised," contains stories about events that intruded into people's routines and left their illusions broken and perspectives enlarged. These events presented them with a choice to open up or shut down, stretching their worlds so suddenly and completely that turning off the intrusion was hardly an option. With hearing attuned, they could hear a cry for help.

Chapter Two, "You're It!," portrays what people saw when they looked to see who had cried out. These are stories about personal experiences in which people were touched and found themselves in the center of the circle, like the "You're It!" moment from a childhood game. Having experienced a "You're It!" the authors responded with "I'm the one." They shouldered reality, picked up responsibility, and were given the courage to deal with the unexpected circumstances that followed.

Chapter Three, "Out Over The Edge," is about living in spite of discomfort, fatigue, uncertainty and fear. These stories tell of coping with political intrigue, terrorists, untried projects, new technologies, personal limitations and above all, being given the courage to move mountains.

Chapter Four, "Whatever It Takes," deals with moving mountains. The stories focus on relating to other cultures, overcoming ancient fears and prejudices, drawing out women to realize their full potential, handling the nitty-gritty routines of service, and not taking "no" for an answer. They describe how a team can help enlarge one's capacities and how unexpected outcomes can surprise us.

Chapter Five, "Beyond Expectations," recounts stories about setting in motion strategies to impact the lives of people and communities, then embracing the surprising turns of history that result. These stories emphasize the ability to let go of expectations, to work with resources at hand, to be touched and shaped by the people one meets, and to celebrate beginnings and endings.

These five chapters describe what happens when we let life in. When we let life reach into us and open us to others, we experience the call to serve. When we embrace the calling, we are thrust beyond the known and given the wherewithal to thrive in the resulting chaos. In that unfamiliar, wild place, we are empowered with energy greater than our own and accomplish more than we dreamed possible. Sometimes in the midst of our expenditure and sometimes decades later, we are given the opportunity to see the creative outcomes of our labor, the heart to know the greatness of the lives we have touched, and the grace to embrace the peace of completion. This experience—opening, call, risk, expenditure and fulfillment—is symbolized in the metaphor, "The Circle of Life." It is a holographic reality that can occur in every moment and describes the journey of a lifetime.

All the stories in this collection describe experiences common to human beings in every culture and nation. They are drawn from the lives of people who belong to many of the great faith traditions and to none in particular. They are about everyday life, albeit in fascinating places and circumstances.

These real-life dramas recall the challenges we all face when we decide to be of service. How do I handle the barrage of newness that assaults me? Where do I fit into the larger universe outside my door? What effort is worth my life? How can I complete what seems so impossible to begin? Where will I end up? Will it be worth it? None of the stories gives a pat answer to these dilemmas but together they contribute to a frame of mind that allows one to see the power of spirit at work in the ordinary affairs of daily life.

Some stories are about doing startling things, some are about amazing people; some are frightening, some are funny, and all are thought provoking. They revolve around the challenge of helping expand people's imaginations and helping them to accomplish things they thought impossible. They deal with the unexpected, sensing the demands of history, personal risk-taking, cooperative action, and surprising fulfillment.

These vignettes derive from the life and work of staff members and volunteers with the Institute of Cultural Affairs (ICA) in twenty-five countries between 1960 and 1997. The ICA's diverse international network holds two things in common: a mission supporting social innovation and a foundation in the transforming power of spirit in history and human affairs. To learn more about the evolution of the ICA over the last four decades, turn to the appendix at the back of the book.

The stories were written and collected during 1997 to celebrate the 80th birthday of one of the ICA's founders and most gracious of grande dames, the late Lyn Mathews Edwards. Lyn pointed out that it was one thing to share the tools of human transformation (the ICA's focus since its beginnings in the 1960s) but quite another to share stories reflecting the hearts and minds of people who had to put their bodies on the line to effect that transformation.

As the stories flowed in, it became clear that they contained engaging insights about living a fulfilled life and sustaining oneself and one's colleagues in service. Thus, this is also a book of metaphors about the life of service. Not everyone will build a dam in an Indian village, cast out demons from a team of African colleagues, or endure the terror of the *desaparecidos* in Latin America. But many people know the need to hold on to precious resources, to transform destructive energies in an organization, or to endure the terror of seeing one's life work go down the drain.

Finally, these stories are about the dynamics of life itself and the spirit capacity that sustains people when they give themselves to a great cause. We hope that you will identify with the challenges and victories, the discoveries and adventures contained in these pages, and the promise that your life will be blessed beyond expectation.

David Dunn

Chapter One

Shocked and Surprised

It is a shocking time,
when falling is flying,
letting go is taking charge,
and anticipation
is the memory of tomorrow's promise.

Consensus

Because I was only three hours away by car, I frequently drove to Chicago to visit the Ecumenical Institute for one event or another. I was still an English professor in Kalamazoo and spent many weekends teaching the Institute's Religious Studies courses around the US. One weekend during 1967, I had an interesting experience watching the staff form a consensus.

Joe Mathews and his brother, Bishop Jim Mathews, listening to the discussion

I arrived at the West Side campus and had the chance to join an evening meeting of the community. A serious discussion about something related to the Institute's work in Fifth City was taking place and people were assembled downstairs in Room A, where we often did our public courses. Many people were active in the conversation to which Joe Mathews listened silently. I had been clear from early on that the Institute used "consensus" somewhat differently from anyone else I knew. It did not seem to quite fit the Quaker usage of the term that I'd experienced while a college student in Ohio. So I felt that this was a fine opportunity for me to observe the dynamics of the group as a colleague without the same level of personal investment as the rest of the people in the room.

The discussion had gone on for forty-five minutes after I arrived and I found myself thinking, "Here's a good example of how this group makes a decision." People had talked thoughtfully about the situation. It was clear to me that the group had looked carefully at the alternatives and had decided that they needed to do "X." At that point, Joe finally spoke up. He said, "I think we've talked about this long enough. It's time to state the group's consensus. Our consensus clearly is that what we need to do here is 'Y.'"

I do not recall many times when such a dead silence fell on a room. Having worked with Joe on a number of occasions by this time, I sat and waited, glancing surreptitiously around the room to see how people were taking his pronouncement. No one was looking at anyone else. McCleskey was studying the carpet closely; others were staring at the paint on the walls.

Finally, a young man named Carlos, who had recently joined the community, broke the silence. He said, "Joe, I don't think you've been listening to what this group has been saying." Now Joseph was a lion of a man when it came to group discussions and consensus building and I thought, "The kid's got a lot of courage or brashness or both." Carlos continued, "Everybody who's spoken has said that what we need to do here is 'X.' If you're going to state this group's consensus, that's what it is."

Well, you could just see the old man internally saying, "Oh, thank you, thank you, Carlos!" What he said however, in a rather thunderous voice, was "No, Carlos, it's you who have not been listening to this group. If you had been listening to it, and had really heard what it was saying, you would have noticed that everyone who spoke was avoiding the spirit issue that they know is at the heart of this question and absolutely must be addressed. Every last person in this room knows, in his being, what the necessary deed here is." He went on to spell this out in more detail and then added, "Now, you're new here, Carlos, and you've got to learn to listen at a lot deeper level in order to read the consensus of this group."

There was another long silence. Joe was speaking, not just to Carlos, but to all of us in the room. You could see everyone thinking about what Joe had said and doing a silent internal audit. I found myself thinking, "Either this is a case of the old man blatantly imposing his will on the group, or I am watching something quite marvelous happening here."

Then, one by one, people began to speak, saying things like, "I hate to admit it, but Joe is right." Over the next few minutes, I watched as the group shifted into a distinctly different mode of reflection, one that brought them out at a very different place—their consensus was "Y." When the meeting ended shortly afterwards, I knew I'd participated in a far deeper level of group consensus formation than I had ever experienced before.

Gordon Harper

All Life Is Open
Tune: Guantanamera

All life is open,
Embrace the future with vision,
Die your death for the living,
The mystery has received all.

Our knowledge falters and crumbles,
Our thoughts turn banal and senseless,
Our feelings food in to drown us,
Our hearts cry out, "Push no further!"
But don't stop now, lead us onward
To what we know yet cannot see.

The real word bursts in upon us,
Our cares are ruthlessly tromped on,
Yet our desires are unceasing,
The power pushes us further.
Is there no end to this chaos?
Must separation be final?

Illusions trap us and bind us,
We can't endure endless struggle,
We need our promise of greatness,
Or must withdraw isolated.
Then life demands we embrace all,
That all is good and accepted.

Both Sides

> The experience of the riots set many women's hearts on fire.

I remember the night of the riots when Carol and my husband and I were taking the weekend course called Cultural Studies One. It was my husband's and my first weekend attending courses together. Sitting on the floor of Bethany Hospital on the west side of Chicago, where we waited for the National Guard, I recall thinking, "Gee, all I wanted to do was to make curtains for poor people. Now look where I am." Thanks to several friends and Joe Mathews, now I have to save the world!"

We all felt that the situation was too dangerous to leave the children at risk, so the next night we drove in from the suburbs again and brought the kids out until things cooled down. When Carol's children helped bathe a "dirty girl," they discovered that underneath the dirty clothes was a dirty boy!

Soon after the riots, one of the young boys went to school and reported, "Someone set my bedroom curtains on fire with a big stick that was flaming at the end!" He was reprimanded for telling a lie.

The experience of the riots set many women's hearts on fire. Several of us got together and called ourselves "The Few." Then we changed our name to the "New Women's Forum" and decided that we could change the world, day by day, then weekend by weekend. We came into the inner city to assist in the preschool and in the other structures that had been created for the self-sufficiency of the Fifth City neighborhood. Our husbands got involved in teaching courses. My husband and I went to Montreal to teach a course. We slept on cots, and having forgotten our alarm clock, had to dress hastily while participants hung around outside the door, waiting for the course to begin.

We were suburbanites in a process of being stretched into a larger world. We were led to explore child care arrangements that enlarged our children's worlds as well. For four or five years, our children went to camp with others who lived in the inner city. The year that our two boys, Drew and Cory, went to the camp in Ottawa, my mother invited her minister and his wife over for dinner to hear about the kids' experiences. They heard about the camp rituals, about the meals which the children learned to cook themselves, and about the big car that had been a hearse which took the children into town to do their laundry. Our guests got an ear full. What was an adventure to our seven and eight year-old boys was clearly not our guests' perception of "church camp."

At the same time, the adults spent many weekends at a colleague's farm, working and playing hard, creating methods to be used in local churches and parishes, playing charades and eating. We did everything with gusto. We created the first Living Effectively in the New Society (LENS) course at the farm and taught an early pilot version in Caracas, Venezuela. This part of the world was lush with new sights like live orchids and blessed with colleagues who were part of this worldwide "spirit movement" that had caught our imagination.

Elizabeth Hill

Growing Up

My wife and I had been involved with the ICA less than a year. I was working in the international office where Nan and I were creating plans for an International Training Academy (ITA) scheduled for Singapore. It still had to be recruited and in a meeting, Joe proposed that he take a trip throughout Southeast Asia, the Pacific islands and India to invite participants. He added, "Someone like Justin should probably go with me."

I did not know what to make of this. I had never been out of the country, let alone away from my family, for three months. Furthermore, I did not know what the "job" entailed. If I had had any sense, I would have asked others who had been on the "global trip" circuit. But I did not. I had very little contact with Joe at this time and he was a little intimidating, to say the least!

Joe did want me to accompany him; it would be just the two of us, with no third or fourth persons to share the intensity or the wonder. I was terrified. We left in February of 1969. Joe obviously intended to instruct, probe, goad, and test me, causing my rapid descent into the world of spirit. I had no way of knowing that it would be the most awesome, educational and spirit-evoking event of my life.

Our first stop was American Samoa. For a "boy" who had not lived outside of the US, Samoa was something! People really did live in grass homes, men really did wear skirts, and bananas really did grow upside down on trees! I learned, as well, that Americans really did have power. I saw how much we could control and how we got attention that the local people did not get. I also learned how excited churchmen could get over the possibility of a real challenge.

We traveled to Australia. Every place we went, Joe was getting commitments to the International Training Academy in Singapore. At the same time he was calling forth the church renewal movement and forming core groups in Perth, Adelaide, Sydney, Brisbane, and Melbourne.

My education continued. After each gathering or meeting with individuals, Joe asked me to reflect on peoples' commitment, their gifts, and their spirit. I do not think he cared what I said, as long as I probed my own being and became sensitive to my surroundings and the people. Sometimes it irritated me! On an airplane, once, he called me to account saying, "I'd like it a whole lot, if you would use more than 10% of your brain!" In thirty years, I have never forgotten that moment!

We traveled to Singapore to talk about setting up the ITA. We continued on to Malaysia and arrived at 4 P.M. during a total curfew at the height of the Malay-Chinese conflict. It was scary. In Malaysia I learned how much Joe loved rain storms. One afternoon a great downpour started. Joe, wrapped in the sarong which he wore whenever possible, jumped up from the table, ran out the door and danced around the yard in the deluge.

"I'd like it a whole lot, if you would use more than 10% of your brain!"

> "This is not a slum, this is the middle class."

We went to Japan where I met several Japanese and American colleagues for the first time. Perhaps Joe saw that I loved Japan. The following year my wife and I were assigned to Japan and stayed for three years.

We went to Korea where we met more colleagues. I could tell that Joe liked the spirit of the Koreans. He was more at home in Korea than in the carefully crafted framework of Japan. It was here that I saw the way liberal churchmen could be treated by a totalitarian government. We had to talk quietly and in the right locations, lest we be overheard. Some people whom we wanted to see were in prison. When Joe spoke to the Presbyterian seminarians, who were late high school age, I saw the power of his style. As he paced back and forth in the chapel he said to them, "If you do not have passion to care for the world, get out now." He continued to pace, actually waiting for someone to get up and leave. None did.

Joe and I separated here. He was going to Sri Lanka and he sent me on to India alone! I arrived in Calcutta's broken-down Dum Dum Airport at 2 A.M. I gave a Sikh taxi driver the name of my hotel and off we went. I saw animals in the streets and people sleeping on the walkways. People were sleeping all around the front of the hotel where the driver stopped. I did not want to be seeing what I was seeing. I said, "This cannot be my hotel." He said simply, "It is."

I got to my shabby room in this "top rate" hotel. The water was in bottles. I was genuinely frightened.

By morning, after a few hours of rest and some breakfast, things looked better. I had a contact with the Missionary Brothers of Charity, the companion group to Mother Theresa's nuns. I went to visit Brother Andrew at their order house. Andrew turned out to be an Aussie priest. The locale looked a lot like 5th City, so I asked, "How long have you been working in this slum?"

He looked startled: "This is not a slum, this is the middle class. Tomorrow we'll visit the slum."

I was in awe and wondered anxiously, "My God, what am I going to see?"

The next day we went to the slums. I walked the alleys with lepers. I sat on the ground with people in their cardboard huts. I even ate food offered to me, although I was sure I would die. I could not understand why, with all this suffering, I did not meet sorrowing people. I had not read *The City of Joy*; it had not yet been written. This experience, of course, became the heart of my trip; it was why Joe sent me to India alone. This odyssey of discovery had to be done as a solitary. A guarded heart can only be exposed alone.

I met Joe again in Hyderabad and all our subsequent visits were with middle and upper class people. At one place we stayed in a missionary guest house run by an old white woman missionary who misused and disregarded people. Joe could not stand it and we moved out. We went on to Bangalore, Chennai (Madras), Mumbai (Bombay), and Delhi. The rest of the India trip was uneventful, apart from the fact that my tongue was in constant pain from the hot spices. It made my experience in Calcutta all the more vivid.

I left Joe in India, went to finish my travel in the Philippines and promptly became ill. My spiritual odyssey had simply drained all of the life energy out of me. I did not think I would ever want to go back to India. But I have gone back several times and now I miss it.

Justin Morrill

Absolutely Other

During the late 60s, thirty-one of us who lived in the North Shore area of Chicago had formed a task force of "people who care" to engage the world in creative ways. In 1970, one of our projects was a Global Odyssey—ten countries in twenty-eight days! We wanted to stop in highly symbolic places in order to know what was going on in the world. We were very serious in our preparation and had spent six months planning an itinerary, deciding what we wanted to see and learn in each country we visited. One of the places that we planned to visit was India, so that we might be exposed to the lives of people known as the poorest of the poor.

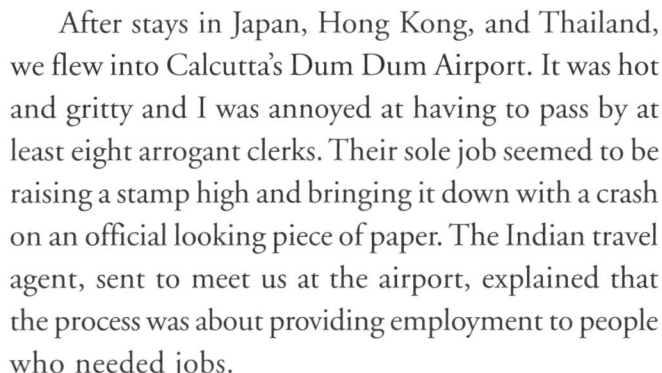

Calcutta rickshaw

After stays in Japan, Hong Kong, and Thailand, we flew into Calcutta's Dum Dum Airport. It was hot and gritty and I was annoyed at having to pass by at least eight arrogant clerks. Their sole job seemed to be raising a stamp high and bringing it down with a crash on an official looking piece of paper. The Indian travel agent, sent to meet us at the airport, explained that the process was about providing employment to people who needed jobs.

As we left the airport, we were informed that there were demonstrations in the streets. The air was thick with smells from literally thousands of people who live, cook, eat, work, reproduce, and die on the street. As our taxis drove through the city on the way

I kept watching the dance floor, imagining that any moment a time warp would occur…

to our hotel, the impression was one of color and energy and life. That taxi ride began my relationship with India—both attracted and repulsed.

Our colleague, Joseph Mathews, Dean of the Ecumenical Institute in Chicago, had visited Mother Teresa in Calcutta during 1969 and had wanted us to see her Home for Dying Destitutes. When we arrived at the Oberoi Grand Hotel, we were greeted by Brother Andrew, who had been sent by Mother Teresa to facilitate our visit. Brother Andrew was in charge of two leprosy camps and was in Calcutta for the week. He was a quiet, imposing man, a beautiful Australian with a handsome, sculptured face, lighted by bright blue eyes that bored into us as if we were saying the most important words he had ever heard.

When we were sufficiently reassured that the demonstrations in the city were peaceful, we persuaded Brother Andrew to take us out to see them. The protests that we had supposed were dangerous riots consisted of well-organized lines of middle class young men carrying briefcases and shouting slogans in Bengali. They were all recent college grads who could not find jobs. They had done everything by the book of success which told them you had to have a higher education—but no jobs were available. Their eyes seemed hopeless and angry, their faces listless with the betrayal they must have felt. My eyes filled with tears as I experienced with them the despair of being thrown back into the struggle for survival instead of catapulted into self-sufficiency by the simple fact of a steady job.

Several days later, my husband George ran into the challenge of sustaining India's huge population from another angle. He was paying a courtesy visit to one of India's great industrial companies—Tata—for a client of his, the DeKalb Seed Company. His host described how, at the request of the government, the company had agreed to take one hundred intern engineers for one year. The company placed one advertisement in the paper and received over sixteen thousand applications. The next year, they would be asked to take another group of interns. At the time, it seemed an impossible challenge.

That night, we intended to dine in the hotel ballroom. The Oberoi Grand Hotel, built at the time of the British Raj, had been magnificent in its day. None of us had ever seen so much marble, but it was a faded glory. We were eager to experience this memento from another era, but our daughter Holly, then ten years old, was exhausted and was not feeling well. We considered whether to go down to dinner. When we called the front desk to ask that she not be disturbed while we were away, we were reassured: "We will take care of her." By the time we had finished dressing, Holly was sound asleep. We carefully closed the door behind us and walked down the long, marble corridor toward the elevator.

Dinner service was very formal. but after dessert had been served, a band appeared, dressed in cowboy outfits and ten gallon hats. George was enthusiastic: "Great, they're going to play country and western," which he adored and I tolerated. There were similar mixed reactions among the other members of the group. Raising their instruments, the band began its set with "The Colonel's Lady's Waltz." It was unbelievable! In boots, chaps, vests, plaid shirts and ten-gallon hats, the band at Calcutta's Oberoi Grand Hotel played waltzes all evening. Not one country and western. I kept watching the dance floor, imagining that any moment a time warp would occur and we would be transported into a room of red-coated officers dancing with elegant ladies dressed in the attire of the early 1900s.

On the way back to our room, we looked out the large picture windows that lined the corridor from the ballroom to the elevator. A huge hole was being dug in the dim light of flickering torches. A line of men carrying empty baskets walked down a ramp on one side of the pit, disappeared, then reemerged with baskets full of dirt, walking up a parallel ramp on the other side. At the top of the ramp they disappeared into the darkness. This slow, circular line never stopped. One of the staff informed us that this was to be an Olympic-sized swimming pool.

Further along the corridor, we passed a small group of men on their hands and knees scrubbing the wide marble hallway with a gritty substance that kept up a continual scratch, scratch sound that we heard throughout the night. These workers were using tools and methods that had been around for thousands of years. Arriving back where we had left Holly sleeping, we discovered a bearded, old Sikh sitting cross-legged in front of the door. He announced that he had been sent to "guard little Miss." After a day of continually pinching myself to remember where I was and what century I was in, my mind was ablaze with bizarre images from these first encounters with India.

Georgianna McBurney

…my mind was ablaze with bizarre images from these first encounters with India.

Visiting Mother Teresa

At the orphanage run by Mother Theresa's Missionaries of Charity, women with babies and small children lined up in what seemed like an endless line. These were women so desperately poor, they were forced by their own compassion to give their children away, rather than see them starve to death. The mothers held up their children, crying out, "See how strong she is; she will be a good worker." The nuns took the children they could. Those who could not be taken finally disappeared with their mothers into the crowded street. Their mothers would probably return another day.

We saw the suffering of the mothers and the compassion of the Sisters and wondered, "How do they choose? How can they say which child will live and which will die?" The questions tore at our hearts.

The Missionaries of Charity also care for dying people. Each day workers go out from Nirmal Hriday ("Pure Heart") Home for Dying Destitutes to bring dying people in from the streets. They pick up people too frail and ill to move or care for themselves, place them on their carts, and wheel them back to the place remembered all over the world simply as the Home for the Dying. The Home was formerly a Hindu temple; it was given to Mother Teresa in gratitude for her work. The temple is a huge oblong shape divided down the center. On the floor are pallets with the most pitiable human beings I had ever seen. One man's body was so broken and distorted that he looked like a spider on his back.

I walked with one of the Indian nuns as she fed her patients. She knelt by each one and gently crooned, "You are safe. It's all right. I have food for you." As she spoke, she gently ran her hand over the person's cheeks and forehead. She slowly fed tiny bites of food to the starving ones. The love and compassion shown by these nuns transformed them; I thought I had never seen women so beautiful.

I was full of questions. "What happens to these people?" I inquired.

The gentle sister answered, "Many die here. Those who regain their strength are sent back to the streets."

Then it hit me that when I first entered the temple, it had seemed dark and unattractive, even repulsive. Now, I looked back as I was preparing to leave, and the temple seemed amazingly light and clean, the nuns radiant, and the dying peaceful. It was very still. No street noises invaded this special place of beauty. A transformation had occurred in my awareness. From that point on in our trip, I did not see India as a hot, dusty, dirty, poverty-ridden place to be judged. I saw living, breathing people in a society being transformed. Mother Teresa said before we left, "Until groups like yours transform India, my order will minister to as many people as we can."

Georgianna McBurney

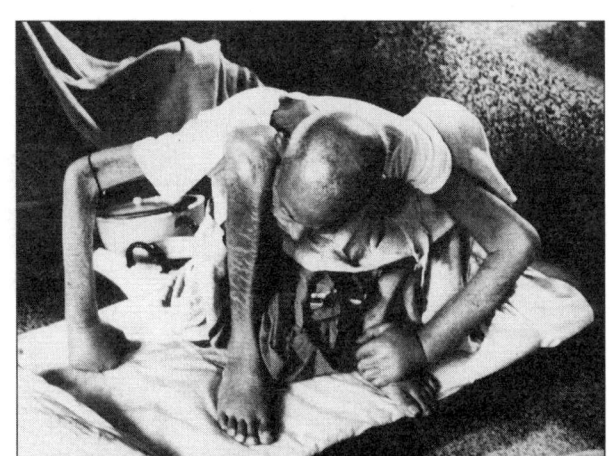

At the Home for Dying Destitutes

Precious Memory

We spent the morning visiting Mother Theresa's Home for Dying Destitutes and the nursery for the children whom she rescues from the streets. The nursery was filled to overflowing with beautiful little children. Some were playing and laughing, some hovered near death. All were cared for by happy, loving sisters.

We returned to Mother Theresa's religious house. Sitting cross-legged on the floor, we talked with her about the spirit life of her community. She was wonderfully gracious. We were all deeply moved by her devout and selfless concern for the human suffering she was attempting to address. When it came time for us to depart, I did not want to go. I had not been able to absorb all that I could feel emanating from this very spiritual woman. I wanted to sit at her feet a while longer.

We gathered in the small courtyard of her community and said our goodbyes. Then we sang to her the song I remember as the "Eagles" song:

> "Those who wait on the Lord shall renew their strength.
> They shall mount on their wings as eagles.
> They shall run and not be weary.
> They shall walk and not faint.
> Help us Lord, help us Lord, on our way."

Mother Teresa was the spiritual model for this song and the words, "Those who wait on the Lord...," had never before felt so right!

Laura Grover

"Those Who Wait On The Lord"

I'll never forget the first time I heard "Those Who Wait On The Lord." We were attending an outdoor worship service on Little Badger Creek on the Blackfeet Reservation soon after James and I went there, during the summer of 1959. The lead singer was a woman who accompanied herself with a tambourine—yes, a tambourine!—and sang-chanted in a minor key. We were touched to the core with that song and brought it to our colleagues, who embellished it, adding verses and melody.

MaryLynn Bell

Metamorphosis

An India scrapbook

My two American colleagues, Jan and David, and I were in India, on our way from Mumbai (Bombay) to Pandur, a poor village in southern Maharashtra state, to attend a week-long village planning consultation. We had been invited to join a team that would help the village improve its life and prospects. We rode all Friday night on a crowded Indian bus, three to a seat. There was a full moon and from what we could see out the window, the countryside was mountainous and wild, like a landscape from another planet. The bus bumped and careened and we jostled against each other. The regular passengers talked or snored. I had made an impromptu decision to extend my stay in India for this unexpected adventure and I was too excited to sleep. It was 1978.

The bus arrived in Ratnagari, a market town two miles from Pandur, by mid-morning. How to get to the village? I had on a pair of sturdy looking sandals like those in the stores now, with wide bands and substantial heels. Luggage was not a problem; I had one sheet, a towel, a long skirt, and a couple of shirts. We decided to walk. But it was hot and dusty, and the road was rough. In the heat of the day the glue gave out and the sandals fell apart. I do not remember what I wore on my feet for the rest of the week.

We finally found our way to Pandur. A set-up team had preceded us to prepare for the consultation. There was a core staff of young Indian villagers recently trained in human development methods at an International Training Institute, and one American. Arrangements had been made for us to stay in the house of one of the village leaders. Water had been provided in a large container by the door and a latrine had been strategically dug not far away on an open hill between two major cross-village paths. The 2 ft. x 2 ft. x 3 ft. hole was equipped with two planks, but there was no screen or cover. We made it clear that this was not acceptable to our sense of modesty. Poles were brought, large banana leaves were skewered and a makeshift green wall was strung together to provide cover. The problem was that the ground was so dry and hard that the poles would not stand up. As the week proceeded, we preferred to use the latrine under cover of darkness, but we discovered that it was possible, in an emergency, to balance on the two planks and hold the screen up with our elbows. The village children loved to race up and down the paths, pointing at us and shouting at each other.

Saturday afternoon, Jan and I set up our base camp on the floor of the kitchen, which seemed to be the highest and driest place in the house. But our host was dismayed, because his household gods lived in the kitchen. There was a brief negotiation. When we agreed to respectfully remove our shoes, he reluctantly approved the arrangement. In the waning light, we went off to dinner cooked by the project staff. It consisted of gritty rice, vegetable *dal* (lentils), and hot *chai*. When we returned to the house for the night, the owner proudly pointed out that the electric light had come on. It was just light enough to see that the mud walls were crawling with inch-long black ants which lived in the cracks and had come out to bask in the glow. We looked at each other and decided that the cow dung veranda outside looked like a more hospitable alternative. We made up pallets with half our belongings under us and the other half on top and stretched out for the night. The house was surrounded by palm trees quietly standing guard in the moonlight. We settled in for a week of village living.

On Sunday morning the village was preparing for the consultation. The week's meetings would be held in the Hindu temple, a large structure, open on three sides with a clay floor and a roof, but without furnishings. Because the event was to be a sign of new possibilities, our colleagues had decided that everyone should sit at tables. Since there were no municipal tables and chairs, we went door to door to persuade residents to lend tables and chairs from their homes.

In the meantime, the floor of the temple was being prepared. A young girl arrived with a mixture of cow manure and water in a large bucket. She used a mop to apply the pungent mixture with enthusiastic, sweeping strokes. By Sunday evening, the floor was dry, the tables and chairs were assembled, the blackboard was positioned, and all was ready to begin.

Early Monday morning the village participants arrived. There were about seventy-five eager people sitting at the tables, most of them young women, dressed in colorful saris with flowers in their shiny hair. Most of the men had gone to the city because there was no work in the village. A few elderly men sat cross-legged on tables around the back of the temple.

On Monday and Tuesday the villagers talked about their village and what they wanted and needed. The discussions were conducted in Marathi and English and recorded on the blackboard for all to see. Many of the young women had some schooling and could read. Gradually, a picture began to emerge. Crops, farmed by the women, were the only source of income for the village. They had no shops, and went to the city for all their supplies, failing to turn over any income within the village. The men were absent for months at a time, sending what income they could back to their families. We suspected that there was a kind of barter system, but so far as we could tell, residents could not buy so much as an egg near home.

On Wednesday, teams fanned out into the village to gather information that would help people find ways to improve their lives. One section of the village was

The village temple

Daramuthi and Louise

the home of the Harijan community—the untouchable caste. A Harijan woman came up to me to show me her finger. It was cut, covered with black mud and badly swollen. At one time, she said, a doctor had come to the village from a nearby clinic, but had stopped coming. Clearly the swollen finger was infected and needed attention. We arranged to get her to the clinic in one of the few vehicles in the village.

On Thursday and Friday, we were joined by several businessmen and government officials who came to offer their expertise and assistance to the village. Plans were made which the village would carry out with the assistance of the young Indian human development staff assigned to the village. Jan and David stayed on the next week to document the consultation and help get the work started.

During the week I tried my hand at threshing beans from the chaff, did research on why coconut trees were not producing, inspected the irrigation system, joined a wedding celebration, and watched a small green lizard with a curling tail making itself at home on my foot one night. On Saturday there was a village celebration with music, food, a parade and colored streamers.

I left India and traveled on to Oxford, England. By contrast to the sensuous color of India and Pandur, Oxford seemed gray and rational. My interior, it seemed, had been permanently altered by new rhythms and images, by the villagers' graciousness and by my glimpse into their daily lives. The difference between my own world and the world of the village was so striking it hit me in the face—I could no longer relate to people overseas with abstractions. I'm sure they will remember the week of the meeting in the temple with tables and chairs, with its discussions and dreaming and planning about what they wanted for the life of their village and their families. I suspect, like me, the village was never quite the same again.

Louise Singleton

Smell The Jungle

"Fly the ocean in a silver plane.
Smell the jungle when it's wet with rain."

I heard something close to these lines sung by a Filipino singer in a cafe somewhere in Southeast Asia around the time of the ICA's Sudtonggan village planning consultation. She rendered the song with an understated intensity that made it hover in my subconscious, returning later carrying images from my experiences in the Asian Pacific. The song evoked the many times I had flown the Pacific in a silver plane. I almost always landed in a gleaming airport, drove into a modernized capital city, stayed at an international hotel and attended meetings in shiny new skyscrapers.

The song eased my memories back to the plane flights where often, as we began our descent, I would look down at the country I was visiting and see something very different from the routine of a quick, urban business trip. Sometimes it was a green jungle with a village on stilts, sometimes a lovely beach lined with palm trees and a graceful fish net sweeping out hundreds of yards into the blue water, that became symbols of life lived close to the edge of survival on nature's offerings. I always wondered about the "real" country I was landing in but never saw. The mystery and adventure that had lured me to Asia seemed to lie somewhere beyond the city limits.

Attending the planning consultation that launched the Sudtonggan Human Development Project changed all that. My most vivid memory is a village wedding, not all the hard work. The foreigners were welcomed and the entertainment was multicultural and spontaneous. A very passable party brew that one can always find in the Philippine countryside reminded me of a sweetened Four Roses or some similar blended whisky. It made for great ambiance and the experience of warmth and joy in the village celebration mitigated any feelings of helplessness, guilt, or alienation provoked by harsh conditions typical of the impoverished 75% of the world.

We worked hard, and the two weeks spent launching a development demonstration project on a tiny island in the Philippines inverted my perception of the world. It was hot, there was gritty, bright white coral all around, but the island was bordered by a sparkling blue sea reflecting a deeper blue sky. I remember looking up during one of our workdays to see a silver jet far above, possibly beginning its descent into Manila. I realized that I had flown over this very village many times. I wondered if there was anybody like me gazing out of the round windows of that silver plane at the jungle, the coral beach, the blue water and the sweeping fish net, pondering the mystery of touching the earth in a faraway Philippine village.

The line, "Smell the jungle when it's wet with rain," is a memorable image of human feeling and connection and possibility.

Jeff Coolidge

> I always wondered about the "real" country I was landing in but never saw.

Panic

The word *panic* is my word. When I arrived in India I always had the sensation that I was going to panic. There were so many anxious moments, I always had to say to myself, "I am not going to panic in this situation." Sometimes I had to sit on the floor of a train by the men's urinals or go to some place where I did not know exactly where I was going. Sometimes I did not even know which bus I was supposed to board. All of these situations were terrifying, but I practiced "no panic."

I discovered that there were people who helped me in the process. That was a gift in India. Many people speak English and they showed up at just the right moment and asked, "What do you need?"

But the gift of India went deeper. One night I was sitting on the floor of a third-class carriage of a train, surrounded by men. I felt more and more uneasy as the night went on. At one point, one of the elders who was on the train did something that shifted the mood of the whole situation. I do not know what he did, but from then on, everything was fine. I knew then that it was more than just the English-speaking Indians who were looking out for me.

Jeanette Stanfield

I do not know what he did, but from then on, everything was fine.

When You Are Aware
Tune: When You are in Love

When you are aware, the whole world is a mountain of care.
Skies constantly weep, over all of the tragedy there.
Then your life belongs, to the suffering found everywhere,
When you are aware, the whole world is a mountain of care.

Bearing the weight of the world,
  and the dread of its crushing demands,
Joyously burdened to know, that there's no other world on your hands, and,
Your heart starts to soar, with the wonder that's filling the air,
When you are aware, the whole world is a mountain of care.

An Egyptian Hello

We had been invited by a Coptic priest, Father Mateus, to work in his village, El Bayad, two hours' drive south of Cairo. The foreigners who were to stay in Egypt, plus our new Egyptian project staff, had moved into the village. After the planning consultation that launched the El Bayad Human Development Project, the expatriates were still floundering around, wondering what and where we were going to eat next. Every meal was an event.

One day, Father Mateus invited all twelve project staff members to come to his house for dinner. Because Coptic priests marry, we were to share the meal with his wife and family. Two colleagues had a fund-raising visit to make in Cairo that day, but were coming to the big dinner a little late. We were all quite excited about the prospect.

On the big day, the staff walked over to Father Mateus' house. While we were all sitting in his living room, anticipating our colleagues' return, Father Mateus was doing his best to entertain us. He said, "Now when the Mr. and Mrs. come, I am going to give them a big 'Egyptian Hello!'" He was such an imposing figure, with his long, gray beard, and his eyes were sparkling with such mystery, that everyone felt a bit nervous about what he meant. He sensed our anxiety and said matter of factly, "I will show you."

He pulled out a revolver. We had heard that everyone in the village had a gun hidden under a rug. All of us said, "Oh no, don't do that! They will feel very.... Don't get the gun out!" We could not imagine our colleagues' reactions.

"No, no, I must give them a big welcome!" Father Mateus insisted.

Just at that moment someone shouted, "They're coming!"

We looked out Father Mateus' front door and saw the two latecomers coming up through the village. They had crossed the Nile by *felucca* (sail boat) from Beni Suef, and in order to get quickly to Father Mateus' house for the dinner, had borrowed a donkey at the boat landing. One latecomer was sitting astride the donkey and the other was leading them both up the narrow, uneven lane. The scene struck everyone as positively biblical, like Mary and Joseph entering Bethlehem. We nearly doubled up with laughter.

Father Mateus reached into the pocket of his *galabiya* (robe). We all shouted, "No, no! Don't shoot!" Father Mateus was not dissuaded.

"Oh yes, I must do this!" Whereupon, he pulled out his revolver and shot several times into the air!

When the two reached the house, their faces were as white as a sheet!

Judy Gilles

Father Mateus listens while Joe addresses the planning consultation

I'll Bet You A Dollar

Since the late 1970s, El Bayad, a small Egyptian village sandwiched between the Nile and the desert, two hours' drive south of Cairo, has been remembered as the place where villagers created a miracle by building their own water system. In the process, they overcame a cloud of despair and broke deeply-held images of impossibility about what villagers could accomplish.

The drilling tripod behind the El Bayad pumphouse

I was working with the Bayad water team, finishing up a new well in a neighboring village, Sheik Ali. Our drilling rig consisted of a tripod of sturdy pipes with a mechanical winch hung in the middle. The men began a well by digging the mud and sand out from within a twenty foot length of pipe that was about six inches in diameter. As they dug, the pipe sank deeper and deeper into the earth. When the digging was completed, they dropped a well casing into the larger pipe, which was then pulled out of the ground.

One day in 1980, Ike, our new Project Director, arrived from the city at our digging site next to the Nile, just as our strong-armed team leader, Abdul Hamid, was tying the rope connecting the pipe to the winch in order to pull the large pipe out of the ground. Ike surveyed the tripod, winch and rope. Ike did not yet know Abdul Hamid, who, though he had no formal education, was a man with a penetrating intelligence about ropes and pulleys born of a lifetime piloting a *felucca* (sailboat) on the Nile.

We could see Ike's mind calculating his prospects. He finally observed, "There is no way on earth that that rope can possibly grip that pipe strongly enough to pull it out of the ground!" Abdul Hamid just grinned, and bet one Egyptian pound (about a dollar) that he could do it. Ike took up the friendly wager.

With exaggerated nonchalance, Abdul Hamid wrapped the rope three times around the pipe, not even bothering to pull the it tight. Then he looped the rope around the hook attached to the pulleys and began pulling. The large pulleys provided tremendous mechanical advantage and the rope steadily tightened, gripping the pipe like a vise. The tension increased to the breaking point and Abdul Hamid's muscles bulged with the strain. Then suddenly, nearly invisibly, the pipe began to move. The tension on the ropes eased and the pipe slid easily up out of the ground.

Ike laughed and laughed and admitted defeat. Abdul Hamid's face had a smile that stretched from ear to ear. We had all learned a valuable lesson. While those of us from outside Egypt knew many things, we could never underestimate the canny intelligence of the villagers. And concerning ropes, pipes, and pulleys, we should never make a bet with an Egyptian boatman!

Tim Wegner

Unforgettable Characters

After graduation from college, I was fascinated like anybody else with work in an international organization. I especially looked forward to training, traveling and language practice. During my first week, I visited the ICA offices in Egypt. One of the visits was to the small loans program. Patrick, a former staff member, and I went to El Hamraya village. We left the main road south of Cairo and went into the desert. We stopped by the home of a man who had only one leg who lives with his wife in a tent. He had gotten a loan for sheep and was paying the monthly installment.

There was nothing to sit on except the floor of the tent, but he insisted on presenting something to us to show his generosity. He prepared tea, but it was a big problem. The kettle was an old rusty salmon fish can with a metal handle. There was only one small glass for the four of us. Despite that, a smile was always on their faces. I left this tent in tears.

My style in life changed. I read a saying in a book: "Worry almost killed me when I lost my shoes until two days later I met a man with no legs." This saying is now a principle supporting me in difficult situations. The visit to the desert helped me in dealing with poor people, in the way to speak to them and how to approach them. I learned satisfaction and humility.

The villages are full of strong people. Raya, for example, is a housewife and a widow, with children to raise, who lives alone in a simple house in El Warsha. She worked in the health caretakers' program and helped the Loan Team to market their program, following up on loans and collecting payments. In spite of being old and short, she had character and strength.

One day, the Loan Team went out with the camera to take pictures of the loan recipients: a woman who was raising sheep, a woman with a sewing business, a woman with a small supermarket, and a woman with a bird project. When we visited a widow selling snacks in front of the school, we found a group of adults and kids had come to her house and wanted to break our camera and damage the film. The leader of this group was the son of the woman with the bird project. Though this young man was blind, he attacked us with sticks. Raya defended us and tried to calm him down, but he continued in his stubbornness to get the film. She became very strong and threatened the young man to speak in a good manner. Raya showed courage in convincing the young man to stop. She said that the picture of his mother was for the loan program. We promised the young man to give back the picture and the negative. On the next visit we gave him the picture and negative. His mother's face did not appear in the picture, only her hand, as she opened the door of the bird room.

I will cherish these memories as long as I live because they are the beginning of my work in the development field.

Nagwa Abdel Moneim

Selling vegetables in El Bayad

Drunk Shrimp

> "Don't worry, soldiers can eat anything."

Chen I An, a Taiwanese colleague, Ed and I were raising money for the Human Development Project in the center part of the country, near the old capital of Taiwan. There was a gentleman who ran a print shop in the town of Taijung, who had previously given money to the ICA and to the project, so we went to visit him. In China, business is centered around the meal and that normally means going to a restaurant. The gentleman invited us to share a meal at a very special restaurant that served Japanese food.

In Taiwan, business meals also provide an opportunity to see if a guest loses face. I was confident. A Taiwanese colleague, Peter Hu, had taught me to eat Chinese food while we toured the island on his motor bike. I had always asked Peter, "What will we have for breakfast?" Peter, ever the commanding general, would say, "Don't worry, soldiers can eat anything." So I had already eaten many different kinds of Chinese food and felt that I knew about the kinds of things I would be served when going out to dinner in China. Besides, Chen I An, our representative in Taiwan, was at my side. I figured I could do anything with him along.

After we went into the restaurant, our host made it clear that this was a famous restaurant. The meal started with hors d'oeuvres of a pickled clam accompanied by a fine wine. Then the first dish was brought to the table in a silver bowl with a special cover. The host said, "This is a specialty of the house, and the most expensive dish on the menu." As soon as the dish landed on the table, it moved. Obviously, whatever was inside was alive.

We hesitantly asked, "What do you call this?"

Our host picked up the cover. Twenty shrimp were lazily swimming around in a clear liquid. "This is 'Drunk Shrimp.'" The chef had taken rice liquor, added live shrimp, and left all twenty creatures to relax. Of course they got drunk. With the four of us sitting there, we knew that each of us had to eat five shrimp. I quickly learned how to grab the head and tail, put the loop of the shrimp into a horseradish and soy sauce, bite the loop off, and spit out the shell. I felt like a trooper and must admit they were good.

After that experience, I never worried again about what was being served for breakfast.

Doug Druckenmiller

Mother's Advice

We were celebrating Bhimrao's birthday in the Chikhale Training Centre in India one night. I had started to ask him questions about the significance of this particular birthday. As he was dutifully answering, out of the corner of my eye I caught a glimpse of a snake moving behind his chair. I remembered my father's warning to me as a child: "Nancy, when you encounter a snake or another dangerous creature, remain still and calm."

I quietly whispered, "Bhimrao, there is a snake behind your chair." In a fit of terror and with an unbelievably loud clamor, my friend yelled and instinctively jumped onto the table.

It was immediately apparent that Bhimrao's mother had given quite a different warning to her children: "Bhimrao, when you encounter a snake, get as far away from it as quickly as you can and send someone back to beat it to death with a stick or rock." He seemed fascinated, though, as if he were watching himself and the rest of us in the room, and was amused with what he saw.

It was an emotional event that impacted our minds, bodies, and spirits and was indelibly imprinted in our memories. We never got back to the birthday questions, but to this day, Bhimrao and I cherish this shared experience rediscovering the differences in our cultures.

Nancy Lanphear

Shantumbu

In November, 1976, the grass along the dirt road east of the city of Lusaka, Zambia, had turned to a brown straw that grew six feet high. By the time the leadership team arrived in Shantumbu, five hundred villagers from the surrounding nine villages were expected at the planning consultation. We had to chop down nearly ten acres of grass to clear a space for a large meeting tent and several small staff tents. The villagers helped to arrange the space. We put up the large tent at the bottom of a small hill and pitched our own tent on the top of the hill. Our two small cots left just enough room for the pole in between. We could see the staff tents and the plenary tent below.

We were regularly surprised and amazed at the wisdom of the villagers. They showed us how to make home-made toilets. First they dug deep holes along the hill outside the big tent. Then they took large empty oil barrels and cut them in half with an acetylene torch. The torch was also used to cut out a hole large enough to squat over. They turned this barrel upside down over the top of a mound of dirt surrounding the pit. Then, for privacy, they tied the straw we had cut to a bamboo framework to create a round house with a round, tapered roof to ward off the rain.

The planning consultation was moving along with great excitement every day with five hundred villagers crowded together under the big tent. Many of these villagers had walked fifteen to twenty miles just to get to the consultation, often arriving hours before the workshops began! One day, in the middle of a

The planning consultation was moving along with great excitement every day with five hundred villagers…

> *"Good boy!*
> *Good boy!*
> *Try again!*
> *Try again!"*

plenary session in the big tent, we heard the cry, "Fire! Fire!" We all raced outside. One of the home-made toilets was disintegrating in a great swoosh of solid flame that shot fifty feet into the air. As we stood and watched, listening to the straw framework crackle from the intense heat, we learned that someone had cleaned the toilets with kerosene. A smoker had obviously decided to use the public facilities and thrown a match into the toilet. Where was this person now? During the fifteen minutes it took for the flames to die down sufficiently for us to poke around in the ashes, we anxiously counted heads. We decided that no one had been in the toilet when it went up in flames. Rejoicing, we went back into the tent to continue our work.

Barb was terrified of the African cattle. They were huge Brahmin bulls, standing seven to eight feet tall with long, pointed horns. They seemed to be everywhere! The first night I was lying awake brooding about the next day when Barb said, irritably, "Bill, stop snoring!" "I'm not snoring," I said. "I'm wide awake." Heavy snorts continued from Barb's side of the tent. We had unwittingly pitched our tent in the middle of the path which the cattle used every night to go down to their watering hole. We were surrounded by a herd of bellowing cattle unable to fathom why this strange canvas structure was sitting in their path. They could have stampeded in anger or fear, but fortunately, they just seemed to be snorting in puzzlement.

We were surrounded by enthusiastic villagers who were eager to go to work. A team stayed on in Shantumbu for a few weeks after the planning consultation, helping the villagers begin the projects they had planned. A preschool program, for example, was started the day following the consultation. Village women were trained in the evenings and gathered under the trees with their classes during the day. While we wrote up the development plan in the tent, we heard the deep, brassy voices of these village women saying: "Good boy! Good boy! Try again! Try again!" Their affirmations were an encouraging litany that echoed antiphonally from tree to tree.

The village's first projects progressed and members of the leadership team began preparing to return to their regular assignments. Judy, who had come to help us from India, had brought voluminous notes from her experience in orchestrating planning consultations during the previous year. She had spent hours writing out all these notes and kept them in a large briefcase on the ground in the team space. When she went to gather up her notes, she grabbed the handle and the whole case came apart from the bottom! Zambian termites had eaten through reams of precious notes! A thousand hungry creatures had left her holding the handle while they scurried off to digest our colleagues' considerable wisdom on human development.

Bill and Barbara Alerding

The Falling Lizard

My husband, Jack, and I left windy Chicago and arrived in the heat and humidity of Hong Kong in August, 1980, on our way to Nam Wai village. I still remember being slammed by the heat when we walked out of the airport. It took our breath away!

After we were settled, the staff was having a planning meeting one hot summer night. The community center for the project was a temporary building with an unfinished ceiling, furnished with fluorescent lights. It was a very hot evening so the windows were open and the lights were on. The staff was seated around the tables, set in the characteristic rectangle with Jack "up front." He made a rather profound statement, which escapes me at the moment, but there was a certain awe in the room. We were all engrossed in our work.

Just then, a gecko—a small lizard—fell from the light fixture and landed right on Jack's balding head. The whole meeting room was in a turmoil as everyone, realizing Jack was only shocked and not injured, started laughing uproariously. The gecko, which has been on the earth longer than most other creatures, had inadvertently given a timely lesson in humility.

Louise N. Ballard

Pigs In The Bedroom

A severe earthquake had hit the village of San Miguel Conacaste, Guatemala and many homes had been destroyed. Early in the summer of 1978, my husband and I arrived for the consultation to launch the Conacaste Human Development Project. Housing arrangements were of great interest to us. Though some rebuilding had begun, new houses in the village had only cement block walls and tin roofs. Vacant openings remained where doors and windows would be—once they were installed. In the meantime, village families were living in one-room huts made of sticks and mud.

We shared one of the unfinished houses with another couple participating in the consultation. Just like the other new homes, our unfinished house had no doorway, but the four of us looked at each other bravely and said, "We don't need a door." The single large room had been prepared with boards across the windows for privacy from the outside and sheets slung down the middle of the room on a rope for privacy on the inside. With four bunk beds, everything seemed quite satisfactory. Until it began to rain.

Rain transforms a dusty village, and the torrential rains that began soon after our arrival were harder and longer than any I had ever experienced in the US. In the best of times, animals roamed throughout the village, so it was common to meet a dog, a cow, a horse, or a mother pig and her litter along the village paths. But the night it rained was the worst of times and the mother pig and her piglets headed for the nearest shelter—our unfinished house.

…the four of us looked at each other bravely and said, "We don't need a door."

Our only recourse was to choose peaceful coexistence.

The pigs crowded into our bedroom, soaked and squealing. My idea of decency did not include sharing my bedroom with a mother pig and her piglets. I insisted that my husband get up and shoo the pigs away. No sooner had he climbed back into his upper bunk than the pigs reappeared. After trying valiantly and failing miserably to go back to sleep, I again insisted that my husband get up and rid us of the pigs. He again succeeded, and for good measure, he barricaded the door opening with boards from the window. Again, he climbed back into the upper bunk to sleep.

Not to be daunted on her search for shelter, the mother pig knocked down the boards, ushered in her children, and settled them down for their own much deserved sleep. By now we knew we were sharing the room with the pigs whether we wanted to or not. Our only recourse was to choose peaceful coexistence. We were so tired, it worked. By morning, the rain had stopped and Mom and her piglets had left. We awoke, refreshed from our sleep.

This brief encounter with Mother Nature at her most powerful and Motherhood at her finest, left me with some degree of shame at my own expectations of what was "right" and a profound respect for anyone with the ability to adapt to the needs of the situation. I was humbled by the experience of making do and awed by the experience of sharing my space with creatures of the earth who required the use of my home for their survival.

Leila Crandall-Frink

Baboons Direct the Buses

We were driving along in a little bus, when we saw a baboon out in the middle of the road. He was standing there waving. The driver pulled off to the side of the road to stop, so people could get off to "go to the bathroom" in the bush. When we got over to the spot, there were about six other baboons.

The driver opened the door. The six baboons got on the bus and started going up and down the aisles. People were throwing bananas and all the baboons had their hands out. I wish I had had a video camera because nobody really believes it. After they got their bananas, they all got off. Everybody else got off for their rest stop and then got back on the bus.

When we got ready to go again, that same baboon was waving and directing the bus. I think that was a regular stop for this driver.

David Coffman

The Cyclone

It was Christmas Eve in Darwin, Australia. After camping out for a few days near Darwin, we had planned to treat ourselves to a Christmas getaway at a motel near our home. There were news reports that a cyclone (hurricane/typhoon) was in the area, but since four or five cyclones threaten Darwin every year, it did not seem like a big deal. When we arrived at our house, we changed our clothes and went out to dinner. We thought it strange that there was no one else in the restaurant. We did not realize it at the time, but other people were taking shelter.

After dinner we checked into the motel just four blocks away and a quarter mile from the shore. We set up our Christmas decorations and as we got ready for bed, listened to the radio news. People were very blasé, talking about the cyclone as if it were any other day. I'll never forget the last report before the radio went off the air: "Cyclone Tracy is located six kilometers north northwest of Darwin and is heading south southeast at twelve kilometers an hour."

I said to Margaret, "I think it's going to hit us." Two hours later, driving rain started seeping into our room. By then the radio was out and nobody knew how bad everythng was.

When the wind died down a little after midnight, I went out to go check on a guest who was staying in our house. There was not a lot of damage, so I drove up to our house. A few tree limbs were down, but no houses had been destroyed. I checked our house and it was okay. I decided I would drive through the shopping center parking lot where we had recently built a playground. So I drove in one of the six entrances to the parking lot. I looked around and everything seemed to be okay. But I noticed the wind was coming up and started back to the motel. One after another, I tried each of the entrances to the shopping center parking lot. All but one had been blocked with debris of one sort or another, so it took a while to get out. By the time I returned to the main road, the wind was really starting to come up. Sheets of roofing were flying through the air and down the road. I had not realized that the relative calm at midnight had been the eye of the cyclone!

I went back to the motel a different way from which I had come. That was not smart, because I found power lines down. I ended up having to drive across somebody's lawn to return to the motel. By the time I returned and parked the car, the wind was lifting the car off the pavement. I managed to get the door open and get into the motel.

Shortly after my return, we were startled by a knock at the door. There stood a man, naked except for a sheet wrapped around his body, with big gashes in his knees. He had been blown off the second floor of his house across the street. That was when we really knew it was bad! We tore up sheets from the motel bed to bind his wounds.

At first light the next morning, we saw that the ocean had risen to within only one hundred feet of the motel. Not a single leaf remained on any of the

He had been blown off the second floor of his house across the street.

trees or bushes in what had been a tropical neighborhood with dense vegetation. Normally, if you looked at somebody's front yard, you could not see through to the next house. Now, you could see straight through the whole subdivision. There was nothing there. Cyclone Tracy had virtually destroyed Darwin, Australia. Of twelve thousand living units, only five hundred were livable. Our home was one of the five hundred survivors because it was not located in a densely built-up area.

Kit Krauss

> *There was nothing there. Cyclone Tracy had virtually destroyed Darwin, Australia.*

Shocking

Ijede village is in the Ikorodu district of Lagos State, Nigeria. Being close to Lagos, everyone was very familiar with electrification, but the national electrical grid had not yet reached them. Because Ijede was a good-sized village with a lot of activity, residents wanted to extend commerce and improve personal safety. The community had planned for a lighting project during the consultation that launched their development activities, and in 1979, soon after the consultation, everyone wanted to set up street lights.

The street lighting system had been designed by one of the chief *Are* (pronounced "Ahray"). *Are* is a role designation in the complex traditional Yoruba chieftain structure. We thought of the chief *Are* as the Minister of Defense. He was actually an electrician and a group of people from the community had been working with him. It had been a long campaign, and despite the fact that they were quite dedicated, some of the commitment in the community had dissipated. But there was always a core focused on the project, and participation of our team members, Charles and Hubert, gave a final boost to their efforts.

The community built a small building for the generator and Charles Olasanlola and I built the concrete pad and set the bolts. When they brought the generator in, it fit perfectly.

The *Oba* (King) was going to dedicate a whole series of things that had been developed over the past several months and a major day of celebration had been planned. This was a significant deadline and the pressure was on to be ready. In Nigeria, "dedicate" means carrying out a series of traditional rituals and it was very big stuff to have the *Oba* bless something. It meant that a project was recognized as the real work of the community and would be integrated into the local culture. We wanted to finish the system, but it was very complicated and no one on our team was an electrician.

On the day of the dedication, Charles and two villagers were still stringing wire. Full-sized, termite-proof electrical poles had been donated by the company which made poles for NEPA, the Nigerian Electrical Power Authority. Charles was working at the top of one of the all-teak poles, checking the connections to make sure they were all secure. At the same moment, in another part of the village, someone was working on our donated generator. It was a big one with a diesel engine. They were setting up the wiring and wanted to test the motor. Someone started the motor without checking the switches.

On the other side of the village, two hundred twenty volts immediately shot through Charles' body. For a moment he appeared frozen in mid-air, like Freddy Kilowatt charged with lightning. Under the circumstances it was difficult to stay in one place and Charles was suddenly airborne. Then he fell in a heap at the foot of the ladder.

In those days, we placed ourselves in physical danger on a regular basis. We were used to it and flirting with danger was "a young dude's life." Charles was rattled, but, being young, strong and dedicated, he got up, cursed those at the generator shed, and went to make sure the switch was off. Somehow he climbed back up the pole and finished the job just in time for the *Oba* to come and bless the electrical system.

The celebration was a great one. The *Oba* was a natural thespian and played his role as Chief of the Village and "Symbolizer of Great Deeds" to the hilt. He was in top form that day and dedicated several things. It was a time of real pride for the village and there was a lot of drumming, dancing and partying.

No one knew about the unintended drama of Charles' shocking illumination and flight. The next day we began work on our next project.

Wayne Nelson

> The *Oba* was a natural thespian… and "Symbolizer of Great Deeds"…

Considerations of the Whale

In 1977, I was swimming in a pool at the foot of the cliffs Australians call the "jump-up" at a place not far from Oombulgurri called Nungi. Two weeks before, the pool had been a crater of dust and stone, eight to twelve feet deep and thirty to fifty feet in diameter. Then the wet season had come and the rains had begun to fall as regularly as clockwork every afternoon at 2 P.M. As if by magic, there were fish in the pool where there had been only a dust bowl two weeks earlier. The dip was a welcome relief, for the temperatures were well above 100°F during the day and did not drop below 90°F at night. We lived and worked in a village without climate control.

The jump-up soared a dramatic one hundred to one hundred fifty feet above the rambling flood plains of the Forrest River. The hills, which the jump-up announced, formed the watershed for the fresh water that flowed into the Forrest River during the three-month wet season. For nine months of the year these hills lived on the thirty inches of rainfall that occurred within that three-month period. There was an initial flourishing of flora and fauna when the wet season arrived, then a period of dormancy during "the dry," the long Western Australian dry season.

The wet season was coming to an end. The daytime and nighttime temperatures had moderated. Though we would have been regarded as workaholics, we succeeded in justifying this trip away from the village of Oombulgurri one Sunday afternoon. We left after lunch and went about as far "outback" as non-natives were likely to go, because we were not bush-wise. The sand was uncomfortably warm, even through the soles of my shoes. (The Oombulgurri people are accustomed to going barefoot, though when the sun is at its zenith, even they do not go out because the sand is so hot. Nevertheless, whenever the barge came in at noon, there were always Oombulgurri residents helping to unload it, in spite of having to walk on the barge's frying pan-hot plate-steel deck.)

My colleagues and I had made the one-half hour walk to Nungi one hot afternoon. We changed into our swimming suits, played, talked, relaxed and relished the water. The water was inviting and refreshing. It was cool and invigorating. It was natural and soothing. It was harboring and protecting. It was comforting and nourishing.

As the afternoon wore on, our minds wandered from the refreshing coolness of the pond, as one by one each of us began anticipating the responsibilities awaiting us back in the village. We knew we would emerge from the comfort of the water, replace our swimsuits with our clothes, and return to work in the harsh wet season climate.

The Oombulgurri residents had extended us a year-round invitation to "go bush" and revel in the way the Outback sustains life. We were so busy administering the Oombulgurri Human Development Project, we had declined the opportunity to abandon ourselves to their care.

"Camera Pool" on the Forrest River

Now it seemed natural that I did not want to leave the water. But more astounding to me was that I had a sense of remembering—remembering what the whale must have considered when she decided that she would not leave the sea and attempt life on the land, but instead remain within the comfort and protection of the deep.

Suddenly I knew that the whole evolutionary process had been recapitulated within the cells of my body. Evolution is about trillions of conscious and unconscious choices which I had grasped as a part of my own memory. I was part of an environmental family; the whale was my relative, a cousin if you will.

As we walked back to Oombulgurri, the whale seemed to say, "Extract yourself from consuming. Live lightly on the earth. Care for all of creation."

David Zahrt

Oombulgurri from the road to Nungi

Meant To Happen

Amidst the complexity and crush of Hong Kong, one of the world's great cities, the question was, "Where can we find a site for a Human Development Project?" The group had made a great deal of effort to find a place and had chosen a poor district on a mountainside that reared up within the city. The planning consultation had been scheduled and all the provisions of the government had been lined up. But when Joe came, he immediately determined it would not work as a Human Development Project because it would not be a visible demonstration.

We had to make a huge turn. The question immediately shifted to, "Where shall we go now?" Joe decided that each of us would be given a part of Hong Kong, and we were to search. We had no car, so my team was assigned to take a bus and go to a certain area. We got on the bus and all three of us promptly fell asleep. I remember waking up and hitting the buzzer hard to stop the bus because we knew we were way beyond our stop! We piled out of the bus, and literally ran into a signpost that said, "To Nam Wai." So we followed the sign and walked down the road. We were shocked to find the most perfectly insulated little village you could ever imagine. We looked at each other and agreed immediately: "This is it!"

We came back, reported on our find, and by god, that's the village we selected. I understand that Nam Wai is a great tourist attraction now. I do not know how much of the village's success has to do with the Human Development Project, but I suppose the project got it all started.

With all the emphasis on planning and methods, sometimes we think things happen because we plan them. I'm amazed at the historical inadvertence of how things sometimes happen. I think "inadvertence" is another way of saying that God decides when to strike and where to intervene in history.

Pat Moriarty

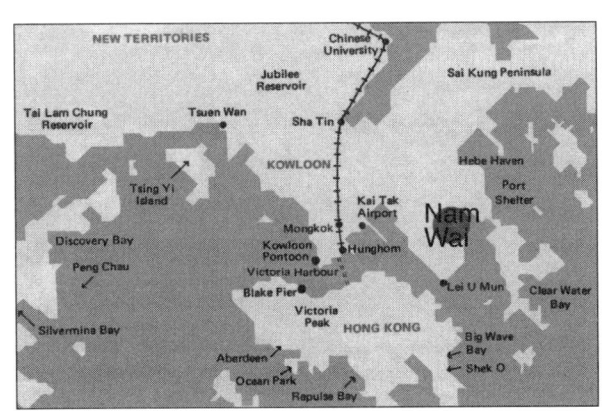

Map of Hong Kong

Chapter Two

You're It!

It was as though a great arm of history
reached out across the planet and embraced us.
We could not refuse to go,
and having gone, we could not return alone.
Having touched, we cannot forget,
and remembering, we will always dream together.

Moth To A Flame

> "I just wanted to say hello and I'll be leaving now."

My first memory is from Austin, Texas, at the Christian Faith and Life Community (CFLC). Joe Mathews had taught a college weekend seminar in Big Rapids, Michigan, which was so exciting that I drove to Austin on my spring break. Having grown up in Austin, I knew several ministers from the CFLC and had had some Sunday school experiences and seminars with them when I was in high school. But it was so different after that weekend with Joe! I looked up the CFLC address in the phone book, but when I drove by, I was too scared to go in. Finally, after driving up and down the street in front of the building, I walked into a place that had books and files everywhere on the floor and stacked against the wall. Someone said that Joe was in a meeting, but that Lyn, his wife, was there.

Joe had given a lecture in which he referred to Lyn as "the wrath of God in [his] life." I assumed that if Joe could shake me up so much, then Lyn must be twice as awesome. Lyn came down some stairs and as I looked up, I saw what seemed like a six foot tall, majestic and frightening woman. She welcomed me in a kind voice. I remember stuttering and perhaps communicating that I was just driving by—1100 miles from Michigan to Austin. "I just wanted to say hello and I'll be leaving now."

By some magic, Lyn got my feet moving in the direction of Joe's office. He came bounding out, greeting me as if I were his long lost relative. I had nothing to say, nothing to contribute and was feeling quite the lowly college student. I was loaded up with a lot of the newsletters, including issues that talked about the unusual meals served in the religion courses, an issue on the movie "Judgment at Nuremberg" and an issue about music.

This short meeting impacted me so much that I began sending $25 a month to the CFLC. I sent my check faithfully for the next three years and after the staff moved to Chicago, I sent the $25 to the office in Evanston. I visited the group yearly to get renewed and I had my second and third meeting with Lyn.

By my second meeting with the staff, they had moved into the old Bethany Seminary on the west side of Chicago and Lyn had become shorter than the six feet I had remembered from Austin. She again took me up to Joe, who asked me about my fondest hopes for the future. I could not answer. Joe never asked why I had come. I just wanted to be a part of this vitally alive group. Lyn took me downstairs for lunch, saying, "I hope there is some food left." There was some stale bread and peanut butter and jelly on a table. She said with great delight and enthusiasm, "Oh, look, there is food left." Little did I know how much that statement could have told me about the next twenty-five years of my life. I just thought maybe Lyn had a fetish about peanut butter.

I came several times, including the day President Kennedy was shot in 1963. Joe was engaging some children in conversation and asked me to join him. We had the greatest conversation about death and JFK. It blew my mind. By the third meeting with Joe, I had graduated and moved to Chicago, in hopes that I could be a part of the Ecumenical Institute. Joe talked to me and said, "We never ask anyone to join." I understood this to mean that I had no chance of getting in. Later, I decided that it meant that I had to do the asking, but I was not too bright in those days. He said once, "Well if you move in, we'll put you in the Preschool. We just got a grant to start one." In April of 1965, it was called The Headstart Program. In September, Sargent Shriver, President Johnson's Director of the Office of Economic Opportunity, came to visit. The staff got very busy, re-did the gym and started the Preschool curriculum.

I think Joe finally got tired of my not asking to join and asked point blank if I had ever thought about coming to live there. I said, "When?" He told me to give my phone number to Lyn and then the leaders of the group would meet me for lunch. They would meet afterwards and decide about me. Lyn would call me in a week. The lunch went okay. I remember being asked for a three-point plan for China and if I were willing to clean toilets. Both were great signs of things to come.

Two weeks went by and no one had called. I was in agony and finally, when I could not stand it any longer, I called Lyn. I can hear her voice today. "Oh, I'm so glad you called. I lost your number and Joe is so mad at me. We want you to come."

So I did. I moved into Mae Hall, later called Faculty West. On the day I arrived, I was shown how to do the solitary worship which we did together in the chapel every evening. We had a form to use with a list of everyone in the community, so that we could pray for different people each day. I do not remember my first daily worship. The whole year was such a new experience that I must have been in a continuous daze. I do remember that evenings were free and we did a lot of sitting on the porch, watching the Sears sign blink. I also remember Lyn saying that she could see herself and Joe at 80, rocking on rocking chairs on that porch and looking at the Sears sign. For some reason, that was very comforting to me and I could see myself in my old age on that porch. Needless to say, we evolved a bit since that time, but I can still remember the vitality and excitement of being with people who had visions of change, who were willing to live among the poor, who made plans together and who laughed a lot.

Preschoolers on the lawn on the West Side campus

Kay Hayes Gadway

Lured By The Mystery

There I was in the middle of the Amazon jungle in Riberalta, Bolivia, sometime in 1979. Someone was calling by radio-phone patch. There was so much static I could not understand what was being said. The Maryknoll brother operating the radio told me it was a call from Chicago from a Lyn Mathews. She wanted to know if I could be a member of the "panacea." Knowing it was Lyn on the other end, I guessed that she wanted me to be a member of the *Panchayat*.* In spite of very poor communication, the meaning came through loud and clear: could I become a member of the international leadership team of the ICA? While I said "yes" because Lyn was a trusted colleague, I also knew that it was the Mystery trying to communicate with me. Even more, I said "yes" because I trusted the Mystery.

That "yes" eventually led me on a *Panchayat* trip to India in 1979. In one of the places we visited, the Sikror Human Development Project near New Delhi, I met a young Indian man in blue, the symbolic garb of ICA staff. That evening, because there was no other accommodation available, we slept on the cold floor of a house in the Muslim village. In the morning, as I spoke with this young man, I learned that he was a Catholic from Kerala and a catechist who wanted to do more than just teach the message of Jesus. He wanted to respond in a practical way to India's poor. His village priest had given his blessing to work with the ICA. He was married and his wife had returned to their home for a few months during her pregnancy.

I asked him three questions.

"How do you feel as a Catholic Christian, living in a Muslim village?"

My new young friend answered without hesitation, "Did not Jesus say that we are all brothers and sisters?"

"Your wife is expecting a baby and you are far away and living in such poor conditions. Why not be at home and help?"

"Did not Jesus say that we must be poor and be with the poor?"

"The ICA is worldwide and they may decide to send you to Asia or Latin America or Africa. How would you feel about leaving your home and country?"

"Did not Jesus say that we must go to the whole world?"

This young Indian man caught me each time with the simple wisdom of a committed disciple of Jesus and a true man of the spirit. His answers were a profound address to me as a Maryknoll missionary priest.

Rafael R. Davila

She wanted to know if I could be a member of the "panacea."

---

* *"Panch"* is the Hindi word for five and *Panchayat* is used across India to indicate a group of elders.

Being A Mother

My husband and I were asked to travel to Japan and await further directions concerning our next assignment, which, at the time, was to have been Indonesia. We had to decide whether to accept the assignment.

I could not imagine leaving our daughters and needed to talk with Lyn Mathews Edwards. When we met, she reassured me about my role as mother and the importance of thinking about my daughters' welfare as we considered our assignment. She said, "There is no one else who will really care for them like a mother, so continue being a mother to them."

From that conversation, I decided to leave for Japan and to write to each of my daughters one day a week. I'd write to Margaret on Monday, Laura on Tuesday, Debra on Wednesday, Nancy on Thursday, and Carol on Friday. Keeping to that schedule did not always work out, but that was my decision.

One of my daughters referred to her collection of letters. She has said that she wished I would use them to write a book for her!

Muriel Griffin

"I'm The Greatest!"

Fifth City is a neighborhood on Chicago's west side, most of whose residents are African American. Many struggle with economic poverty. A neighborhood woman who taught in the Fifth City Preschool, was telling me about the approach of Imaginal Education in dealing with the depth human problem in a community. She illustrated Imaginal Education with a story about a government official who had visited the preschool and was startled by an encounter with a five year old student.

The visitor asked, "Who are you, kid?"

The child replied, "I'm the greatest!"

The official asked, "Where do you live?" expecting the child to say, "In this ghetto," or "In that crummy apartment over there."

The boy said instead, "I live in the universe."

The man, surprised by the answer, fired back another question: "What are you doing here?"

The little boy said, "I'm going to bend history!"

The official was flabbergasted and went to the teacher. The teacher explained, "We want the child to have an image of who he is. He will change history."

From its inception, neighborhood women who taught in the preschool did innovative curriculum building as a key part of their teacher training. Because of this pioneering work, the Fifth City Preschool was recognized in 1970 as one of the top preschools in the USA.

Vinod Parekh

Preschoolers at the statue of the "Iron Man"

In the midst of that dark numbness, it dawned on me that I cared.

Anger Transformed

I drove over fifteen hundred miles from the far north of the state to Perth, the capital of Western Australia, with several Aboriginal people. We were going to a summer program to train community leaders. We stopped at every Aboriginal community along the way, to tell the Aboriginal people the good news about what was taking place. We experienced ceaseless pain.

Our first stops were delightful, as people gathered around the car. But as we went on, we saw many little children with runny noses who smelled badly. The huts were a shambles. People lived like animals. First I felt sorry. Then I got angry at what other people had done to the Aboriginal people. Then I got angry at the people themselves for living the way they did.

Finally, as we got closer to Perth, I found myself just wanting to stay in the car. On one occasion I made excuses, dropped the Aboriginal people off and drove on into town to get a cup of coffee. As I sat there, cup in hand, I began to get ahold of what was going on. I was angry at the world. I was angry at the white Australians. I was angry at the black Australians. I was angry at my wife because she had not come on the trip with us. In the midst of my anger, a numbness settled over me. I did not wish to listen to music, to talk to anyone, to drink coffee or do anything. I just wanted to sit there and be numb. In the midst of that dark numbness, it dawned on me that I cared. We're all driven into care and then cut off and then driven back to care again. Endlessly.

George Holcombe

Letter From Caño Negro

January, 1977

Dear Dallas:

Here's the story from Caño Negro. I've been here for only two weeks of my one-year commitment, but last night I was ready to buy my return ticket to Kansas City.

We're not actually living in the village yet because there still is no good water there. In the meantime, we're staying in Tapipa, a bigger town (bigger than Caño Negro's 350 souls, that is) a few kilometers down the road, at a place called Hacienda San Jorge. You may be tempted to conjure up the picture of a large, inviting Latin American ranch with arched doorways leading to cool interior patios, manicured flowering hibiscus and the like, but don't be. This is a long-deserted old farmhouse with chipped turquoise paint and cobwebs hung at the windows instead of curtains. The kitchen is a lean-to where we heat water in the morning over an open fire to make coffee. The bathroom is a large open space with a toilet at one end and a shower head stuck on the wall at the other. The concrete floor dips down to a large round drain in the middle of the room.

We swept out the cobwebs and made one room into the women's dorm and the other into the men's. I have a top bunk, which concerns me greatly. It seems there is a bug to be greatly feared in the jungle known as the *Chipo* bug. During the night, it falls out of the thatched roofs like we have here at Hacienda San Jorge, and onto the sleeping person's face, which it then bites. That wouldn't be so bad, but while the *Chipo* bug is biting you it is also defecating on you, giving you a disease which attacks your bowels! Gradually, you become unable to defecate yourself. And there's no cure! You can imagine my terror as I climb into my top bunk at night. I look up into those dry palm leaves for a split second, then carefully wrap myself with the sheet which I tuck in all the way around the mattress, including over my head. It's hot as blazes, but at least I have some protection from the *Chipo* bug.

Yesterday was especially traumatic. In the morning several of us piled into the beat-up blue Fiat for the dusty ride into the village. When we arrived, Pablito and Ramon, two Caño Negro boys, ran up to the car and waved a long snake at the end of a branch right in my face as I stared out of the car window. This is a snake they call the *Macagua* here. It is very poisonous and every year there are deaths from its bite, especially on the plantations where the villagers go to farm the cacao fields. They were very proud to have killed it with a machete. To add to my dismay, soon after we unloaded and started setting up for the planning session with the villagers, a man came running down the road from the direction of the cacao field, screaming, "Se murio. Se murio." "He died. He died." He told how a *Macagua* had just fallen out of a tree and bitten his compadre. The friend had died right there in the cacao field!

Chipo bugs and *Macagua* snakes. Down here, they fall right out of the sky to do you harm. You always have to be on the lookout. Can you imagine me with my fear of snakes in this setting? Out of sheer emotional exhaustion, I decided to call it a day earlier than the others and got a lift back to Hacienda San Jorge. I wanted to be by myself, to read a book or to write in my journal. I figured I would sit on a lower bunk. But first a shower, though cold as always, would be refreshing. So I went into the bathroom. While I was sitting on the toilet I saw a snake in the middle of the floor. I don't know how I managed to get out of that bathroom and away from the Hacienda San Jorge all together, but that's when I decided to buy the return ticket home.

I felt giddy this morning as we bounced up the dirt road. I was thinking about getting out of this godforsaken place and anticipating the simple pleasure of sleeping with my face exposed, without fear, to the night air. Of course, it was still my secret; I hadn't told anyone yet that I was leaving Caño Negro.

We pulled to a stop in front of the little mud hut with the corrugated tin roof we call the community kitchen. Rigoberta and Izidra, two women from the village, approached the car with somber faces. "Se murio la niña de Esteban y Luisa por la noche." The baby daughter of Esteban and Luisa died during the night.

"But how could this be, she was only one year old?" we asked. They explained that she had been so

Down here, they fall right out of the sky to do you harm.

full of parasites that she had suffocated. The worms had cut off her breathing passage.

At that moment, I knew I wouldn't be buying the return ticket.

That's how it is in the jungle.

Love, Donna

P.S. Sometimes I think about the yummy cheesecake at Putsche's Coffee House and how we love to go there and talk. You can't imagine what a luxury that would be in a place like this. But, for now, Caño Negro is the right place to be.

Donna Ziegenhorn

> At that moment, I knew I wouldn't be buying the return ticket.

The Cost Of My Care

Tune: Anniversary Waltz

Given the chance to do life in the deeps, to
 serve humankind is the gift that I be.
To care for the world is the burden I bear,
 invent with my life, 'tis the cost of my care.

Chorus:
Strange aweful power is dancing through
 me, buoyantly forging impossible be.
With all my heart I'm poured out
 endlessly; I'm burdened eternally.

Wholly engulfed in unbounded rapport,
 doomed for the world, my life wholly
 outpoured.
Always encumbered, tomorrow is here,
 molding the future the cost of my care.

Burning with wisdom, empowered to do: the
 weight of the world on us all everywhere.
Guardian of all, to all history an heir: absurdly
 in charge, 'tis the cost of my care.

You've Got To Be Crazy

When I came to India, Slicker was running the replication plan of the *Nava Gram Prayas* (New Village Movement). We had troops galore and dozens of people were running madly from one end of Maharashtra state to the other, trying to implement the incredible expansion plan that Slicker and his team had developed. We called him "General Joe." I arrived in the middle of November, 1977, right after Joe Mathews, our founder, had died, and was given the assignment to be on the Economic Acceleration Team. I had no idea what that meant, but it was my job to figure out how to triple the income of the villages.

Though I had never so much as seen a village, I was an obedient soul and set out from Maliwada on a trek to visit the villages of Maharashtra to figure out how in the world we could triple their income. I felt like I did not know anything about anything, let alone village economics, but there I was with my assignment. I felt a little smug to be on one of the special teams. My life was extremely interesting and I felt quite privileged to be serving on a team which made it possible to learn so much about local people. The Agricultural Team and Health Team had vast amounts of work to do and constant deadlines to meet. Members of the Economic Acceleration Team just roamed around freely trying to figure out what to do. But the further I went, the more clear I became that I was not going to be a great success and the less clear I became about how the villagers would benefit from all my trekking about.

When I got back to Maliwada, we were in the midst of intensive preparations for expanding the number of villages involved in *Nava Gram Prayas*. It was like the moment in wartime when the last great battle has begun and all the cooks have to pick up the rifles and shoot. Slicker turned to me and said, "You're doing a village planning consult."

I said, "I am? That was not my assignment. I was supposed to do economic expansion."

Slicker said, "We need everyone we can get and your village is Narayan-Chincholi. You are to run the consult and the person running it with you is Cyprian."

So I had to go out as part of the advance team. Narayan-Chincholi was a broken down, decrepit village when we found it. Jim was the person in charge of preparing the village and he had been arranging the consult. A second person had been sent along with me as a translator, because I could not speak Marathi, the local language. He was an alcoholic and a thief. In the middle of the night, I found out that the man had stolen my money, stolen my boots and disappeared. There I was in a strange village with no shoes, no money, and a consultation to run. I thought, "No problem. Cyprian will save us."

We were ready for the consultation, but Cyprian was nowhere in sight. Now I was worried. The village was primed and excited about doing the consultation. Arrangements had been made with local officials to come to the village to speak. And I was the only one there, supposedly in charge of running the consult. I

There I was in a strange village with no shoes, no money, and a consultation to run.

have never in my whole life wanted so badly to find a rock and crawl under it.

I began to panic because there was still no sign of Cyprian. I decided to send a telegram to Slicker saying, "Help! You need to come here. I cannot do this." I sent a telegram even though the consultation was the next day! Later on I found out that the telegram had arrived a week later in Mumbai (Bombay) and two weeks later in Maliwada.

The morning of the consultation, Cyprian walked casually into the village and said, "Okay." He was doing his first consultation too. Furthermore, he spoke only Hindi, whereas Narayan-Chincholi was a Marathi-speaking village. I despaired. I had spent my time trying to train workshop leaders, most of whom spoke very little English, to lead the village teams. Every night when I went to bed, I wanted to cry. I just said, "You're crazy, Slicker; you are crazy!" I was cursing and muttering, "We have gone too far. We have reached the limit of human capacity and we have got to stop this machine because clearly we are at the end of the rope and the rope happens to be around my neck."

When the consultation was about to begin and we discovered that we had no place to hold it, we started anyway, using the side of a building for our workshops. Cyprian read the villagers' input from large paper sheets in Hindi and someone else translated it from Hindi into Marathi. We tried to stick tape to the bricks that stuck out, but had to hold the papers anyway. Throughout the week, every time a mischievous wind whipped up the sheets with the villagers' input, off they flew into the nearby fields. We chased after our data again and again, bringing it back to the group. All of the villagers were wide-eyed and eagerly participating! In spite of everything, the consultation was a great success and Narayan-Chincholi became a demonstration village.

When we returned to Maliwada, we told General Joe, "Enough! We cannot continue this pace."

But his response was, "Is this one of those experiences when your humiliation and your weakness becomes your glory?"

It was a glorious, glorious experience.

Jack Gilles

Celebrating the launching of 232 demonstration villages across Maharashtra state

A New and Fearful Task

We held the first Human Development Training Institute (HDTI) in Kenya in April, 1979 in Kawangware. There were people from seven Kenyan tribes and from Zambia, Nigeria, Egypt, India, and Australia. One young couple was from Western Kenya. Grace, who had never been to school and her husband, Titus, who had only a few years of formal schooling, had been part of the Urban Agriculture Manager's program. They were attending the HDTI to learn about community development and the ICA. At the end of the eight-week program, participants reflected on their experience at the graduation feast. When Grace's turn came, she rose and spoke in broken English about the opportunity she and Titus had been given and the fear and fascination each felt about their future. This was just the beginning of the journey for this couple, and especially for Grace, who was just beginning to discover her greatness.

After graduation, Grace and Titus took a staff assignment in a village which was part of the project replication scheme in the Machakos District. Soon after their arrival, another staff member suggested that Grace could facilitate the writing of the Weekly Report on Friday morning. Grace probably felt that the task was impossible for her. The conversation went something like this.

"Grace, could you lead the staff meeting on Friday morning?"

"I have never been to school. I cannot even write my name, so how could I lead this meeting?"

"Well, Grace, have you ever considered that you could facilitate the meeting and assign someone else to write out the report?"

This is exactly what Grace did. She discovered that she could not only facilitate a meeting but also could think for herself and make choices.

Grace told the story from her own perspective at the ICA's global gathering in Chicago in 1984. She stood confidently and spoke dramatically about her experience in 1979. "I said to my husband, 'Titus, I have never been to school and you know I cannot read or write, but if I need to do this job, I will do it.'" The group to whom she was telling her story was moved to tears. Here was a woman who had imagined little or no future for herself. In 1979 a window had opened onto a future of which she had never dreamed. I think that Titus was always very supportive of Grace, especially when he realized that she was being so affirmed by their colleagues.

There was nothing more exciting in my life than to have one of my colleagues take on a new and fearful task and make it work in a significant way. Though the tasks were sometimes ones I took for granted, when we offered new possibilities to colleagues, again and again we saw the impossible becoming possible before our very eyes. These great human beings were wonders of transformation.

Nancy Lanphear

"… but if I need to do this job, I will do it."

A Small Miracle in Salzburg

…I proposed that we reach a group consensus…

I will never forget being selected to represent Egypt at the Salzburg Seminar in 1997. This program, which has been operating since 1947, is one of the most renowned leadership development seminars. An article in *Newsweek* magazine said, "There are hundreds of seminars in the prestige-conscious firmament of academe, but few can rival the eminence of the Salzburg program."

Mid-career professionals from all over the world are selected as Fellows for each session through a meticulous selection process. Fellows then work with a distinguished international faculty—people like Mikhail Gorbachov and Hillary Clinton—who donate their time and expertise. Previous Fellows from Egypt included ministers, members of cabinet and parliament, ambassadors, mayors of major cities, professors, leaders of NGOs (nongovernmental organizations) and leaders in the various professions.

I participated in session No. 351 of the Salzburg Seminar whose theme was "NGOs: Leadership and Civil Society." Sixty-five Fellows and ten faculty members, representing forty-five countries, were present. The session was an excellent opportunity for all participants to discuss the complex nature of NGO leadership through exchange of knowledge, skill and experience. It provided the ground for understanding some of the cultural, social, economic and political settings of many of the participating countries. In addition, the diversity among the group members, who represented governments, businesses and NGOs, greatly enriched the discussions.

During the working groups, the discussion of the effects of globalization on NGO work went in all directions. This was helpful at the beginning; however, it was not focused enough, so I proposed that we reach a group consensus on three main issues: major challenges facing NGO leaders, advantages and disadvantages of globalization and how NGOs can empower communities. I suggested that we divide ourselves into sub-groups to arrive at some proposals for those issues using the ICA's *Technology of Participation*® workshop method. Members of the group got very excited and found the method helpful in identifying specific issues and brainstorming ideas. They said the workshop was miraculous in allowing them to draft specific conclusions and proposals. I was selected to present the group's results to the plenary.

Dina Raouf Khalil

And Then It Hit Me

My family joined the ICA staff when I was five years old. I became interested in electronics when I was nine, during my stay in Manila where my mother was teaching an International Training Institute (ITI). After thirteen years growing up with the stories, songs and symbols of the EI/ICA, I entered college to study Electrical Engineering. Four years later I was hired by Texas Instruments to design high frequency, analog circuits.

During my first three months on the job at Texas Instruments, I learned about the frustrations of the newly hired engineers. Retention of engineers was an important company goal because it is so expensive to recruit and do background checks on new engineers. One of the department managers visited with me and shared some of the items that other engineers had offered, such as building break areas and restrooms closer to the work area, and providing free lunches. He mentioned other benign ideas and then asked if, as a "new hire," I shared any of the others' frustrations and had any ideas about what could be done to improve our work life.

Without hesitation I said that the items that were on his list were not really getting at the root of the problem and that he should gestalt them and find the underlying issues. He paused and stared at me, and then said that it sounded like a good idea to him and would I lead the meeting to do it. I agreed.

And then it hit me. I did not quite know what I had described to the manager. I learned to brainstorm and organize my ideas from my exposure to ICA's work, but had always done it with others who knew the process and how to lead it. I did not think my peers would know what I was trying to accomplish. So I picked up the phone and called my dad in Brussels. I told him about the discussion and asked him what I had described to the manager. He told me that it was called the "workshop method."

My life took a turn that day. I began to receive materials about methods from my parents. I received care packages about facilitation from my family's colleagues. They included bits of wisdom from the woman who had taught me to count in Spanish in an ICA afterschool program when I was a child.

During the next five years, I began to consciously relearn the lessons about facilitation and being a change agent that I had absorbed unknowingly while growing up. The local changemasters group became a "guild" where I became reacquainted with the old methods and added new methods, principles and values for facilitation. Without these mentors, I would not have learned so much so fast! I eventually changed my career to become an internal change agent. I earned my Masters Degree in Organization Development to solidify my career change and now facilitate project teams and lead Transformation Management activities for Lotus Consulting.

Rick Walters

> *He paused and stared at me, and then said that it sounded like a good idea to him....*

Miracle in Gunfoundry

Gunfoundry is a small area within the city of Hyderabad, India with a population of about ten thousand people of all castes and creeds. It is a mixture of rich and poor, educated and illiterate, of Hindu, Moslem, Parsee and Christian. We were working with four churches: St. George's, Centenary Methodist, Ramokte Methodist, and St. Joseph's Roman Catholic. The miracle took place smack in the middle of this area.

The Gunfoundry miracle did not just happen. We had been meeting in a room given to us by Miss Strettle for about three months. We had sixteen people, including three Hindus and one Moslem. With only candlelight in this stuffy room, we started training and planning. We wanted to do a cleanup miracle with local residents and participants in the International Training Institute (ITI).

About thirty hours before the workday, we knew we had to select the site for our miracle. We wanted to remove an eyesore in about 180 person hours. It needed to be located in a central place to impact the maximum number of people, and must be so dirty that not even paid sweepers would attend to it.

There was a public latrine in the Gunfoundry community that had served about five hundred people for many years. Such an abominable stink emanated from this public place that most people avoided the area. Bordering the latrine was a huge rubbish dump that had been festering there since my childhood, fifty years before! The Community Hall, which unhappily was located along side both of these disasters, had been used only two or three times in ten years because of its surroundings. We decided that it was essential to clean up the rubbish dump, but I was very reluctant to go ahead in that awful spot. I could not imagine the priests and nuns in the ITI cleaning latrines! It would be a powerful symbol.

On the morning of the workday, I went down to the site about 6:30 A.M. to find that a lot of the garbage had already been removed! A couple of other people arrived and were furious to see the symbol being carried off before all the workers got there.

Many residents and a few municipal officers had gathered when the ITI participants arrived singing. We all went to work, cleaning, shoveling, loading, scraping, painting. Everyone was digging with precision and excitement, laughter and determination. One of our group had the neighborhood children working along side us. A crowd began to gather. The onlookers were obviously wondering what was happening.

I witnessed people expending their energy and soiling their hands with the dirt of the land. Four hours later, the latrines were cleaned and painted, the Community Hall was painted, and the huge rubbish dump was transformed into a park with plants and a fence around it. We had found an effective way of communicating with God. We had performed a miracle and had won! It was the most powerful prayer.

Mali Balm

> *Everyone was digging with precision and excitement, laughter and determination.*

The Altar Guild

The women in Caño Negro are strong women. Members of the Altar Guild, when they are out cleaning the front lawn of the church with their machetes, smoke their cigarettes with the lit side in their mouths so the rain from the jungle will not put them out. They can carry fifty to sixty kilograms of cacao (the beans from which chocolate is made) through the forest to their homes. When you dance with one of these women and you hold her with your hand on her back, you reach past two inches of muscle before you touch her spine. These are really strong women.

In about 1981, a cluster of new *viviendas* (houses for people "to live in") was being put up by government agencies with the guidance of a board of directors in the village. Juan Pablo and Domingo were two of the ancient traditional people in the village who ran things. Just as the new public construction was getting underway, they had allowed a private house to go up at the end of the road where the public *viviendas* were being built. This was against the law. Immediately the public construction was shut down out of concern about material being siphoned from a public job to a private owner.

All the new *viviendas* were intended for women who were raising families. When construction was stopped, there was a little revolution. The women gathered in front of Juan Pablo's and Domingo's houses. They did not ask, they told Juan Pablo and Domingo that they had to solve the problem.

Juan Pablo threw up his hands and walked away, saying, "I am not responsible," although everybody knew he was.

Domingo, however, said, "I am responsible and I will take care of it." And he did. Two days later the private house was buttoned up and its construction shut down.

The women, gentle souls, 50% of whom were members of the Altar Guild, got their manifest will into history.

Rod Worden

When construction was stopped, there was a little revolution.

The Company Store

Widen, West Virginia was a coal mining town in one of America's richest mining districts. Mining is a foundational industry like agriculture and fishing, only maybe older. It is important to civilization. Some call the smell of burning slack heaps pollution, but it is filled with nostalgia for any who grew up in West Virginia. It was a deep experience to attend a community consultation in my home state.

Widen was isolated and the coal company saw to it that it stayed isolated. The company brought in everything people needed: a fine gymnasium, a beautiful lodge in the forest, even popular entertainers. Roy Rogers had come once and ridden Trigger through town and into the gym. People said that many good things had been done in Widen to keep the residents satisfied and happy.

In Widen, you could get everything from a wedding gown to a casket at the company store. You could go to the company store to buy groceries and automobiles and gasoline, so there was no need to leave the valley. We heard that many cars were bought and driven in and around Widen until they wore out. They never had state license tags because they were never driven on state roads. People spent their money there and were always in debt to the company store.

Rather than expanding people's consciousness, people were being compressed and made smaller. The owners of the coal company had kept the people contented, like the kept rabbits in *Watership Down*.

People resist being domesticated however, and violent labor strife broke out in the 1950s. A new company took over in 1959, but in 1963, the mines were closed and the community stagnated. The coal company sold the houses to the people, but retained the land and limited what owners could do, since their houses sat on company land. People were a mixture of free mountaineers and vassals.

Still, for years, the men all talked about going back into the mines. To be a man, you had to be a miner. The local people told us the children blackened their faces with soot to look like miners when they played.

On the opening day of the planning consultation, in the early summer, 1978, people showed us around town. On Monday, they were slow to come to the work sessions. One fellow wanted to come and find out what was going on but stayed away because of peer pressure, maybe just imagined. There is a strong old image in that part of the country to be self-reliant and independent. It was a good image for mountaineers, pioneering the wilderness in the 18th century, but not very helpful for a dying community in the 20th century. What this fellow did was to send his wife for the first three days. By Thursday, he came along as well. He said he had decided to come, "to bring her."

Richard D. Whanger

Widen, West Virginia wall mural

A Meeting In Worcester

I attended a meeting in Worcester, Massachusetts one evening. There was a fellow at that meeting who came off and on. I forget what we were talking about, but all of a sudden, he said, "I'm sitting here thinking about an evening in the forest before the Battle of the Bulge in World War II. I remember that our outfit was asked, that evening, to volunteer for a special mission. All my buddies went, but I stayed behind. I never saw one of them alive again. Ever since then, I have regretted that I did not go. Perhaps, that's why I can't stay away from these meetings. I'm still hoping I can make that decision."

Ronald Clutz

At The Center Tranquil

Tune: Shenandoah

Universe, illumination, all unknown, absurd assurance.
Everywhere is found life's meaning, and I,
    I am the way, at the center, tranquil.

There's no hope, yet all is hopeful, then no cares, there are no problems.
No enemies, no earthly foes, and I,
    I am the struggle, at the center, tranquil.

Pulsing exhilaration, everything's become a blessing.
Embraced by joy, a dance of rapture, and I,
    I am the stillness, at the center tranquil.

Gloriously, condemned to die: life is new, a great resurgence.
Community, with all the faithful, and I,
    I am forever, at the center, tranquil.

> "I'm sitting here thinking about an evening in the forest before the Battle of the Bulge in World War II."

Bald-Headed Tom Sawyer

Soon, I had a plastic bag filled with paper…

In the northern-most part of Sumatra, Indonesia, there is an isolated village called Bubun. A thirty-mile boat ride downstream in a little chug-chug river boat was required to reach Bubun at the mouth of a river northwest of Medan.

The staff and villagers involved in the Human Development Project in Bubun were working hard to increase the families' incomes in spite of their remote location. A villager had been sent to the Kelapa Dua ("two coconuts") Human Development Project on Java to learn about that village's duck project. Project staff had also arranged a two-year bank loan so that local fishermen could buy small motors for the boats. We heard that the bank had not expected to see its money again, but, because of their increased profit, the fishermen had repaid the loans in less than one year.

I arrived for a brief stay in Bubun by river boat one night. After breakfast the next morning, when assignments were made for practical support, I volunteered to pick up the trash around the house. The Bubun house was at the center of the village, next to the main public dock. It was on a corner where the two main village footpaths crossed. About a dozen skinny, barefoot children, ages five to eight and dressed in shorts or shirt dresses, were playing in front of an open-air stand that served as the village's general store just opposite the house. The old woman sitting behind the counter was very stern when I first walked by.

Because their village was so remote, the kids in Bubun had never seen a bald-headed white man before. Several of them started to point and one giggling little girl came right up to me and pointed at my head. I have always had a little bit of fuzz on the top of my head that you cannot see, so I bent down and rubbed her hand on my head. This set them all off and they all wanted to rub my head. The old woman in the store was watching the whole proceeding intently.

I picked up some candy wrappers that were scattered on the ground, held up ten fingers, and motioned for the children to start picking them up. It was quite obvious who had thrown the candy wrappers on the ground and they got the point. Soon, I had a plastic bag filled with paper along with a very sticky, dirty head.

As the children laughed and the candy wrappers disappeared, a wide and wonderful toothless grin spread across the old woman's face. It was the funniest thing I had ever seen.

David Rebstock

A New Day Dawning

During the summer of 1976, we made the decision that one of the twenty-four Global Social Demonstration Projects would be a Native American project. I remember being called into Joe's cubicle early that summer to discuss the task of finding the project. We wanted something "west of the Mississippi," which covered a lot of territory. The Blackfeet in Montana had been ruled out because of my long history with them, but Joe wanted me to visit likely reservations and do an initial site selection. We were looking for several things:

1. obvious poverty and lack of services
2. accessibility to an airport and infrastructure
3. high symbolic power related to a name or historical impact
4. a place that looked absolutely impossible

I gathered my maps of reservations: there are twenty-five in the western states of Montana, North and South Dakota, Utah, Washington, and Idaho. We charted a route that would take me from Billings, Montana, through each of these states. I began my journey in August, traveling by car and sleeping where I could. Sometimes a colleague rode with me and sometimes I traveled alone. I picked up my son, Jim Ed, from the Denver office and we traveled through New Mexico, Arizona, and Utah together. We tried to time our arrival at a reservation for early morning in order to visit as many villages as we could in one day. Usually we knew by dark if we needed to continue our search, or if we were ready to travel on, usually by night, to the next reservation. We began to get more and more excited as we spotted likely places in New Mexico and Arizona.

We found several more likely prospects as we drove through Utah, Nevada, Washington and Idaho. Back in Montana we worked out of the Billings office to explore Montana and the Dakotas. We intended to narrow the choice down to six or seven villages which Joe would then visit with us when he joined us to make the final selection.

Toward the end of September we got a call from the Rapid City office, asking us if we had been to the Standing Rock Sioux Reservation in North Dakota, in and around Fort Yates. They had just held a Town Meeting in Fort Yates and said we should come over and look at a place called Cannon Ball, North Dakota. According to them it met our criteria for a project. We agreed to come over and look, but Joe was already on his way to Montana for site visits.

Joe, Charles, Bob, and I left the Billings office before dawn one cold fall morning. We drove through the Crow Reservation, then the Northern Cheyenne, then north to the Rody Boy Reservation in central Montana, then to the Ft. Belknap Reservation among the Arapahoes. We entered this reservation on a gravel road and traveled up and over a mountain pass. My old '66 Dodge was dragging bottom most of the time. Though we had seen several likely sites by now, we still had not had the "aha!" that signaled our intuitive recognition of the right village for a future project. We decided to go to North Dakota and look over the

It was called Inyan Wa Ka Gapi, "Place of the Sacred Writing."

Standing Rock Sioux Reservation south of Bismarck. At this point, with the intended planning consultation date of December 15 just ahead, time had become a high priority and we decided to fly. We drove to the Great Falls airport, arriving as night fell. We parked the old Dodge and Charles ran for tickets. We scrambled along with our bags and barely made the last plane for Bismarck. We landed in Bismarck about 9 P.M., rented a car and headed south to the reservation. We were in luck as it was a moonlit night. With the help of a map light and flashlight, we spotted five or six villages besides Cannon Ball and decided to visit them first.

Cannon Ball office, ca. 1977

Wakpala, south of Fort Yates, looked very promising as did Little Eagle. Fort Yates itself was too large and too close to the Government Agency. Two other villages were more cowboy towns than Indian villages, so we pressed on. All this was done by moonlight. Usually we turned our lights out and cruised around the village as quietly as we could, stopping in out-of-the-way places to assess what the place was like.

Finally, long after midnight, we cruised quietly into Cannon Ball. There were only seven or eight streets, so we completed our grid of the village layout really quickly. As we looked at dilapidated housing, junk cars, stray dogs, and a rundown school, we began to get excited. Broken glass and empty liquor bottles were everywhere. A large gymnasium and community center were trashed and abandoned. There were two small churches and a small government health clinic. A tiny post office sat next to an old auto garage, which appeared to be the only place of business. We estimated a population of six hundred. We pulled up to the top of a hill on the south edge of the village where there was a water storage tank. We parked there for a long time, talking into the small hours of the next morning about what we had seen. As we organized our thoughts in the moonlit darkness, we had our corporate "Aha!" Cannon Ball, North Dakota, was the village we had been seeking! As soon as we had reached this decision, we turned on our lights and hightailed it out of town.

We dragged into Bismarck before dawn. Charles, Bob and I were completely pooped, dirty and hungry, but wanted to go to a motel to bathe and crash before breakfast. Joe called us a "bunch of sissies" and said to let him off at an all-night diner. We stopped for breakfast. Joe took his big brief case, set up office in a corner booth, and went to work. The rest of us ate, and leaving Joe behind, went to rent a room in the old Bismarck Hotel, where we slept as best we could for a few hours. It was still early morning when we pulled ourselves together, picked Joe up at the diner, and headed for the airport.

I sent the others off while I stayed on the reservation with the rented car for two more days of visiting and getting the lay of the land. My headquarters, the

Bismarck Hotel, was a glorified flop house, and I was happy to be on the road. I visited the Tribal Offices, the clergy on the reservation, and the leaders of the recent Town Meeting in Fort Yates, gathering as much information as I could. With every visit, I was becoming more and more excited.

It was late September. The December 15 planning consultation date loomed closer and winter was coming. I turned in the rented car, flew back to Great Falls to collect my clothes from the Billings office, and immediately returned to Bismarck. For the next two and a half months, operating out of my Bismarck Hotel "headquarters," we secured financial backing and located donated resources, lined up sponsorships, and put together the framework of support and local authorization we needed to launch the project.

We also learned Cannon Ball's ancient name. Modern Cannon Ball takes its name from Cannonball Creek, which flows into the reservation near the town. This little tributary of the Missouri River rolls and smooths limestone rocks into round balls about the size of a cannon ball, thus the name. As the time for the consultation grew near, Thomas, the village elder, took me to see some markings on a low mesa about a mile and a half from town. The lines and hatch marks and dots I saw were on a flat rock about three feet long and a foot wide and looked to me like tracks from a small, three-toed dinosaur millions of years ago. They seemed strange and not of this world. Native peoples had seen this also and believed them to be writings from the Great Spirit, though no one understood the message. Thomas said that it had been a place of prayer for the people since ancient times. Over the years native people had smeared the writings with red ceremonial paint and there were beads and tobacco offerings around the area. It was called Inyan Wa Ka Gapi, "Place of the Sacred Writing." It became clear to all that the project should be called the Inyan Wakagapi Human Development Project.

Fall gave way to an early, cold winter. The elements were daring us to proceed. Everybody believed it would be impossible to launch the project any time soon in such harsh winter conditions, so we did it anyway. By God's grace and with the faithful support of colleagues, we held the consultation and launched the new project, in spite of blizzard conditions and -40°F temperatures. Thomas summed up the spirit that was released under such improbable circumstances when he said, "All these years my people have been suffering in the darkness, now we see a new day is dawning at the end of this tunnel. A new day of hope has come to my people."

Many and great were the events which filled those wonderful years of expenditure and servanthood, but none will ever surpass finding Cannon Ball, North Dakota and participating in its recreation.

James Bell

The elements were daring us to proceed.

Oklahoma 100

Keeping circuit teams on the road was no mean feat.

It has been more than twenty-two years since the amazing events that occurred as part of the Bicentennial in the USA and it seems like time to tell one of the stories. I was in the ICA's Chicago office, when we got word that Bill and Marianna in Oklahoma City had developed a proposal to conduct one hundred town meetings on the same day in the state of Oklahoma. They had arranged for Governor David Boren to proclaim a certain day "Oklahoma Town Meeting Day." We noticed the news, mentally wished them luck, and kept on with what we were doing.

But about six weeks prior to the announced date, news coming in from the field began to get interesting. The Delta Pace, Mississippi planning consultation was scheduled for a week just before Town Meeting Day, and the leadership had assigned everyone in the area to Mississippi to help set things up. This was no problem for the Oklahoma folks, who simply developed a more rational phasing plan to show the governor and then prepared to head for Mississippi.

When Joe heard of the change of plans, he hit the roof. "We do what we say we will do!" was the mildest of his comments during the 5 A.M. session in his cubicle. "And we will do it if we have to send everyone in Chicago to make sure it happens." I was scheduled to lead the staff planning meeting that morning and I remember beginning it with the song "Oklahoma!" from the musical. The opening comment was, "Before noon today, ten people now in this room will be on a plane to Oklahoma." That woke everyone up.

It actually turned out that a large number of people in the room had substantial roots in Oklahoma, so finding people willing to go was no problem. After this meeting, Oklahoma 100 became a major theme for the Chicago office, and a very large state map was positioned on the wall visible to everyone coming in the front door. It soon became obvious, however, that simply sending people to set up Town Meetings was a necessary but not a sufficient strategy to make sure one hundred actually happened. I was sent to Oklahoma to see if we could work out a system that would ensure success.

After discussions with Bill and Marianna in Oklahoma City, we mapped out travel circuits and teams, put a team on inkind to handle transportation and food, and got down to the business of setting up Town Meetings. Bill and Marianna took the most difficult places and at least one town held three town meetings to decide whether or not to conduct a Town Meeting. It was that sort of experience.

In a couple of days, Bill and Marianna had to head for Mississippi and the Delta Pace consultation, while the rest of us kept on with the Town Meeting set up. I remember having about six circuit teams operating in various parts of the state. One team, exercising the "quick win" strategy, went for schools, figuring that if we could get one hundred schools to conduct Town Meetings, the job would be done. The rest headed for the turf, looking up graduates of ICA training courses, family members, school friends, mayors, ministers or anyone else we could imagine who might have an interest in supporting a local Town Meeting.

Once the system got set up, I returned to Chicago, thinking the job was done and only the harvesting needed attention. That was not the case and about a week later I was back in the Oklahoma City office, this time for the duration. Keeping circuit teams on the road was no mean feat. Colleagues around the state were the most helpful, providing transportation, advice, and whenever possible, people to call with the teams. There was a limit, however, and the big day was rapidly approaching. I vividly remember having to camp out in the Oklahoma City office, because it was so full of Chicago people on Town Meeting set-up and development/inkind teams. I spent the duration working with very little sleep.

Strategizing about circuit logistics was complicated by the need to think about practical arrangements for the great day itself. Where were the facilitators for one hundred Town Meetings coming from? The area could provide some, but not nearly enough. So we began calling colleagues all over the USA. We got positive responses everywhere. Clearly, something extraordinary was afoot and people wanted to be part of the action. People agreed to drive in from Los Angeles, from Chicago, from Albany, New York, and from almost anywhere you could imagine. We tried to ensure that every vehicle was fully occupied and we worked like travel agents to arrange pickup times and places. We worked on accommodations, briefings, materials and all the other logistical nightmares that went into those early Town Meetings.

All the furor was taking its toll on the staff and volunteers. One evening, the directors of the Oklahoma City office and I had a discussion about whether or not to have our regular Thursday evening study session. I was passionately opposed, since we had loads of urgent work to do; they were as passionately for it, since we all needed the energy a change of pace would provide. I do not recall how the disagreement turned out, but I do recall a couple of hours of increasing volume from the basement where this "private" meeting was held.

The circuits went on, sometimes with humorous results. We tried hard, with varying degrees of success, to keep things coordinated. One circuit team, on its way out of town after trying to set up a Town Meeting in Boise City, the farthest point in the state out in the western panhandle, met another circuit team coming into town. They had coffee together at the local McDonald's, our main food supplier, then continued on the road.

I was making daily reports to Chicago, where Joe was closely monitoring the results. We were asked several times, "Have you considered geographic coverage?" We later spoke of "golding" the counties, but at this point, systematically reaching every county and coloring the completed counties gold on a large wall map had not yet become our modus operandi. In our phone calls with the Chicago office, our

"Why don't you go for one Town Meeting in each county?"

> *Our cheering and singing and celebration must have rivaled Paris after the French soccer team's World Cup victory.*

colleague Betty insisted that Joe wanted us to think about touching all the counties. "Yes," we said, "coverage is being attended to by having circuits assigned to different parts of the state. No, we haven't considered counties as a particularly useful screen; we're looking more for the right size places, and most of all for people who can and will say 'Yes.'" Next day, we were asked the same question, "Have you thought about geographic coverage? Why don't you go for one Town Meeting in each county?" I think it took about five days to get through my exceedingly single-minded density that this campaign was about more than numbers. We finally began to consider covering all of the counties, but even so, that was not the main focus of our effort.

Throughout the month, I was trying to keep the efforts coordinated and to ensure that nothing crucial was being forgotten in the frenzy. All my military training came back into play, and I remember dreaming about maneuvers and military campaigns during rare moments of sleep. As the Town Meeting Day approached, we had briefings ready, assignments made, materials prepared, and everything ready as people poured in from all over the nation. On the day itself, everyone who could walk went somewhere in Oklahoma to conduct a meeting.

We gathered afterwards for a systematic debriefing. The Oklahoma City office was bulging at the seams. Everyone wondered if we had held all one hundred Town Meetings. Reports poured in and a big chart was constructed to track the results and tabulate the victories. There was a surge that quickly brought the total into the nineties, but then reports slowed to a trickle. A couple more teams were still out, but several events had been canceled at the last moment, and no one knew the total for sure. Then we got to ninety-nine. There was a long pause. Finally, one of the men looked up and said, "Oh. I haven't reported yet." His report brought the tally to one hundred.

Our cheering and singing and celebration must have rivaled Paris after the French soccer team's World Cup victory. We were hysterical. It was done.

The Chicago office invited me to report on our victory after Oklahoma 100 was completed. All I remember after chronicling how we did it, was to say that we ought never to do it again.

Predicting the future has never been my long suit. Within the year, virtually every region was launching a one hundred this or a one hundred that campaign, and the magic worked. We gave Town Meetings to every county in the USA as our Bicentennial gift to the nation. Oklahoma had been the forerunner of many adventures to come.

John Epps

Chapter Three

Out Over The Edge

We were imprisoned by not knowing,
held hostage by fear of meeting face to face,
then came at last to break our bonds
with a desperate longing to find the truth
and courage to embrace it.

Charged souls so long apart
must feel somewhere deep within,
so great a need to be united,
they will do foolish things
to find each other's electric arms.

Who Would Have Guessed

In the early 1960s, I was a mother with small children, and I was eager for them to have the best chance in life. I shared that concern with others in my neighborhood, and we decided to do something about it. We heard that there was an idea to organize some kind of day care in our neighborhood, and we were invited to be a part of it.

Ruth Carter and Fifth City Preschoolers

I had never done planning and I was surprised when I was asked to be on the organizing team. It was a big job. We interviewed many of our neighbors, asking if they were interested in having a day care. Many people said yes, and we signed their kids up. We asked several of the parents to help us.

We worked with the staff of the Ecumenical Institute to develop the curriculum. We knew that our kids were smart and that with help, we could be teachers. In those days, there were no books to tell us how to set up a school for infants and toddlers. This was all before Headstart and there were not even guidelines for care for three and four year olds. We wanted to care for all the children, so we created our own road map.

We had curriculum planning sessions, we wrote songs, we designed a playground, we asked for donations, and we decided to have uniforms. We were creating all of this from scratch! It was great to have community people and volunteers from outside the neighborhood working together to do all this.

We did amazing things with those kids! We gave them lots of love and attention. We read to them, sang with them, did role plays, and finger painted with chocolate pudding. We took them on field trips. One day we went to O'Hare Airport and toured a plane!

One of our favorite songs was about our own neighborhood and the world:

I love Fifth City,
I love the planet Earth,
I love this day in time,
I love the universe,
I'm always ready, to see this world of ours,
I tell you man, I like it here, I tell you man, I like it here.
(Boom Di Yada, Boom Di Yada, Boom Di Yada, Boom Di Yada)

After all this hard work and fun focused on our own kids, you can imagine how surprised we were when we were asked to come to New York City to give our advice to a group that was planning a new television show. We went and had a wonderful time telling those folks what we had done with small kids and how we had done it. Their show became "Sesame Street."

Sesame Street has just celebrated twenty-five years and our preschool is about to be thirty-five years old. The kids still keep us young and eager to learn.

Ruth Carter

A Rock Through The Window

After the death of Martin Luther King in 1968, many African Americans rioted in neighborhoods across the United States, including the West Side of Chicago, where the Ecumenical Institute staff lived and worked. As it happened that week, we had a full schedule of courses on the West Side campus and we had to decide whether or not to hold them. We decided to go ahead. As we began the evening, we could see the fires moving in our direction. I was teaching the course called Cultural Studies One (CSI) in Room E. Just as I got into the first few minutes of my science lecture, a rock came through the window. That was the shortest CSI lecture ever delivered in the history of the Institute. I think I finished the entire forty-five minute lecture in fifteen minutes flat.

I went over to the room where Joe, Frank and Harrison were sitting as the control committee to decide what to do in case we were hit. Betsy and several other people with walkie talkies had been stationed on the roof to watch the approaching fires as they came closer and closer. For some reason, I decided to go out to see what was happening and headed in the direction of the stairs. Just as I arrived at the stairwell, the doors burst open and a man came in with a big pistol which he stuck in my nose. It looked to me as though it was about twelve feet long.

He said, "We are going to burn this ?#@$&!! building down. You better get your #@$&! out of here! I walked calmly back to the control committee and said, "They're here!"

Joe turned to Harrison, an ex-football player and an member of our staff, and said, "Go talk to them."

For a moment, Harrison sat paralyzed at the table. Frank made a beeline for the telephone and called the Mayor's office. We had recently visited Mayor Daley and made a presentation on the work we had been doing in the Fifth City Development Program. The Mayor's right-hand man had given us a phone number and said, "Any time you need any help, just give me a call." So we gave him a call!

Within minutes we knew that something had happened, for just as we finished evacuating the building and moving into Bethany Hospital next door, we heard shotguns going off. That was the way the police announced their arrival on the scene. At the sound of the shotguns, the rioters left.

I was sent to make sure that all the staff families were out of the faculty apartments. I discovered that the rioters had set little fires in many of the rooms. As we searched the apartments, Tony calmly followed behind me with a fire extinguisher, putting out the fires.

Frank's quick action with the Mayor's Office, and Tony's with the fire extinguisher, saved us from being burned down and saved our teaching notes as well!

George West

> That was the shortest CSI lecture ever delivered in the history of the Institute.

He almost had to knock the door down to wake me up…

The Flames Leapt Up

My husband was out of town and the West Side was burning after Martin Luther King's assassination. I awoke about twelve midnight that night, looked out the window of our apartment, and saw the fires burning over on 5th Avenue. There were huge fires with flames leaping up. I was so naive that I did not realize what was going on. I went back to bed and went to sleep. The next thing I knew, a colleague was knocking on my door. He almost had to knock the door down to wake me up and to get the kids out of there.

The first thing I did was hand over our daughter, Teresa, who was a babe-in-arms. Bob ran down the hall with her, and our grade school aged children, David, Wayne and Kathy, ran after him. Then I saw a man trying to take over the building. He was shoving David out with a bayonet in his back. I rescued David and we made it over to Bethany Hospital where we felt a little bit safer.

Ruth Archibald

Learning To Read

I have lived in Texas for seventy years and have often driven back to West Virginia through Mississippi. Each time my wife got depressed just looking at all the shacks along the way. They call them "shotgun houses" because you can shoot a shotgun through them without hitting anything. My wife wanted to just get through the area in a hurry. But I'm here to tell you some wonderful people come from those houses. One evening we attended a neighborhood meeting in the home of a family in Delta Pace, Mississippi. The view was quite different from the inside.

It was interesting to see people using the same methods being used by people in the Kawangware project in Kenya or the Sudtonggan project in the Philippines. They, too, were picking up responsibility for doing things needed in their town.

Right in the middle of the meeting, someone came to the door and there was a lot of greeting going on. It was the parents of some of the people at the meeting. It was about nine o'clock in the evening and they were returning from an adult education program run by the project where people were learning to read and write. They were at least seventy years old and were excited to learn to read and write. I cannot imagine what it would be like to be seventy years old in America and just learning to read and write.

Richard D. Whanger

Awesome Encounter

Mt. Kilimanjaro is a wonder. It is the tallest solitary mountain in the world rising from a plain at three thousand feet to a height of nearly twenty thousand feet. It stands more than a full kilometer above the highest of the Alps. A mere two hundred miles south of the equator, snow glistens on its peak year round. It was impossible to keep my eyes off Mt. Kilimanjaro when I saw it for the first time on a clear morning in early 1987. I fell under its hypnotic power and decided that I wanted to see the view from the top. That's when I began mentioning to people that I planned to spend my fortieth birthday amidst the famous snows of Kilimanjaro.

Pamela, my wife, and a close friend, Sandra, both decided to join the expedition. Sandy said she was looking for a once-in-a-lifetime adventure to mark her entry into the last decade of the twentieth century.

On the 17th of February, 1990, the three of us came from different directions and descended upon the small town of Moshi, just south of the Kenyan border in Tanzania. Pamela came directly from Arusha, where she was a delegate at a UN conference on the role of "popular participation" in the development of Africa. Sandy flew in from Nairobi, immediately following her orientation in New York to her new position as the Nairobi-based regional training director for CARE. I arrived from Zimbabwe, where I was meeting with Swedish administrators to discuss the future of our co-op development project in Kenya, Tanzania, and Zambia. In part, our desire to climb Kilimanjaro came about because of schedules like these.

Two omens appeared on my way to Moshi. First, when I went through the immigration and customs formalities in Dar-es-Salaam, I discoverd that I had left my Cardinals baseball cap on the plane. It was gone when I returned to look for it. I had worn it on successful climbs of Mt. Kenya and Mt. Yubari and hated to lose my favorite good-luck charm. I tried to persuade myself that this was no big tragedy, but I asked an airline official anyway and to my shock, the Air Tanzania steward found the cap and returned it to me. Second, on departing the Moshi airport, both Kilimanjaro and Mt. Meru, a sister mountain near Arusha, were perfectly visible on the way to the hotel. Though I had traveled the same road many times, I had never before seen either mountain from that splendid vantage point. Both signs seemed a good portent for the climb to come—or at least I thought so.

At the hotel, I found that Pam and Sandy had met a French journalist from *L'Express* in Paris and had invited him and his seventeen year old daughter to join our little expedition up the mountain. It was his second time to try. We planned to follow the Marangu route to the top. It called for us to spend five days and four nights on the mountain. We were all glad to be climbing in the middle of Kilimanjaro's driest season of the year. Each night would be spent in a "hut." Originally, a hut was merely a set of sheltered bunks in a small frame building. Such simple

Both signs seemed a good portent for the climb to come—or at least I thought so.

huts remain on Mt. Kenya, but Mt. Kilimanjaro is now quite developed in order to attract more tourists and the huts are really small camps that can accommodate large numbers of people. The Marangu route was outlined in the guide book.

Bright and early on February 18th, we started our climb. Because we arrived early at the gate to the national park, we were able to avoid a long delay in registering and made Mandara by early afternoon. We passed through thick dark trees draped in moss and crossed pure, gurgling streams. Surprisingly, there was no bamboo on Kilimanjaro, nor did we see any "tusker plops," the telltale signs of elephants, both of which we had seen in abundance on Mt. Kenya. We did see many monkeys and birds. Many of the birds had gorgeous fluorescent feathers, usually in various shades of blue. I was especially taken with one black bird that exposed brilliant red tips on its wings when it flew. Africa, like most places, was full of shocking, unexpected beauty which I had seldom noticed for want of taking time to see what was around me.

We maintained this slow, observant pace during our whole stay at Mandara and it helped reinforce our feeling of harmony with the environment. As the sun slid silently below the clear horizon, one of our fellow climbers, a middle-aged man from Japan, quietly serenaded us on his bamboo flute. It was a moment that made us glad to be in this particular place at this particular time.

The next morning we took a little detour in order to see the peaks from Maundi crater. The mountain has two peaks. The sharp, lower one is known as Mawenzi. At seventeen thousand feet, it is as tall as the peaks of Mt. Kenya. Five miles west northwest of Mawenzi, across a barren desert at fifteen thousand feet known as the saddle, is Kibo, the flat-topped, snow-covered volcanic peak that is most often erroneously thought of as Kilimanjaro. Mawenzi could be seen, but clouds prevented us from seeing anything beyond it except for the lower snow fields on Kibo. The view, however, promised memorable scenes to come.

Soon we were in alpine meadows above tree line. The higher we climbed, the more pronounced the distant hills became. Clouds prevented us from seeing much of the peaks above, but the air below was clear as we looked back. One of the pleasures of mountain climbing is looking down on hills and cliffs that required an upward gaze only hours before.

About three hours into our climb through the heath, the air changed and clouds quickly rolled down upon us. As they approached, I remember thinking to myself that those clouds were probably going to bring rain. We were not worried; like all good scouts, we were prepared with ponchos!

The Marangu Route

Day One: park gate (6,000 feet) to Mandara Hut (9,000 feet)—four hours' walk through a heavy rain forest

Day Two: Mandara (9,000 feet) to Horombo Hut (12,000 feet)—five hours' walk past the tree line and into an abundant heath

Day Three: Horombo Hut (12,000 feet) to Kibo Hut (15,000 feet)—five hours' climb through thinning heath, moor and a high altitude desert without vegetation

Day Four: Kibo Hut (15,000 feet) to the top of Kilimanjaro (19,500 feet), then return past Kibo Hut to Horombo Hut (12,000 feet)—six hours' climb on a moonscape of boulders and scree up to the summit; two hours' walk down the peak; four hours' hike back to Horombo Hut

Day Five: Horombo Hut to the park gate and the hotel—six hours' return through the rain forest

But did it ever rain! It poured. Then it hailed. The trail turned white with quarter-inch hail and became a rushing torrent on the steeper grades. Then we made a new discovery. The gentle, shallow streams that we had been crossing easily in the sunshine had became roaring, violent rivers in the rain. I had carefully greased my boots with waterproof oil before starting the climb. This was to no avail, of course, when fording rushing water two and three feet deep. We feared being swept off our feet as we crossed each of these fast streams. We did not falter, though, as we sloshed along.

After an hour and a half or so, the heavy rain and hail diminished to a light drizzle. By now we were feeling quite proud of ourselves. We had learned through firsthand experience that the mountain could become cruel at an instant's notice and felt that we had responded rather well as we fought through some of its adversity. We were not far from the destination of the day, Horombo Hut. Tired as we were, we had almost made it. We knew that after a few more miles, we would be drinking hot tea. But just at that moment we were cold and walked with our arms under our ponchos in an attempt to keep warm.

Then disaster struck. Sandy tripped on a small rock and fell face first onto a sharp boulder without breaking her fall. Blood was all over her face when I reached her. Pam had a cloth out and was pressing the wound above Sandy's eyes to stop the bleeding. Pam kept mouthing the words, "it's deep," and the bleeding showed no sign of stopping anytime soon. We were all a little scared because we had no idea how bad the damage actually was. A group of Austrian climbers eventually came up the trail and helped us bandage the wound, once the bleeding finally did begin to slow. They shared some hot tea with Sandy. Their guide said he would continue on to Horombo Hut and send back a rescue team. Having offered what help they could, the Austrians left us to wait on the trail.

By now, the cold was really becoming a problem. Sandy is prone to low blood pressure and she feared that this would become a complicating factor when combined with the cold. We quickly realized that waiting for assistance in the cold and damp was a losing strategy. We decided to walk on to Horombo. This turned out to be a wise move in spite of our slow pace. We had nearly reached the huts when the rescue team finally appeared. It consisted of three men, two of whom were carrying Pam's and Sandy's bags balanced on their heads in the traditional African manner. Since no stretcher was in sight and the third man had no baggage, Pam suggested that if circumstances required that Sandy had to be carried down the mountain, perhaps it was his intention to balance her on his head.

At Horombo Hut, we were lucky. One of the climbers there had a large supply of top notch first aid supplies and he redressed the wound. He told us that it was indeed a very deep cut, but that it was also clean. Though Pam and Sandy considered continuing up the mountain, we decided that the two of them would turn back in the morning in order to visit a proper

Then disaster struck.

> They ceremoniously gave me the remains of the Oreo package…

clinic. They held me to the agreement we had made before we left the base of the mountain: if anyone had to turn back, the other should not be deterred. I would continue up the mountain on my own.

I did not sleep well that night. Besides Pam's and Sandy's departure, I was worried about the rest of my journey. I had only one extra pair of jeans and hated to risk getting them wet by wearing them on the following day. I decided that if my jeans were only mildly damp the next morning, I would wear them and preserve the dry ones. I fell asleep eventually and spent the night dreaming about reunions. I was at a family reunion where both sides of the family mingled with each other and then I was at a high school reunion (class of '68) where it was a surprise to see so many people I had not seen in years. The dreams were somehow anticipating my fortieth birthday.

The next morning, the damp clothes gave me shivers for the first few minutes until they dried out. Meanwhile, I was being handed a package of Oreo cookies. When first planning the climb, Pam and Sandy thought it would be just the thing to take some Oreos which they had been saving from a trip to the US. We would eat them at the top of Mt. Kilimanjaro. Now their plans were frustrated. They ceremoniously gave me the remains of the Oreo package and I was commissioned to take a picture with them at the top. Pam and Sandy bid me farewell.

A chill drizzle began just a half hour after my departure from Horombo and continued throughout the day. After a couple of hours in the scraggy heath and boggy moor, I came upon the high desert plain between the two peaks. It was disappointing to know that I was in the midst of spectacular scenery which I could not see. The drizzle limited visibility to about 50 yards. The thin air at 15,000 feet and the long hike in the rain were also taking their toll. My fingers and toes were all numb and I breathed laboriously on even the smallest of inclines. By the time I reached the hut at the base of Kibo's snowcapped peak, five hours after leaving Horombo, I was exhausted and freezing.

As soon as I arrived at Kibo Hut, people began relating stories from the previous night's climb. A group of Germans had gone to bed in fine condition but awoke with severe nausea and headaches caused by the high altitude and aborted their attempt on the peak. Three Australian women had turned back after climbing for five grueling hours when they were only half way to the peak. The plan called for us to eat dinner at 5:00 P.M. and then to go to sleep in anticipation of a 1:00 A.M. departure for the final assault on Kibo peak.

I was depressed as I lay in my sleeping bag, still cold, brooding on the challenge before me the next morning. The peak was nearly 4,500 feet above Kibo Hut in air so thin it was like breathing with one lung. Instead of sleep, I wallowed in dark, anxious thoughts. "If the Sears Tower is over 103 stories tall and each story accounts for nearly fifteen feet, then—My god! I'm going to have to climb the Sears Tower three times! On one lung! In the span of a single morning! Why had I not thought to consider the implications of these numbers before? I'll never make it. Instead of marking my fortieth birthday by conquering a formidable challenge, I'm going to enter the second half of my life with a humiliating defeat."

I was still wide awake when the knock on my door came at a quarter past midnight on February 21, 1990. Fifteen minutes into my fifth decade, I put on my damp jeans one more time and went to confront the beckoning silence of Kibo.

Fifteen of us from four different groups trudged up the steep, dark slopes with the help of our trusty electric "torches," the word left by the British to describe what I've always called a flashlight. A half hour later we passed a little stone monument with a cross marking the spot, our guide told us, where a Japanese man had died of a heart attack a few weeks earlier. We heard several references to other deaths on the mountain, but nowhere did we see any statistics on the matter. There might be as many as three or four a year, perhaps even more, from heart failure, strokes, falls, or foolishness. A couple of years ago, a man died while trying to ride a hang-glider down from the summit. Such statistics are probably bad for the tourist trade.

I cannot recall much about the climb to Hans Meyer's Cave, named for the first European who climbed the mountain in 1889, which serves as Kibo's half-way marker. I lost almost all sense of time. I once asked my father about forced marches in the army. He said that after a certain period of time it just became a matter of putting one foot in front of the other and emptying your mind of anything else. That pretty well describes the first half of the night: a constant rhythm of picking 'em up and putting 'em down. Three of my fellow climbers decided that they had had enough once they got to the cave and turned back. A little further on, a fourth climber also decided to call it a night and turned back.

The second half of the climb up the peak was far more memorable than the first because I could not keep a sustained pace. I began counting steps. Five hundred steps, I told myself, and I'll reward myself with a brief stop. That number quickly declined to three hundred, then two hundred fifty, then one hundred, and finally a mere fifty steps between rest stops. The effort had become a tortuous eternity. The one single thought I had beyond the minimum that it took to complete my fifty steps, was that I did not care how long it might take to reach the top, I was now without doubt going to make it. It was absolutely impermissible, at that point, to even consider that I might turn back.

I arrived at the summit at 6:45 A.M., just a few minutes after daybreak. A number of plaques were strewn on the ground to commemorate different occasions and to serve as memorials to a few of the people who had died in route. Nearly a mile below was a sea of clouds with only Mawenzi peak jutting into view. I had a feeling, shared by others, that I was

It was absolutely impermissible, at that point, to even consider that I might turn back.

> ...Kilimanjaro was a journey into realms where human pioneering is still a challenge.

in a strata usually reserved for airplanes. It was exhilarating and I readily confess that I was extremely pleased with myself. I hauled out Pam's and Sandy's Oreo cookies, held up four of them to indicate my birthday, and had the guide snap a photo for posterity. In spite of being out of focus, the snapshot successfully recorded the spirit of the moment, silly grin and all.

After five minutes on the peak, I began my journey down. This included an hour of "skiing" on the scree—jumping from side to side on loose volcanic cinders. This was followed by the long hike back to Horombo through drizzle and fog—the beautiful "sea of clouds" I had seen from above. By the time I crawled into my sleeping bag in the late afternoon, I felt like I had spent a pretty full day celebrating my fortieth. For the first time in three nights, sleep finally came easily. All together, I had been climbing or descending for over twelve hours.

The trip down the mountain was admittedly anticlimactic and many people like myself mistakenly underestimated its unique requirements. Pam, Sandy and I had missed this part of the trail on our way up because of our detour to Maundi crater. When I entered the forest, just before Mandara, I was convinced that I was just moments from my destination. But the track narrowed through a heavy dark forest and we were forced to scramble over and down a steep, gnarled tangle of exposed tree roots. The hour that it took to pass through this surprising purgatory seemed much longer. Later, Sandy said that this part of the descent was one of the most surrealistic experiences of her life. She and Pam had reached the clinic too late for her to receive stitches, and though her wound was healing nicely, she will carry a visible reminder of our rocky adventure for the rest of her life.

It's hard to maintain an illusion of pioneering realms where no human has gone before, when enterprising guides and porters have established a kiosk at fifteen thousand feet to sell beer and candy bars. But Kilimanjaro was a journey into realms where human pioneering is still a challenge. It was a reasoned pause from larger vocational commitments and tackling serious social contradictions. It did require vision and persistence, from the preparation to the last fifty steps on Kibo. It did involve risking the unexpected, but it was not a gamble on a frivolous, untested stunt. A hang-glider from Kibo never crossed my mind.

Terry Bergdall

Terror At 36,000 Feet

My participation hit the "what-the-hell-am-I-doing-here?" level in April, 1980, the day that a certain phone call came to my desk in the lab of an R&D department where I was working. Rick wanted me to go to New Delhi, India, to facilitate the course, Leadership Effectiveness in the New Society (LENS). I said, "Yes."

Why Rick asked me and why I agreed to go are both a mystery. Jack, my team partner, and I later agreed that I had little training or skill. I flew to Chicago the next Friday. On Saturday morning, when I went to breakfast before leaving for the airport, the conversation buzz was about the failed rescue attempt in Iran the night before. The helicopters that went into the desert crashed in a sandstorm, the mission was aborted—and the Iranian government was livid.

I mentally computed that the route to New Delhi would go near Iran and balked, "Holy Shinola, we can't do that!" Jack reassured me that we would go around Iran, so off we drove to O'Hare Airport. About 2 A.M. Sunday morning, in the blackness at thirty-six thousand feet, I found myself looking out the window of a Lufthansa airliner straight down into Teheran the second night after the abortive raid! I was seven miles straight up from the hostages who were making front page headlines. I offered a very sincere prayer that the plane would not have to make an emergency landing in Iran at that moment, and again asked the question, "What the hell am I doing in this ridiculous situation?"

We made it to Delhi without any problems, but for me, the LENS course was a disaster. I had laryngitis from the Indian dust, not a clue about how to process the data, and, furthermore, was terrified of Jack. Fortunately, Jack single-handedly carried off the workshop.

The most I can say is that I made it back home in one piece where I hid for about three years.

Darrell Walker

...the conversation buzz was about the failed rescue attempt in Iran the night before.

Midnight Danger

No sooner had I shaken this fantasy from my mind, than I saw a line of torches moving slowly across the field…

The second Human Development Project, which we started in the Panvel Taluka, was Paragur, a small Indian village of one thousand people. It was about one mile from the road where the bus dropped us off. In order to shorten the walk to a kilometer, we liked to walk across the rice fields, which were stone dry in February. During the daytime, the walk was delightful, tight roping across terraced mounds which separated the quarter acre plots owned by each of the farmers. At night, the walk could be perilous.

I have walked many times in the night in totally deserted rural places and heard the voices of shepherds or the bell of a wandering cow. A farmer may sleep in the field near his vegetables and chat with a neighbor late into the night. No matter how far I have been from "civilization," I have never felt far from other humans. Rural India at night is an awesome experience; it breeds humanity where strangers expect none.

One night, the bus dropped me off at the path to the village later than usual. It was a moonless night and keeping track of the path was difficult even though it was heavily rutted by bullock carts. The only direction I had, not knowing the stars, was a faint brightness above the city of Mumbai (in 1976, still called Bombay), some thirty miles away in the northwestern sky. I reckoned that Paragur was due north. It was too dark to risk taking a shortcut, so I followed the main bullock cart path until it veered east and then north again, for what seemed too long a time. Finally I decided to head straight for Paragur across the field and turned in the direction of the faint glow in the sky.

I walked boldly through the dark, following Carlos Castenada's admonition in the words of Don Juan: "Totally abandon yourself to the moment." I walked over several terraced hillsides and fell several times, first just a foot, then almost six feet, then three. Before long I was afraid to step forward and found myself crawling, only to end up in the bushes, scratching my face and arms. To make matters worse, I almost lost my glasses during each tumble. For many years my glasses had been my only friend and the only item I had never given up.

My sense of helplessness increased as the night grew colder. There was a dark chill in the air and I almost broke down several times, wanting to cry piteously into the night. If I cried out loud, some villager would have found me, but I feared the worst. Terrified by wails from the night in a strange language, I supposed the villagers might form a posse to identify an intruder. I saw myself huddled wretchedly near a bush, illuminated by torchlight, surrounded by uncomprehending villagers gaping at the strangest sight they had ever seen.

No sooner had I shaken this fantasy from my mind, than I saw a line of torches moving slowly across the field just a few hundred yards away. I was saved! It was a wedding party and they were singing. I jumped up and ran toward the receding lights, falling several times down the terraces. There was no point shouting because of the singing. If they had heard me, I would likely have frightened them away. I gave up again, exhausted.

By now I had no idea where Paragur was. It was cold and getting close to 3:30 A.M. In order to keep warm I had to keep moving, but I could not stray too far because I might be moving farther and farther from the village. I walked for over an hour in circles around the perimeter of a small plot, until the first hint of morning light. I eventually found a small hut and waited outside until the first sign of life. At 5 A.M., a bullock cart finally came by and the villager took me to Paragur, which was about a mile to the southwest. On the way we passed several open wells and deep water holes in the fields. I shuddered at the thought of what might have been my fate the previous night.

After a ten minute ride, we reached Paragur, and I went to the auxiliary house to awaken the project workers. Within an hour, a good cup of tea and the problems of the day ahead made me forget the dangers of the night before.

Bill Staples

You Stand On Your Head

We took the night bus to a village about half way between Mombasa and Nairobi in a part of Kenya the old British maps call "Shooting Area, No. 46." The area had been part of a game park. We got off the bus at about three or four o'clock in the morning and began our fifteen mile hike to the village.

We were walking down a little trail when all of a sudden my Kenyan colleague said, "Did you hear that?" "Hear what?" I asked. He was walking ahead of me and after a little while he stopped again and said, "Did you hear it that time? I think it is a leopard. Just be quiet for a minute."

We waited for a minute and he said: "Here's what you do if you see a leopard: you stand on your head. They always jump for your head. If your feet are in the air, they won't attack. You'll be safe if they can't see your head or your face." We laughed and went on to the village and fell into bed.

At sunrise, a villager came in, trying to wake up all the people who were staffing the project. He said he needed help to find his goats and livestock. They had been stalked and frightened away by a leopard. We went out with the distraught man who led us right to the spot where we had been frightened ourselves the night before.

David Coffman

"You'll be safe if they can't see your head or your face."

My Life Took a Turn

My life took a turn the day that I visited the ICA for the first time and went on a field visit to some families. I saw my colleague sit down on the ground with villagers and drink and eat with them, talking and laughing. It was only near the end of the visit that they asked about the loan repayment which was the reason for the visit. My work since then has been full of memorable experiences.

The person I always remember is Mr. Soliman. He was a member of the Loans Committee from Til Abo Marouz village. He was an ideal model for volunteerism and commitment. He was dedicated to his work in the CDA—the Community Development Association—but his financial situation was not so good and his wife was always complaining that he spent all his time with the CDA, gathering loan repayments instead of working to improve his family's level of income.

We trained animal caretakers to provide preventive health care to the animals, as there was only one veterinary clinic unit serving thirteen villages and settlements. But the situation was really looking bad in 1990. After the animal caretaker training, the doctor of the clinic unit was very upset and complained to the government Veterinary Department that we were taking away his work. He tried hard to stop the caretakers from providing these services to the community in spite of the fact that the services they provided were in support of his work and did not interfere with his role. The caretakers were allowed to continue to provide service to the community and were not stopped. Eventually, the doctor came to appreciate their work and even provided training for them.

We took some village women to a mall in Cairo. It was the first time for the women to use the electric stairs (escalators). I tried to help one woman who was afraid. The others were laughing and tried to encourage her to put her foot on the first step.

During the evaluation of a training event for the CDAs in Beni Suef, one of the CDA board chiefs said, "The things I learned from those [ICA] youth I never learned before in my sixty-seven years."

Azza Shafik

Women and girls at a water tap

The Unforgettable Egg

We set out from Langub, a village in the high mountains of the southern Philippines with plentiful rain and many water buffalo, bound for Kamweleni, a dry, low-land village in the middle of Kenya.

It took three days to fly to east Africa and four hours to drive from the Nairobi, Kenya airport, south and east through the Machakos District to Kamweleni village. The local ICA staff had arranged for us to stay at a large, comfortable resort nearby. When we arrived and saw Kamweleni for the first time, we told the local ICA staff that we always lived in the village with the people. The resort center was out of the question. This threw the local plans awry, but after negotiating with one of the village men, he set us up in a small room attached to his own house.

We walked through the village in the heat of the midday sun and discovered a dry river bed that was the only source of water for the entire village. It was February, in the midst of the dry season, and there was no water in the river. The local people dug into the dry river bed with sticks until they found some green-colored water, which they carefully scooped up and carried home in small buckets. By the middle of the day, the pace of the villagers had slowed noticeably. Everyone seemed to crawl along. People acted as if they had been completely drained of all their energy. We reflected that we had come to a very poor village indeed.

Late that afternoon, while we were busy preparing for the planning consultation, we realized that we had not eaten since before we got off the plane and we were feeling very hungry. There were no stores in the village, we had no transportation to drive anywhere to buy food, and the local staff who were assigned to cook meals had forgotten to show up. It was very late in the day when one of the cooks finally came to set up the kitchen for the consultation in an outside area surrounded by crumbling, stone walls. She started a fire and put a large pot of water on to boil some eggs. The lack of food had drained all the energy from our bodies and we were reacting as slowly as the local villagers.

Finally, after what seemed like an eternity, the eggs were ready to eat. There were only enough for each person on our team to have one. When I bit into that egg, every single cell in my body cheered! The muscles, tendons, molecules and atoms of my body kept shouting, "Hurrah, hurrah," with every bite I took. I will remember that one egg for the rest of my life. Even today, years later, my body still cheers at that memory.

Bill and Barbara Alerding

The lack of food had drained all the energy from our bodies....

Encounter with Desaparecidos*

In 1980, we were assigned to the Human Development Project in Sol de Septiembre, Chile. We came to Chile with a three-month tourist visa which could be extended for three months without leaving the country. As the maximum six-month period drew to a close, we looked at ways of renewing our visa by leaving the country and returning. We had two options: 1) fly over the Andes to Mendoza, Argentina (a forty-five minute flight), wait an hour and then fly right back to Santiago, or, 2) take the bus over the Andes to Mendoza, spend a couple of days being tourists, then return to Santiago. We decided on the second option in order to see the Andes first-hand and to experience Argentina up close.

There was a convoy of three buses, each one with a steward and two stewardesses. Lunch would be served on board after we had passed the Chile-Argentina border station. It was all quite luxurious compared with buses we had known in the Philippines! Who could ask for anything more? Our departure day was bright and sunny and we took many pictures of awe-inspiring views as we ascended the Andes. We were very grateful our driver did not seem to be in a macho mode of driving as we negotiated the "hairpin curves" along the road which ascended the Andes. As far as we could tell, the other passengers were either Chilean or Argentinean and many had lots of luggage. We had heard that Argentineans liked to shop in Chile because it was cheaper. Since the ride between Santiago and Mendoza was normally only about eight hours, a weekend shopping trip was not unreasonable.

Before we reached the top of the ridge where the two countries met, we passed through a tunnel and somewhere in the tunnel crossed the border. Both nations' customs facilities were just beyond the far end of the tunnel. First, we all had to "exit" Chile, which seemed to us a very orderly and systematic process. Then we had to "enter" Argentina, which was an altogether different experience. It was disorganized and chaotic; we had to change the lines in which we were standing several times. But the day was beautiful and sunny and the eastern side of the Andes invited serious picture taking. It was awesome in a gaunt, otherworldly way. The colors, formations and "feel" were different from the western, Chilean side.

About thirty kilometers from the town which surrounded the border and custom locations, we were drowsy and ready for a siesta. Suddenly, without warning, the buses turned off the main road and we made our way to what turned out to be an Argentinian Army outpost. Our buses were directed to a parking area near a cluster of buildings. The bus crew told us to stay in our seats until we received further directions and discouraged even the softest whispers. Tony and I intensified our listening and watching. You could touch the fear on the bus with a feather! Our smoking increased exponentially.

Looking back down the Chilean side of the Andes

The person who seemed to be in charge was someone we later named "Achtung." He was the perfect intimidator! Just in case we were not properly terrified, a simple five-minute display was enough to get us there. Not everyone played this role or acted out this behavior, but Achtung was the one to whom we all paid attention.

After a while we were told that we could go outside the bus, but under no circumstance were we to touch any of our luggage. We could only take our purses and had to stay in sight of the guards. Not long after our arrival, a very pregnant woman became hysterical. She was crying and moaning and no one could understand what she was trying to communicate. There was some concern that she might deliver on the spot, so she was removed to an infirmary, which we were told was not far away. The luggage in and under the bus had been removed to a building where something was going on, though no one seemed to know what. Every so often three or four names were called out and several people went into the building. Time was suspended and stretched out interminably. The people coming back from the building were not talking.

We were not thinking best-case scenarios. We had heard about *Desaparecidos*. This was a perfect spot for us to become one of them! No village nearby. No witnesses. There did not even seem to be flies or lizards or condors. As far as the customs people at the border were concerned, we were on our way to Mendoza. God only knows how hazardous the road is in the best of weather. Name after name was read, but not ours. We were not sure who "returned to our midst." We tried in all the ways we knew and in new ways we improvised, to help time pass—or stand still.

Finally, our name was called. We felt like we were going to swallow our hearts. We were praying hard that we would not be in Achtung's line. We were not. We were told to take out our passports and open up our luggage. An officer gave our passport a cursory glance, then we were waved on and told to retrieve our carry-on luggage. Apparently they were not interested in American citizens that day. "Glory Hallelujah!"

We got back on our bus and waited for further instruction. The bus had been filled to capacity. We were never certain about the number, but the bus never did fill back up. It was late in the afternoon when the convoy set out again for Mendoza. We were all thirsty and hungry, but infinitely patient in light of what could have happened to us. Piecing together all we heard afterwards, we gathered that some passengers were suspected of smuggling certain things from Chile—what exactly, we never knew. It could have been something as innocent as blue jeans!

Ellery Elizondo

Stopping for customs on the Argentinian side of the Andes

* *Desaparecidos* means "The Disappeared Ones."

Almost Caught

She knew she had to get to the bottom of all that money ...

We stayed out of sight during the attempted coup on Kenya's president, Daniel Moi. But a week after the coup had been put down, we turned our attention to paying our Kenyan staff. We had to take about 4,700 Kenyan shillings out of the bank, bring it back to where we lived in Kawangware, a slum area in Nairobi, and then send it out to our colleagues in dozens of villages all across Kenya. Usually, Marilyn would have done the bank run by herself and come home. But the military was still everywhere with their submachine guns, stopping people and checking things out, and in view of this situation, we decided it was best for two of us to go together. So Marilyn and I got on the bus for the ten-minute bus ride to downtown Nairobi.

Marilyn withdrew the cash from the bank account, put it in her briefcase, zipped it up, and we went out to catch the bus back to Kawangware. In Kenya, there are always three times more people on a bus than one thinks can fit. We had learned to cram ourselves in. We rode along, standing in the aisle crunched among all these people, while Marilyn held her briefcase tucked tightly under her arm. We were the only two foreign women on a bus full of Kenyan men. Suddenly the bus stopped and men with machine guns directed everybody to get off.

Everyone piled off and lined up. A military man came by and said, "Let me see your identification." We had brought our passports with us because we knew this might happen. I found my passport easily but Marilyn's passport was buried, out of sight, somewhere at the bottom of her briefcase. As the military man became more and more insistent, she held the briefcase so he could not see the 5,000 shillings while she rummaged for her passport. She knew she had to get to the bottom of all that money without pulling it all out to get there. She began talking to me very quietly in English while this man was yelling in her face. I heard her saying very sweetly to me, "If I can't find my passport, I'm going to give my briefcase to you so you can take it on home. You can find my passport there and come and pick me up." And I heard myself say, "Okay."

Just then she found it, we supposed only a moment before being hauled off. It was pretty scary. We were very relieved.

Patricia Coffman

Will The Terrorists Return?

In the Philippines, early in 1979, we launched a new cluster of village projects around Langub in Davao, and ended up doing two planning consultations at the same time in neighboring villages. After completing the planning sessions, some of us were preparing the document in a village school building.

Suddenly, we heard gunshots and the villagers came running towards us. Terrorists had come to the village intending to shoot a man, but the bullet had ricocheted and killed his mother. Two American doctors, who were attending the planning consultation, took the wounded man to a hospital, where he recovered.

Meanwhile, the terrorists continued on to the next village. Jim and Dick were returning to our village by car on the same road. The terrorists stopped their car. Jim said he made himself as small as he could while the driver convinced the terrorists not to harm them.

My colleagues and I had to stay overnight in the village in the house of the mother who had been killed. We were terrified because the villagers said the terrorists would return to search for guns. Many of the ICA staff thought we would be safe even if we stayed, but since most of us were there only on short-term assignments and did not know the local political situation, it seemed wiser to move us out. While the night ended without incident, the next day everyone moved out of Davao, except for staff who had been living and working there for a long time.

Judith Hamje

Eleven Flights of Stairs

In 1982, we had just finished a training course in the Xerox Building for some of the Xerox staff in Guatemala, and had scheduled another training program that we would conduct over a period of time with their sales department. We were scheduled to begin one morning at 7 A.M. We pulled up in front of the Xerox Building from the village about 6:30 A.M. We were early and decided to go down the street for a cup of coffee.

While we sat sipping our coffee, we heard a very loud boom. When we returned to the Xerox Building, we discovered that it had been hit by a bomb! Everything had been affected in the building and broken glass was strewn everywhere. When the CEO arrived at 7 A.M., we assumed we would postpone our meeting. Instead he said, "No, let's go ahead!"

We walked up eleven flights of stairs, found a broom to sweep the glass off the floor and conducted the first session of our training program!

George West

> *While we were sitting sipping our coffee, we heard a very loud boom.*

Water Tank Miracle

Water was normally carried by "beasts of burden," which, in the rural villages, were the women and children!

We lived in a Kenyan village where we ate *ugali* and *sukuma* (cornmeal and kale), almost no meat, and very little fruit. At a point so near the equator, with twelve hours of sunshine and twelve hours of darkness year round, people worked from sunup to sundown, without labor-saving devices. During the dry season (nine months out of each year with long periods of cloudless sunshine) even trips out of the village consumed great amounts of physical energy—walking, jostling someone in a *matatu* (pickup taxi), or taking a bus. Drinking water became scarce and sometimes disappeared. A reliable source of potable water in a village, let alone in or near a house, was a luxury. Water was normally carried by "beasts of burden," which, in the rural villages, were the women and children!

By contrast, during Kenya's wet seasons, more water was available than could be adequately used. In principle, Kenya experiences two wet seasons each year—one lasting from mid-October through November and one lasting from March through April. In years with two wet seasons, it was possible to raise two crops. Being able to provide a preschool, a village, or a cattle dip facility with a means of collecting water during the wet seasons not only provided an additional source of water, but also made the water more accessible. It lifted the burden of water procurement from women who were already responsible for meals, child care, housekeeping, shopping, and raising a crop.

In early 1976, after only three months in Kenya, with no more explanation than, "Karoki built some water tanks in Maragua Ridge," I was assigned to build water tanks with funds from a grant.

Before my arrival, ICA Kenya had published a *Village Health Care* booklet with tips about how to improve the public health of the village. One of the features of the booklet was a description of how to build a water tank. The water tank was always placed beside a building with a roof that could catch rain water. The foundation was made of ballast (what we call gravel) and cement in which a drain pipe was installed. The skeleton for the walls was constructed of a cylinder woven from the stems of a small "wedlock" tree. The skeleton was nine feet in diameter and six feet tall. Once it was woven together it was reinforced with several strands of heavy wire wrapped around the outside. The woven and reinforced skeleton was placed on the foundation and then plastered inside and out with a concrete mixture made of cement, lime for waterproofing, sand and water.

The original grant called for us to build seven tanks at a cost of 6-7,000 Kenyan shillings per tank (about US$2,000). I doubled the impact of the grant by insisting that while we would provide the capital input (pipe, cement, wire, a lid for the tank), we would ask the village to supply all local materials and labor (the ballast and sticks, the artisans to make the basket and plaster the tank, and the eaves troughs to collect the water). We would also provide the facilitation, but the community needed to build the consensus about the placement of the tank.

I arranged to go with one of our Kenyan staff to Maragua Ridge to talk with our colleague, Karoki, about building a demonstration tank at the training center where we lived in Mugumoini. Karoki took us on a tour of Maragua Ridge to inspect the existing tanks constructed in the village. He detailed the equipment and materials that had to be on-site to ensure the orderly and timely completion of a tank. I arranged with him to have the Maragua Ridge Women's Group supply the sticks and expertise, weaving them into a basket to be used as the skeleton for our new tank.

Then I organized the work into phases, relating and prioritizing them so that completion of a tank seemed manageable. I did a cost estimate of the materials that would have to be purchased and created a budget. I orchestrated the logistics required to hold a residential Village Leaders Conference for leaders from neighboring villages at which a tank would be completed from start to finish. I had to delegate responsibility for recruitment and for preparing a facility to house forty village leaders for two days. There was no possibility of "running to town" to get something we had forgotten!

We submitted the budget to our office in Nairobi, ninety kilometers away by bus. We got the OK to build the tank, but were advised to arrange for credit in order to get the materials. So I borrowed a pickup truck, went around negotiating credit with near strangers, and collected all the local materials, tools, and supplies from the hardware store. I supervised the creation of a curriculum that would engage forty village leaders in the construction of the tank so that they would be able to duplicate it in their own villages after returning home from Mugumoini. I created a rationale which showed how we would provide one half of the cost of the tank (the hardware) if they would provide the other half (the local materials, labor and leadership).

It was not hard to get village leaders to the retreat center. Aside from anything our program would offer, they understood they would get three solid meals and a chance to mix with other village leaders. We had worked directly with these leaders in their own villages, and they were hungry for any and all help available. One Kenyan Agricultural Extension Agent struck up a conversation with me on the bus. He told me of a six-month internship he had done in US. Then he asked, "How long do you think it will be before Kenya can be like the US?" Reading between the lines I took that to mean, "How long do you think it will be before we can over consume and throw away as much as you in the US are doing?"

We borrowed a pickup and brought Karoki and Maragua Ridge Women's Group with all their sticks over, early on Friday. They wove the stick basket in advance of the workshop. The rest of the participants arrived on Friday evening for the opening feast. Karoki made a presentation at the meal and we followed up with a discussion: "What questions do you have about building a water tank that you want to have answered this weekend?"

> *…we got the OK to build the tank, but were advised to arrange for credit in order to get the materials.*

The next morning at breakfast, we told them they were going to find the answers to their questions. We assigned them to work groups that would participate in the completion of the tank by noon. By noon the tank was completed except for the final touches that the *fundi* (cement mason) was putting on the inside plastering. At lunch we asked, "What did you learn about building a water tank?" and "What else do you need to know?"

In the afternoon session we gave them the rationale for placement of the additional tanks. We then divided the leaders into townships and asked them to come back with their consensus on chosen locations for the remaining thirteen tanks. At the plenary, we told the leaders that we would await their invitations to village meetings to explain the conditions for placing a water tank.

When I left in November 1976, we had completed seven tanks and four Kenyans were capable of supervising tank construction. Within a year of the construction of the first tank, ninety-six more had been built. When I heard the news, I was euphoric. It seemed like a miracle and brought tears to my eyes.

David Zahrt

Placement Rationale

1. The new tank is placed in a public spot, e.g., at a preschool, cattle dip, or village square.

2. The project is explained at a community meeting where a consensus to build the tank is established.

3. The ICA supplies the "hardware" and the village supplies the "software."

4. The supplies are delivered when the ballast is in place and the stick basket woven.

Rupert's Vision

In the early 90s, I took up responsibility for monitoring a Canadian International Development Agency (CIDA) grant to the ICA in Zambia. At that time ICA Zambia's energies were focused on conducting a vast number of Community Development Forums across the eastern part of Zambia. But the staff was also doing a project in Kapini, where we began our development work in Zambia, so we went out to visit the village.

A fascinating story emerged. In 1978 and 1979, after Kapini had become one of the ICA's Human Development Projects, the village focused on significant social infrastructure development. When it flooded, the river that ran through the village was a real mess and a genuine barrier, so the community built a stable crossing point that allowed people to deliver their crops to the market at the main road and their children to school. They also built several new community buildings, including a school and a clinic, which have been in community hands for many years now.

I was most impressed by the clinic. It had been transformed and was operating as a sparkling women's center. It was the site for a "mother and child" wellness and educational headstart center, operated, I think, by the Christian Council of Zambia. At the same location, another group was operating a plant nursery. Since many of the farmers are women, this provided a means of introducing improved plant strains and trees to combat desertification.

After its early success in this initial demonstration village, ICA Zambia expanded its work into what was called "The Diamond of Zambia." Work was started in the cluster of communities around Kapini which led to work across the entire nation. For quite a number of years, the staff had not done very much in Kapini itself. Some staff were living in Kapini, but most of the time they were leading community meetings and assisting communities in developing their own projects elsewhere around the country.

In the late '80s, one of our colleagues, Rupert, reappeared in Zambia on one of what he calls his "migrations," and came to Kapini, filled with the fire of sustainable agricultural development. JRB, as he is known locally, has had a deep and lasting passion for agriculture in Africa since his days as a farmer in Kenya. He continues to be actively involved in searching for ways to enable African farmers to develop and use sustainable farming methods. After a great deal of conversation, a team of staff and local colleagues started working again in Kapini. They visited people in the community, at the Ministry of Agriculture, and on the faculty of the Agriculture Department at the University of Zambia. Out of all this, they put together a project designed to help people increase their income, renew the soil, and control pests without using fertilizers or chemical pesticides and herbicides.

Although most of the ideas flew straight in the face of current high-tech practice, the project worked. The team organized and helped form several farmers' clubs. Some were all male clubs, some were made up of all women and some were mixed. When the project was going well, there were about one hundred families in the community directly involved in improving their own farms. They used a combination of new methods, along with some ancient traditional methods like planting legumes to increase soil fertility naturally. They kept rather careful records and discovered that, over a period of three to four years, while reducing their use of expensive commercial fertilizers, they all increased their yields, and consequently, their incomes as well.

Pride in genuine accomplishment was revealed in the faces of everyone I talked with about the project as we walked through the fields. It was Rupert's vision, the on-the-ground, practical passion of our Zambian colleagues, and technical and financial assistance from ICA Japan that really made the project happen. By the mid-1990s, the ICA Zambia staff was replicating the project throughout central Zambia.

Wayne Nelson

> *Although most of the ideas flew straight in the face of current high-tech practice, the project worked.*

Chapter Four
Whatever It Takes

I cannot forget your revolution,
the thrill of the edge, the luxury of feeling history.

Mud was full of magic and life was full of passion,
making love with the magician of history.

Ukrainian Meatloaf

In late fall, when I was still new and not many people knew me, I had the privilege of being assigned to the kitchen to cook meals for people who came to our weekend courses. Some weekends as many as three hundred people came. I had been assigned to get the meat loaf started for the Saturday night dinner. The weekends were on a tight schedule and the weekend before, dinner had not been ready until 7 P.M. and, even then, when people had cut into the chicken, the blood had run pink. I had been warned not to create any more disasters.

I had never made meatloaf. Mom did not like it much, so we never had it. But, hey, I was an intern and it did not seem too difficult. I was alone in the kitchen. As I pulled out the designated plastic bags full of hamburger, I looked for the biggest mixing container I could find. It was a stainless bowl, about three and one half feet across at the top, with round edges. I put all the meat into it and it fit, though it was rounded high in the middle. I did not want to make a mess, so I took down all the large containers of spices I might need and placed them around the edges of the stainless table in front of the stove where I was working. I began to mix. There was no leverage on this large amount of hamburger, so I brought over a chair to stand on and continued mixing. About that time, one of the teachers of one of the courses came in for a cup of coffee and saw me standing on the chair up to my elbows in hamburger.

"Hey, what are you doing?"

"I am making meat loaf for dinner."

"Are you sure you know what you are doing? Have you done it before?"

"No, but it can't be too difficult."

He departed. I continued to mix and season. On the way out, this teacher met another teacher by the coffee urns. I heard scraps of conversation: "Intern…all alone; never made meatloaf before; standing on chair; last week, dinner was not ready until 7 P.M. and the chicken was not done."

The second teacher came over wearing a friendly smile. "Making meatloaf, eh? You know people are very concerned about dinner. Last week dinner was very late and we had to show the movie very late and that was not good. You're sure dinner will be ready?"

"It's meat loaf. Simple."

"Well, be sure it is on time."

I said, "No problem."

The teacher left.

Another whispered conversation was held over by the coffee urn with another teacher who had stopped in. This third teacher came back with a big, warm smile on his face.

"Hi, what's for dinner?"

He gave me a sincere look and then turned to the large mixing bowl where my hands were buried.

I had been thinking to myself, "This will go on all afternoon."

Kitchen duty

I said, "We're having Ukrainian Meat Loaf for dinner. It is my Grandmother's recipe and it is really delicious."

The teacher relaxed.

"Ukrainian Meat Loaf, eh?"

We chatted a bit about Ukrainian Meat Loaf. The teacher left and moments later met someone coming into the kitchen over by the coffee urn. "Hey, we're having Ukrainian Meat Loaf for dinner!"

The next September, a new person was assigned to be in charge of the kitchen. She came up to me and said, "We're collecting recipes for the kitchen. Can I get your Grandmother's famous recipe for Ukrainian Meat Loaf?"

James Wiegel

1000 Single Beds

The Institute staff had been living and working in an old seminary building on the West Side of Chicago once occupied by the Church of the Brethren. But we had outgrown this well-worn facility and had just received an eight-story office building from the Kemper Insurance Company when Kemper moved its headquarters from Uptown on Chicago's North Side to the suburbs. The "Kemper Building" began the process of becoming a new kind of community landmark when it became officially ours in January, 1972. Its eight stories of L-shaped floors seemed like a quarter city block of unconquered urban territory. We sent the first staff to begin occupying our new home in March, 1972, and in May made the decision to hold our annual month-long summer Research Program for one thousand people there. We mounted a campaign to turn six floors of abandoned office space into a residential conference center.

I was assigned to lead a team of six to secure inkind donations to reduce program costs. We conducted a brainstorm with the one hundred fifty staff gathered to prepare for the summer and listed materials which each task force would need. The taskforces estimated quantities and costs for a prioritized list of the most needed, most costly items. When we assigned teams to inkind the items which would realize the greatest cost reduction, my assignment was to secure one thousand single beds for the Kemper Building.

We needed nearly five hundred more bunks in a hurry! I created a concise story about whom I represented

Its eight stories of L-shaped floors seemed like a quarter city block of unconquered urban territory.

I… adopted as an operating principle the power of statistical probability: one out of ten tries would lead me to my goal.

and what special need I was trying to fill. I listed all the possible sources I could imagine, scoured the phone books for phone numbers and addresses, and added new sources from the yellow pages. On each call I made sure to ask for additional suggestions about where I could find beds. I kept all these contacts and comments in a notebook and adopted as an operating principle the power of statistical probability: one out of ten tries would lead me to my goal.

I networked my way from used furniture dealers to scrap metal dealers, neither of which were of any help because they had only occasional odd assortments of beds for which they wanted exorbitant prices. But they mentioned the Great Lakes Naval Training Base. Scrap metal dealers bid weekly on scrap from the Great Lakes Scrap Metal Depot and the Depot sometimes got old metal beds from the Naval Training Base. But the Depot had rigorous policies about who was eligible to buy, and beds that made it to the Depot were in rough shape. In looking for another entré to the Naval Training Base, I discovered that we had conducted courses for Navy Chaplains two or three years earlier. I called the Office of the Chaplaincy to investigate. The Greek Orthodox Chaplain had been in one of our courses, and through him, I learned that the Base was in the process of bulldozing several old barracks and was not bothering to remove the bunk beds.

I asked the Chaplain to help me salvage the bunks from the barracks before they were razed. The Chaplain secured authorization for a single entry to pick up a truckload of bunks. The following day the barracks would be razed. I realized that one truck would hold only 1/5 of the bunks in the barracks, and by the time we loaded, traveled back to the Kemper Building, unloaded, and returned to the Base, we would be lucky to get a second load, even if the Chaplain could arrange for a second entry. So I asked for fifteen volunteers and we rented five trucks.

We arrived on schedule and waited with one truck in the parking lot next to the gate until the appointed hour. Four of the trucks parked around the corner in an abandoned filling station until the appointed time. When we went to the gate for clearance, the other four immediately appeared. I told the man at the gate that we were clearing the barracks. He did not question us since we were all right there and he had the barricade up. Our five trucks cleared security and we entered the Base accompanied by an escort vehicle. We had the barracks empty before noon. That afternoon, they pushed the barracks in with bulldozers and would have destroyed the bunks if we had not gotten them first. But we had come away with only four hundred bunks and we needed one hundred more.

As soon as we returned to the Kemper Building, I called the Chaplain, told him we had gotten all the bunks in the barracks, and asked him if he knew of other places where we could get more. He could not believe we had gotten all those beds and indicated I had used up all his favors. However, within another day or two he called again and said he had found another seventy bunks. I arranged to send another crew, but did not accompany it for this final pickup. While at the base, someone on the crew decided to take a ping-pong table out of storage as well.

A Captain from the Great Lakes Naval Training Base called soon thereafter, in a rage that his ping-pong table was missing. I was sure he intended to press charges against me. I consulted with Phil about the situation. Frank had been in charge of the team that got the Captain's ping pong table, though I never spoke with him about it. I suspect that Phil did some dealing with Frank to get a beautiful old wooden desk, which had come with the Kemper building, released as a peace offering. I arranged to have the table, plus the desk, at the Base freight dock the next day. The Captain was satisfied and I did not go to jail.

There was something magical about the summer. We had enough beds for all one thousand people who stayed at the new conference center. Before the summer was over, I had inkinded two tons of grits, fifty thousand napkins, and a railroad freight car full of green beans! I do not know how I did what I did. I find myself wondering how I could recover the capacity to do such things, which, in retrospect, seem so monumental. Memory of the one thousand beds and fifty thousand napkins has slipped through the cracks of history, but the two tons of grits and the railroad car of green beans became legends and reappeared on our breakfast and supper tables for years after.

David Zahrt

On A Clear Day

On a clear day, rise and look around you,
And you'll see, who, you are.
On a clear day, how it will astound you,
That the glow of your being, outshines every star.
You feel part of, ev'ry mountain, sea and shore.
You can hear, from far and near,
A world you've never heard before.
And on a clear day, on that clear day,
You can see forever, and ever, and evermore.

(Repeat the whole song.)

The City That Works

> The guy said, "Who?"
> I said, "Victor."
> "Never heard of him."

In the summer of 1974, a summer taskforce was organized to further the development of the Fifth City Demonstration Project. Our average age was twenty-two years old. The taskforce was made up of three teams. One team was to raise funds to eliminate a $40,000 debt. A second team was to finish the housing program. Mark, a preschool teacher, and I were to open the Fifth City Shopping Center. Paula and Jane were keeping everything glued together while the entire team worked to hand the Community Center over to Mayor Daley and the City of Chicago.

The first task we had to do, in order to get the shopping center completed for its grand opening, was to get a building permit so Floyd could finish his laundromat and dry cleaners in the shopping center. I asked for advice from Victor, the general contractor who had guided some of the initial conversion of the old Kemper Building in Uptown into the Institute's new office and staff residence. Victor was the general contractor whom we had employed for the Fifth City Shopping Center and for some of the housing units in Fifth City. He said, "Just go down there and talk to the guy at the front desk. His name is Biff or something like that. If you have any problems, just call me."

We said, "Fine." We had never done this before but we figured we were set to get a building permit in a day! Mark and I went down to City Hall.

We got down there, walked in the front door and walked up to the guy at the front desk and said, "Hi, we're here from Fifth City and we need to get a building permit today."

The guy started laughing and told us the waiting period for getting a building permit was from three to six months right now.

I said, "No, no, you don't understand. We have to have a building permit today. Victor told me to come to talk to you about it."

The guy said, "Who?"
I said, "Victor."
"Never heard of him."

So I went running down the hallway to ask a fellow if I could use his phone to call Victor. The guy said, "No, you can't use this phone."

I got to a pay phone and got Victor on the line and said, " Vic, I'm down here talking to your friend Biff to get the permit and I'm getting nowhere."

Vic said, "Get him on the phone."

I stuck my head out and loudly called up the hallway. "Hey, Biff, will you come talk to Vic on the phone here?"

Biff hollered back, "I can't talk to him on that phone. Have him call me on this phone."

So we get Vic's number and two minutes later, Biff answered his ringing phone and we heard him say, "Uh. Uh, yep, yep, right!" and he hung up.

Biff said to us, "All right, start here and go right around the room. So I headed for the electrical desk, the venting desk, the roof desk, etc. I went to the first desk and the guy said: "Oh! you need a permit today? Fine. Let's see. According to the fire code, you have to have those doorways going in instead of out. You're the architect aren't you?"

I stuttered a bit and said "Yeah."

He then said: "Just take out your pen and have those doors going the other way." So I got out my pen and drew the doors the other way.

It was the same story from one stop to the next. Each one of them in their turn stamped the plans. At the end of the day we walked out with our building permit, an accomplishment that caught everybody's attention. The ability to get a building permit in one day in the City of Chicago is why Chicago is known as "the city that works."

Geoff G. Nixon

Right On His Derrière

Right after the planning consultation with the Marshall Islands—the first Human Development Consultation we had done—Joe wanted to make sure that all the people in the Marshalls knew about all the development they would see in the ensuing years. So we decided to take a boat trip to all of the other atolls. We consciously stopped at each of the atolls and Joe did a presentation on community transformation. It was all translated so he could tell the people about the coming events and programs. Many of the people had not seen a white person since World War II.

We ended this two-week trek on Likke atoll, which was the Kings Highway. Our hosts decided to organize a big pig feast. The Marshalls were traditionally a matriarchal society ruled by queens. When guests from the outside world came to the island, the women carried them about, as no one from the outside world was permitted to walk on the land. True to tradition, these women intended to carry all four of us to the spot where we were going to have this party.

They carried Lee, Oscar and me off to the feast. But when they got to Joe, who weighed over two hundred pounds at the time, they picked him up and immediately dropped him right on his derrière! They knew they did not have enough strength to carry him to the feast. Just then, a huge Marshallese woman came forward and lifted Joe right up onto her back! The fine feast which followed lasted for six hours. We had the time of our lives.

Patrick Moriarty

> The Marshalls were traditionally a matriarchal society ruled by queens.

Saving Face

Even though it was only August, it was already chilly on Japan's northern island, Hokkaido. Each winter, more than eight feet of snow fell on the dying mining town called Oyubari. In just a few months, the people of Oyubari would be shoveling snow off their tin roofs to prevent its weight from crushing them. Even though there was no snow during the planning consultation, our team was already thoroughly enjoying the local bathhouse whose boiling hot water warmed every bone in your body. People told us stories about men running naked through the winter snow during their local festival. "No wonder," we thought, "with bathhouses like this one to warm your body, anyone could run naked through the snow and not feel a thing!"

Oyubari was a forlorn place when we arrived. Throughout the town, huge black birds that seemed as big as eagles perched atop the telephone poles. We discovered that people were frightened to death of these birds. During the Second World War, Chinese prisoners of war were brought to Oyubari to work in the coal mines. The mines were very deep, steep and dangerous, and many of the Chinese prisoners died. The townspeople believed that the souls of the dead Chinese prisoner-miners remained in these large black birds and had come back to haunt them. This common belief had locked the townspeople in paralyzing fear!

One of the aims of the consultation was to help people overcome their paralysis and start rebuilding their community. During the week, plenaries were held in the large town hall where five hundred people could meet comfortably. In Japan, this meant that five hundred people left their shoes outside the door.

During these consultations we always had a local translator who instantly translated everything that was said by the facilitator. Joseph was the major translator in Oyubari. He knew the ICA methods very well and was an expert in translating the meaning of our thoughts. In the middle of the consultation, however, Joseph started losing his voice. He had been translating nonstop for three days and the strain on his vocal chords was becoming noticeable.

In order to give Joseph a rest, we called on a young woman attending the consultation who was a professional translator. In the morning, while the facilitator gave the local economics talk, the young woman translated for him. Joseph, who was sitting with the local people, passed a note to me: "Bill, this translator does not understand what is really being said and is totally misinterpreting everything! How can we ensure that the facilitator's words are really understood and at the same time allow her to save face?"

When Joseph and I talked a few minutes later, we decided that he would translate my words at the next session. We agreed that I would give a summary of the earlier talk as an introduction and Joseph could then translate with the proper context. This was done, allowing the translator to save face. It was a win-win situation for everyone and a memorable symbol of the gift of an Eastern philosophy of life for us.

Bill and Barb Alerding

Leading a plenary session

Just Cry

In 1972, my husband Joe and I were assigned to Hong Kong to teach courses and to raise money. The American Chamber of Commerce in Hong Kong was looking for a taxation and legislation expert and the only qualification was that you be an American. I needed a job and looked into the position. There were various magazines and bulletins to be read monthly so that you knew what Congress was doing and you had to go to lunch at the American Club every day and take notes on the committee meetings. I knew I could do those sorts of things with my hands tied behind my back, so I applied and was hired as an expert on taxation and legislation.

It was not long before we were reassigned from Hong Kong to Tokyo. I decided to consult my boss, Karl. He had been with the Secret Service for the U.S. Army in China during World War II. His secretary, Betty, had worked with him in Nanking during the war. When I told her I was moving to Tokyo, she talked to our boss who said, "I think we can set you up in Tokyo. It will be a little more complicated, but it will be a cinch, so just wait here while I make a phone call."

He called Tokyo and said, "Bart? I have a girl here for you." He turned to me and asked, "When are you moving?" When I said, "Next month," he turned back to the phone and said, "So you need to hire her next month. I'll take care of her when she comes back for a visa. Okay?" He explained to me that Commander Jackson, the Executive Director of the American Chamber of Commerce in Tokyo, was a close friend and would take care of me. I was given directions, plus Jackson's office and home phone numbers.

We proceeded to Tokyo. The first day I was there, I called Commander Jackson. He asked, "Can you come in tomorrow?" I assured him that I could. When we met the next day, he said, "You have to go back to Hong Kong to get a visa," and gave me a ticket.

So I flew back and applied for the visa. I waited and waited and waited. I had been waiting more than three weeks and I was getting nervous. Jackson had said that it would be a few weeks, but it had been nearly a month, so I dropped in on the Hong Kong Chamber and said, "Look, I'm getting kind of worried! Do you think the Japanese won't let me in? Is there something I need to do?"

My former boss looked at Betty and said, "Why don't you handle this?"

Betty walked into the hall with me, asked about what I had already done and then suggested a strategy of last resort. "Just cry! Just go into the embassy and cry. It embarrasses them if you cry."

I had tried everything else and was still waiting, so I went back to the Japanese Embassy, and went on and on, wailing about the missing visa and really crying. Finally a man came around the corner and took me to another room. The visa was sitting right there! I returned to Tokyo and began my new job the next day.

Carol Pierce

"I think we can set you up in Tokyo."

A Taiwan Thanksgiving

In the fall of 1978, we were celebrating our second Thanksgiving in Hai Ou, a little fishing village on the west coast near the southern tip of Taiwan, south of Ping Tung. Our work included community meetings in nearby villages. We were leading a meeting in a little farming village inland from the sea about ten kilometers south of Hai Ou.

Simultaneously, we were getting ready for a traditional American Thanksgiving dinner with thirty-six of our Taiwanese colleagues the next day. As the designated American cook, I had been getting ready for this wonderful feast for a week and a half. I had been making rolls from scratch and village women had been coming over to witness this magical process in person. Our most major appliance was a roaster oven, which did not have a second shelf and accommodated only twelve buns, two pies or one turkey at a time. Every batch of buns that came out of the oven had to be shared with the village baking enthusiasts, so only about half of what I baked was left over for the dinner.

In the back of my mind I had been thinking about the turkey. Thirty-six people, I reasoned, probably required more than one turkey. Given the small size of the turkeys, we certainly required more than one bird. Colleagues in Taipei had promised to pick up the first turkey, a Butterball, from the American Army PX. Mr. Wu, the foreign police inspector, had assured me he could supply the second. Mr. Wu's job was to ensure that we were conscientiously engaged in anti-communist behavior and that we did not do anything horrible against the Taiwanese government. Basically, though, he was out for a good time. He promised that he would get me a Chinese turkey; that it would be very fine; that I could prepare it exquisitely; and, furthermore, that everyone would enjoy it immensely. I was suspicious, but he kept reassuring me.

I had finished baking the buns and pumpkin pies. It was the first time I had ever made pumpkin pies with too little cinnamon. In China, cinnamon is a medicine and costs fifty cents a tablespoon.

I turned my attention to the community meeting. It was to be a fine event and our colleague, Bruce, had come down from Taipei. But about mid-morning, the villagers informed us we could not hold the afternoon session; something crucial had to be done in the fields. We rescheduled the afternoon session for that evening. Internally, my anxiety about the Thanksgiving dinner was building. "O god, how will I roast two turkeys and get everything ready for thirty-six people?"

In this frame of mind I was certain that our American Thanksgiving dinner was already in trouble. Turkey and sweet potatoes are low class food in China. The skinny turkeys are generally boiled, leaving them bland and unappealing. Sweet potatoes grow fast and can be eaten without much preparation, and Taiwanese people picture nearly starving people relying on them. Turkey and sweet potatoes are what people eat when they are poor. It felt like an up-hill battle to pull off this dinner in fine fashion.

> *He promised that he would get me a Chinese turkey.... I was suspicious, but he kept reassuring me.*

Mr. Wu appeared at the village meeting, but failed to mention the turkey. When noon came and the villagers left to do their chores, Mr. Wu offered to buy us lunch. We drove to a nearby village to eat lunch together. We drank more rice liquor than we should have, and Bruce, who was at the wheel on the way back to the village, managed to drive the bus into a ditch. With no damage or injuries, we all hopped out and got back to the community meeting in spite of our mishap.

That evening, it was dark as I started my speech at the village meeting. Katherin, as usual, was doing a terrific job of translating. In the middle of the speech, Mr. Wu roared up with a live turkey strapped to the back of his motorcycle. I'm sure that I must have looked dismayed, because someone from the village saw the expression on my face and apparently realized my difficulty. An unknown and saintly woman completely cleaned and dressed the turkey. It was ready for roasting.

Gratefully, I started the Butterball roasting that night, went to bed, got up at 3 A.M., and walked the three blocks to the office where the roaster oven was steaming with the delicious aroma of turkey. The Butterball was done. I put the second turkey in, went back to bed, got up at 7 A.M., retraced my steps and took the smaller turkey out of the oven as well.

A wonderful Chinese colleague who was a Presbyterian minister celebrated Thanksgiving with us. He read the Mayflower Compact and translated the spirit of the celebration for our Chinese guests. People had a good time and even used knives, forks and spoons. They discovered that roast turkey was a clear improvement over boiled turkey. They relished the experience and there was nothing but bones left from both birds. The candied yams with marshmallows were a big hit also! Low class food in Taiwan had never been so presentable and delicious!

Pat Druckenmiller

> *An unknown and saintly woman completely cleaned and dressed the turkey.*

Village Economics

> The proud smile of a business tycoon with a clever gimmick spread across his face.

In Maliwada village, the team working on the economic development of the village was interested in how people earned an income in such a micro-economy. Someone suggested we visit the merchant who ran the government grain store just down the street. He seemed like a good example of a successful local merchant. At the time, we did not even know there was a government grain store down the street.

The grain merchant welcomed us and we went into his front room. He opened a side door which led into an even smaller room. Only four of us could get into it. There were ten 50-kilogram bags of grain (about 110 pounds each). Our conversation went like this.

"How do you get the grain?"

"I go into Aurangabad to get it."

"How much do you get?"

"Whatever the government has rationed for us."

"And how much do you pay for it?"

"All different prices, depending on the price the government sets."

We pictured the people in Maliwada bringing their little pans, which hold about a kilogram, to the grain merchant.

"Then how much do you charge for it?"

"I sell each kilo for 3 *paise* more than I pay for it."

I mentally calculated the margin. He had to sell the grain at the government price plus a very small "mark-up" which amounted to a total of 3 *paise* per kilo. Therefore, for 100 kilos, his profit would be 3 *paise* x 100 kilos = 300 *paise* or 3 *rupees*—only about 33 cents. 3 *paise* per kilo was not a very large margin!

I pictured the grain merchant going into Aurangabad and transporting the grain back to Maliwada at his own expense. There would be losses, through spillage in handling, weighing errors, pebbles in the grain, and always the rats. It was hard for us to believe that the 3 *paise* per kilogram could even offset his costs.

But when I asked, "Is that enough to make a living?" everybody was shocked. They knew it was not and knew he loses more grain than that. The grain merchant tilted his head with a subtle negative movement.

"Well, why do you do it?" we asked.

The proud smile of a business tycoon with a clever gimmick spread across his face.

"I get to keep the bag and I can sell the bag for 3 *rupees*."

This was a surprising lesson in village economics. The grain merchant was not in the business for the mark-up, but for the burlap bag which was the by-product of his business. We were shocked by this revelation and it gave us a whole new "set of eyes" to see how a village's economy really works.

Ken Hamje

The Earthen Dam

By the third Training School, when our staff was doing both project implementation and replication into new villages, everyone was spread a little thin. Ed, for example, was working part time with the Farmers' Guild and part time on project implementation, because we were trying to build a closer partnership with the people in Maliwada village. Ed was concerned that, since we did workdays during the Training School, we needed to do something to benefit the village, not just keep the participants busy. He and Vivian came up with the idea of building an earthen dam. The third Training School was being held during the dry season and a dam would show people that it was possible to catch water during the rains and let it seep into the ground to raise the water table.

Ed and Vivian scouted around and found a dry wash which went through a narrow cut in some rocks. The wash was in a scenic location. You could see the Daulatabad Fort quite clearly from there and there was a tumble down building off to one side that someone said was an old stable for elephants. It seemed to be an appropriate place: it was a wide area that caught the runoff and the tops of the rock outcroppings were probably fifteen feet high. We decided this was where we should build the dam.

The first step was to dig trenches in the bottom of the gully between the two outcrops of rock and then find big, heavy rocks and put them in the trenches to provide a foundation for the dam. It took two or three people to carry these mighty rocks. After we put the rocks in place, we had to fill in the gaps. This meant carrying rocks and dirt, then more rocks and dirt, hour after hour, day after day. People formed a human chain. At one end of the chain, people dug and filled metal dishes with dirt. We passed the dishes from person to person to the front where the dirt was dumped among the rocks. We were all covered with dirt and dust.

We had not realized how hot it was going to be. There was no shade anywhere. The people from the Training School were villagers who knew how to work in the heat, but the staff members were people who were not from villages. We all felt compelled to look as if we were working hard, but we all felt as if we were going to die! The greater challenge for the students was how to work together and the dam building project became an extended team building exercise. It took us four workdays plus two additional half-days during the Training School to finish the dam. I can remember the joy everyone experienced, when the staff came out with lunch—and water! Oh, it was just wonderful! It was very hot out there.

When we finished the dam, we had a dedication ceremony. Everyone in the Training School gathered after supper one night. With lanterns to light the way in the pitch dark, we walked along the road past the village and out over the fields to the dam. We sat in rows all the way across the top of the dam while Ed stood at the bottom, reading poetry to celebrate the accomplishment. Then we all walked back to the village.

James Wiegel

We all felt compelled to look as if we were working hard....

Finding The Center

They created a great symbol that showed the globe sitting on top of an eagle's wings.

Kendur is located fifty kilometers north of Pune, twenty kilometers off the Aurangabad Highway in India's Maharashtra state. It was named after the Hindu goddess Kendra. Kendra in the Marathi language means "center" and usually refers to places of service and care for all the people. A statue of Kendra stands outside the small temple near the village center in Kendur. I vividly remember the remarkable changes that occurred the year I lived in Kendur.

The project had an enthusiastic start in 1976 as one of the first four human development projects in Maharashtra. At first, the head Brahmin and the *Sarpanch* (elected village head man) were for the project. But one of the project workers had made serious social mistakes and deeply offended some of the upper caste Brahmin leaders, which proved to be an early and serious setback. The Brahmins as a class were opposed to the project by the time I arrived in 1977 and our work continued with great difficulty.

In a way, the village and the project had lost their "center" and we had to proceed with a very low-key approach. The project leaders decided on three programs which we hoped would prove effective in rebuilding the confidence of the village leaders. One was a Hindi literacy class which trained more villagers to speak and read India's national language. The second was an evening youth program with after-school tutoring, singing and empowering rituals. The third was a schedule of weekly meetings in the homes of village families. Under the guidance of our colleague Mary, we met with people, reflected on the week, talked over village and family issues and celebrated our life and work. One evening I took photographs from the Hai Ou project in Taiwan to one of these meetings. People were excited to see themselves in a project similar to one so far away off the coast of China. A certain global awareness was beginning to be built in the village.

Through these indirect efforts, villagers began to regain the self-confidence needed to turn the project and the village around. Subsequently, we accomplished two really great projects. The Brahmins had a close relationship with the village elementary school and one of the teachers was one of our best friends. Because of this connection, the project was able to build a model house across the street from the elementary school at the entrance to the village. We also organized an eye clinic in which seventy people had cataract operations at the village's health clinic. The villagers' new-found courage led to the formation of a Community Development Association (CDA) to promote social and economic development in the village. CDA members met as a group alongside the *Gram Panchayat* (Village Council) to discuss the project and what needed to be done. They created a great symbol that showed the globe sitting on top of an eagle's wings.

Most of the village projects that we did in India at that time had CDAs, but with a population of four thousand people, Kendur was large in comparison with most of the other villages where we were working. Because some families lived in outlying *wadis* (hamlets) scattered throughout the various farms, representation in the CDA was difficult and very important. Despite the scattered situation, the CDA became strong and effective. Women led some of the work groups and lower caste people were also active. The full extent of the turn-around in the village became clear the next June when *Gram Panchayat* elections were held. To everyone's astonishment, CDA leaders were elected to many of the offices and the president of the CDA was elected *Sarpanch*. No Brahmins were elected. The new *Sarpanch* was a young farmer from one of the *wadis* who had great vision and determination.

Kendur had set aside the earlier difficulties and begun to do its own development in a bold, new way. The village was known for its onions, one of its major crops. We had hoped that Ruston Hornsby, a company in Pune, would help us market village-grown onions directly to their cafeteria. But I was visited one day by a slickly dressed onion buyer from Pune who offered me a cut of the take if I would stop bypassing the middle men such as him in our onion-marketing negotiations with Ruston Hornsby. I replied, "No, thanks."

Though the effort had not yet succeeded before I left Kendur for other assignments, I have heard that the village is still working in close partnership with Ruston Hornsby in Pune. A scattered, fragmented village had once again found its center. Kendra reigned.

David McCleskey

Women Of The World

When we first taught the Human Development Training Institutes (HDTI) in India, the schools were attended by young village men and a few single women. But at one point, some of the young men began bringing their wives. Most of these young women were only fourteen or fifteen years old. They came to the sessions, but did not speak. The women on the teaching staff decided to do something about this.

We decided to have an all-day Global Women's Forum with these young women during the second week of the Training Institute. During the forum, women staff and the women participants went through the process of getting to know each other. We decorated our room and had a lovely tea together. We talked about our hopes as women and our struggles. Individually and in small groups we looked at a month calendar and marked in different colored pens how we spent our time. We talked about how we could make time to fulfill some of the hopes.

Excitement increased as the young women discovered the energy of possibility and permission. From then on, they fully participated in the HDTI! Even though they were always a minority in the midst of many men, they spoke up in workshops and in the lecture hall amidst over one hundred people. The women became colleagues who had found their voice.

From the first time we held the Forum, we were amazed that a one-day event was such a great happening for the young women. We continued to do a similar forum in many Training Institutes after that. The

The men were a bit suspicious.

"magic" worked every time and the women found their voices.

I also witnessed the Global Women's Forum giving life to village women near Patna in eastern India. After an Imaginal Education course Liz and I had led with a large group of students at a Catholic school, we went with the students to a tribal village where they had set up a Women's Forum. Liz spoke Hindi and was going to lead the event, but the students were going to facilitate the small groups.

"Women of the World"

When we went to the village, we brought a great supply of the photomontage called, "Women of the World." We saw that we were going to be out on the lawn, so we sat down and took the pictures out. Soon the village women came out of their houses and sat down. But almost immediately they all started leaving. We wondered, "What's happening?" We found out that the men had not known that this meeting was going to happen and they were calling their wives back to their homes. The men were a bit suspicious.

We waited and watched. Soon the women started coming back again. Such audacity! This was an interesting turn of events.

Now the men started lining up all around the edge of our circle so that the women had to walk between them to sit down at the meeting. The children were also there standing behind their fathers or their mothers. We ended up having all the women in the village sitting down on the ground inside the circle.

This was a potentially dangerous situation. Liz and I were both shaking in our boots. We knew that every word Liz said would be screened and scrutinized by the men. Did we have the courage to do this forum? We decided "yes" in spite of our jitters.

Since Liz spoke little of the local dialect, we were really counting on the young women from the Catholic school to make this forum happen.

Liz got the Forum started. Then in groups of three or four, the young course graduates led conversations about the "Women of the World" photomontage. In spite of the fact that the men could hear and see everything all the time, the village women fully participated. They saw women in that montage who understood their pain and joy. They shared their own hopes and dreams, struggles and plans for the future. This took a lot of courage.

The young school women who led the conversations were overwhelmed by the insights of "illiterate women." In my heart, I knew that the women's spirit revolution was alive and well.

Jeanette Stanfield

Souvenirs

I moved to Kenya in 1980 and lived for four years in Kawangware, our urban village project in Kenya's capital city, Nairobi. At that time the village movement was not really doing anything for the women who remained in the villages while their husbands and other village men worked in the nearby cities, so a team was created to offer development training for village women. Dorothy and Bernadette were two of the first Kenyans trained in methods of women's advancement, along with Sandra and me.

I have vivid memories of my first Women's Advancement Module. Dorothy, Bernadette and I traveled by bus to Nakuru, the fourth largest city in Kenya, located in the Rift Valley about a hundred miles north of Nairobi. From there we took a *matatu* (pickup taxi) north along a dirt road past the turn-off for the Masai village where we had project staff.* After stopping along a smaller dirt road, we hiked on into the village, another twelve miles away.

The reception from the villagers was as warm as the weather was hot. They had prepared beans, rice and *chapatis* (flat unleavened bread) for us and showed us the hut where we would sleep.

The next two days were spent in workshops on economics, literacy, clean water, and planting hybrid crops. We sat on a small hill with twenty or so women around us and drew charts about the future of the village. Two of the women and I went into Nakuru to arrange for English classes to be taught in the village. When we returned with a blackboard, chalk, literacy books, writing books and sharpened pencils, the women were immensely pleased with themselves; they had actual materials to show off to the others. Sometime later we joined the village women in clearing off a patch of land together, planted hybrid maize seeds, carried water up from the stream and watered them. When the weekend was over and it was time to leave, the women gave each of us a gourd decorated with leather and beads for carrying water.

Months later, when I returned to this village, the maize was growing quite well. The decorated water gourd is hanging on my wall to this day.

Penny Portman

Village women with Bernadette
(far right above);
the souvenir gourd (below)

---

* Later that year, on this very same road north from Nakuru, a *matatu* in which one of our colleagues was riding was stopped by the Army during the riots against President Moi. Two of the men riding in the *matatu* were forced to get out and hauled out of sight. Shots were fired. The two never came back.

Raising The I-Beam

The Isle of Dogs planning consultation in London posed as many challenges as opportunities for those of us involved in preparation and support. We had wonderful experiences. E.F. Schumacher, the famous futurist and writer, came by for several hours of fascinating dialogue. Later, we acquired an old pleasure boat which we intended to dock on the Thames and turn into a shoe factory. But for every delightful or intriguing public accomplishment, there were a dozen rough-edged dramas going on behind the scenes.

It all began with the I-beam. We had acquired a building in the Isle of Dogs, near the old East India Docks. We needed to knock down a wall in the basement to create a large meeting room adjacent to the kitchen. But the wall was a load-bearing wall and there was every chance that the whole huge four-story structure would collapse from the weight of all the good folks who would be working above. That is where the I-beam came in—we needed some serious steel to support the structure above our new meeting room.

We placed an order and the steel I-beam was delivered a few days later. Twenty men were rounded up to lift a ton of steel. They all lined up and slowly lifted the beam up one foot, up two feet, three, then up to shoulder height. But the beam began to win; it was too heavy and began to tilt. Someone called out, "Don't grab it on the far side!" Everyone had time to heed the warning, except Frank. Just as the rest of the men let go: bam! Frank's thumb became quite squashed. The blow was agonizing, but the thumb survived.

With the help of a heavy construction jack, the I-beam was finally hoisted into place. A hole had to be cut into the ceiling when the jack was set up. After we finished, we could not figure out how to extract the jack and it had to be left right there in the ceiling.

There were other dramas as well, like preparations for the opening ceremony dinner. We had decided to roast a pig. The pig returned from the market and was stuffed into our very small oven. As it began to cook, fat began to ooze out onto the floor. Joe stopped by to check on our progress and everyone realized that the pig was not cooking fast enough and would not be ready in time. So out came the leaking, partially cooked pig. It was cut into pieces and the pieces were rushed to several neighborhood pubs to be cooked in their microwave ovens. Dinner was delayed while the pig roasted and the cooking team packed the cooked bits back to the waiting platters. In the midst of all this chaos and uncertainty, members of the cooking team decided to sing as they worked. One song after another sprang up, but the most memorable line was, "We are poor little lambs, who have lost their way, bah, bah, bah." With apologies to the pig and lots of laughter when the cooks realized they were singing to the wrong animal, these poor little kitchen lambs pulled off a small miracle that day.

Further humiliations followed later in the week when a colleague took the cooking team to work on a

> ...the pig...was cut into pieces and the pieces were rushed to several neighborhood pubs....

gardening project. A clump of blackberry bushes needed to be cut back to make room for other projects. The team decided to burn the bushes, since cutting them out required tools which they did not have. Unfortunately, the winds were whipping around at gale force, and the fire threatened the main building that housed the ICA staff and the consultation. Only fast action kept the fire from setting the building alight.

Document writing during the week following the consultation posed its own challenges with fire. In the middle of March, it was still quite cold in London, and of course the rooms needed to be heated for the people typing the consultation results. Like all British houses built earlier in the century, the house was heated with coal-burning fireplaces in all the rooms. The coal that we hauled up periodically from the basement to maintain the fires was so heavy and messy that we had to apply burning tar to the bottom of the fireplaces to keep it burning. But the viscous tar had a way of running out of the fireplace and onto the wooden floors, with a trail of fire not far behind. Only a great deal of vigilance prevented any mishaps.

Jan Latham

Where Is Our Luggage?

The ICA staff in the Philippines were hosting people from all over the world attending the week-long initiating consultation for the Sudtonggan Human Development Project. Our guests had to fly into Manila International Airport, then, from the national airport, they flew on to Cebu. Finally, they rode a pedicab out to Sudtonggan. A group coming from Indonesia included an important national Muslim leader, the son of a General, and a Christian dignitary. We wanted to take good care of such prominent guests.

We had devised a careful transportation plan, since the village where we were working was hidden in a rural area far from Cebu's national airport. My part in the plan was to meet everyone at the International Airport in Manila and get them across the city to the national airport for their flight to Cebu.

We had a good plan, but just as the consultation was to begin, a tremendous typhoon struck the Philippines. The palm trees were bending down to the streets, the rain was coming down in sheets, and I had only one umbrella. Military regulations prevented waiting for arrivals inside the international airport, and the national airport was jammed with anxious crowds. I decided to invite the guests to enjoy a look at crafts at an art center while I arranged their tickets at the national airport. They seemed impressed with my graciousness and I was pleased that I had come up with a tranquil alternative. We hailed a taxi and the driver helped us load the luggage in the trunk in the midst of the driving rain.

> ...but just as the consultation was to begin, a tremendous typhoon struck the Philippines.

I was... still chilled to the bone by what I had done....

We arrived at the art center and I dropped off the guests, then went on to the national airport to do the ticketing. Because of the storm and the congestion at the airport, I got out quickly and told the taxi driver to go on. I was eager to begin the arduous task of ticket negotiation. There were hundreds of people inside the airport, all trying to make plane arrangements. I used the savvy I had gained as a foreigner to find strategic contacts and I was able to negotiate the tickets quickly. I felt very competent, but was anxious to return to my guests. I grabbed a taxi to the art center and went to the coffee shop to meet my group. We greeted each other and they said how grateful they were for my braving the storm to negotiate their tickets. Then the General asked, "Where is our luggage?"

A chill came over me as if I had been enveloped in a wet blanket of dread. Everyone was waiting for my reply. I remembered that I had left the luggage in the trunk of the first taxi I had sent off over two hours ago at the national airport. There was no way to skirt around it. "I'm so sorry. I left your luggage in the trunk of the taxi and I have no idea where the taxi is now." There was a long pause as we stared at each other.

The guests were quiet and very gracious, holding back every urge to blame and be angry. One of them said, "There is a way to find the luggage and we'll just have to figure it out together." I was relieved, but still chilled to the bone by what I had done, wishing that I could start the day again, knowing there was no escape.

I asked our guests for a description of the bags and hoped that they were well marked and distinctive. They wrote on the back of an envelope, "Two brown leather bags and one black canvas bag. There are no identification tags. Inside the bags are four pieces of cut ivory, five pieces of silk from Singapore, a brown box containing precious gems, $200 in dollar bills, and a set of house keys made in Amsterdam." (The keys were the owner's only set.) Once again my heart sank. With such common bags and no identification, I could not imagine how we would ever find them. And if we did find the bags, would we ever recover the precious contents?

We deliberated for some time about what steps to take. Knowing that the deadline to catch the plane to Cebu was approaching, I posed the alternatives: people could stay in Manila to look for the luggage with me or they could proceed to Cebu and the village without their luggage. After further thought, one of the guests stated their decision: "We came to this country to find out about village development. We'll go on without our luggage."

I stayed in Manila and spent the next day on the phone, checking with the hotels, with security officials, and anyone else I could think of who might give me a clue to finding this one particular taxi in all of Manila. I did not have any luck and continued my increasingly desperate search into a second and third day.

One of the young men who worked in our office was the brother of a friend of one of the guests. He began pressing me daily, "Have you found the luggage yet?" Each day I had to admit, "No." Each day he reminded me, "It is all your fault that it is lost!" It was a painful reminder to try harder! I had telephoned everybody on the first day; on the second and third days, I went everywhere I could think of. "It's no use," I thought.

On the fourth day, the bell at the gate rang. A colleague went out and returned, saying, "Keith, you'll never guess who is here."

"I can't. I'm all guessed out."

"It's a taxi driver. Should I let him in?"

"What taxi driver?"

"The guy with the luggage."

Did we let him in!

The driver said, "Do you realize, lady, I have been looking for you for three days?"

I said, "I have been looking for *you* for three days."

The driver was carrying an envelope with our Manila address on it. It had contained a letter with the name and address of my accuser, the young man who worked in our office. The envelope had been sent with one of the guests from a friend in Singapore. The guest had decided to carry the envelope in her suitcase. The taxi driver said, "I'm sorry that I had to look into one of the pieces of luggage after two days. Come with me to my house and I will show you the luggage."

We got into the taxi and drove to his house, still flooded by the typhoon. The water was up to his knees but there was all the luggage, dry and safe. The taxi driver asked, "Is everything here?" A quick inspection revealed that the items people had been worried about—the carved ivory, the silk, the keys, the precious jewels, and the $200—were all there. I was amazed.

We loaded the bags back into the taxi and returned to the office, listening to the driver relate his story about how he had spent three days looking for me. I related the details of how I had looked for him. His tale was far more dramatic and we knew that there was no way to reward him for his integrity. We tried to convey our appreciation with the money we could spare and many words of gratitude. For him it was enough; for me it seemed hollow compared with the gift that I had received. The experience became a talisman, a touchstone, much more than a memory.

The guests who lost their luggage were ecstatic when they read the cable message that their luggage had been recovered. They surprised me by asking me to keep it in Manila! They were getting along just fine with clothes that villagers and other consultation participants had lent them. They were learning over and over again about the goodness of people. I walked away with the treasure of knowing that when I am in a tight situation, I will be supported and sustained by others.

Keith Packard

On the fourth day, the bell at the gate rang.

He Slowed Down A Train

> "Could it slow down a little more?"
> "I don't know."

Rupert and Slicker had been doing site selection for replication of our village work. Several of us had been "walking" those villages to confirm their suitability for human development projects. I pointed out to Larry how many of the villages our colleagues had selected were on the top of hills. I knew because I was having to climb all those hills. We were looking for key villages, especially from the point of view of visibility, so that when transformations began to take place, they could be seen by neighboring villages. One of the reasons everybody knew about Kamweleni village, for example, was that it could be seen for miles when its generators were running in the evening, especially from the main tarmac Machakos-Kitui road across the Ikiwe River. Naturally, villages on top of hills were especially visible.

One day, Rupert and Slicker were to take a night train for the eight-hour overnight trip from Nairobi to Mombasa on Kenya's south coast in order to visit government officials and do site selection nearby. They had purchased their tickets in advance to give each of them a top bunk in a three-tiered berth. They were to meet Larry at Mombasa.

We still needed to pick up Rupert at a friend's home in a suburb of Nairobi and were bringing his newly-cleaned safari suit for the trip. Slicker was still pouring over all the maps he had been using and we were running late. When we arrived at Rupert's friend's home, I took the safari suit into the house with Slicker's urging that Rupert dress and come without delay. A Lutheran minister was visiting the family. I gave Rupert his suit and returned to the car to wait with Slicker. Several minutes passed and no Rupert. Slicker began to fuss and fume. He honked the car horn. He shouted, "Rupert, we are going to be late!"

The minutes dragged on and we were approaching train departure time. Finally, Slicker shouted out as loud as he could, "Rupert, damn it! Come on!"

We heard commotion in the house. Rupert appeared and climbed into the car at last.

We got to the Nairobi train station just in time to see the train pull out. Without blinking, Slicker said, "The first stop is about ten miles down the road. This train does not go very fast, so let's go on down the road and we'll catch it at the next stop!" We hurried back to the car and arrived at the Athi River Station about twenty minutes before the train arrived. We dropped Rupert and Slicker off and drove back to Nairobi.

When Rupert and Slicker got to the platform, they asked the station attendants what time the train would arrive. They were told that the train did not stop at that station.

Slicker asked, "Does it slow down?"

"It does have to come around the bend here, so it does slow down a little bit."

"Could it slow down a little more?"

"I don't know."

Slicker persisted. "What do they do here?"

"They have to get the mail pouch. There is a man on a bicycle with the pouch, and the men on the train catch it as they go by."

Slicker had a plan. "Well, why don't you make it a little hard for them to catch?"

The two station attendants were in their sixties and the cyclist was a young man of about nineteen or twenty. Slicker talked them into slowing down the train with the bicycle! The young man with the mail pouch rode alongside the train as slowly as possible, forcing the train to slow down more and more.

Rupert and Slicker, with their two suitcases, just made it onto the steps of the train by the skin of their teeth. Later we heard that the people inside the car finally opened the door and helped them. Everybody cheered and Slicker became known as the man who conned a guy into slowing down a train.

David Coffman

The View From The Train

Rupert and I ran alongside the train and finally jumped onto a sleeping car's steps. Rupert was on the front part of the car and I was on the back. The train doors were locked. No one inside the train knew we were outside or that anything unusual was going on.

The train was picking up speed as it pulled out of the station. It was frightening. I had my bag under my left arm with my hand hanging onto the hand rail. My briefcase was in my right hand, so I tried kicking on the door with my right foot and hitting the window with the briefcase, and knocking my head against the glass in the door window. By this time the train was moving rapidly and we were in darkness except for light from the train windows. Finally the car porter heard us and let us in.

Joe Slicker

I tried kicking on the door....

Casting Out Demons

We were facing a crisis in Nairobi. There was still no funding in sight and without funding, there could be no program. The only thing to do was to work on the training center facilities, but without program funds, it seemed silly to upgrade facilities. Besides, a needs assessment, equipment lists and trips to the nearest large regional city to seek donated goods seemed futile under the circumstances.

Water boiling on the jiko

The staff Council had made decisions to deal with the situation, including reducing the number of ICA village offices from ten to five, closing some project houses and consolidating or relocating others. Everyone knew that there would be hard times in the coming months because of the loss of program momentum, the reduction of project houses and the uprooting of families as staff members were relocated. The Council had also approved a plan for a leadership meeting once a month that would approve a disbursement of funds to the houses every two weeks. In spite of our careful planning, we were painfully aware of the drop in morale.

One Thursday, the Nairobi staff was anticipating spending the next day in careful preparation for one of the monthly leadership meetings when the phone rang. Evans was calling from Saba Saba, the town with a telephone nearest to Mugumoini village. He was calling on behalf of the Mugumoini Office to register his concern about a disagreement between two women which had turned into a confrontation and the threat of physical violence. No amelioration seemed possible. Later in the day a second person called, indicating that the disagreement had escalated. Everyone in Nairobi knew that something must be done, but no one was eager to send off any of the leaders needed to plan the monthly meeting. Our Regional Director told me everything he knew about the situation and asked me to go to Mugumoini. I wondered if I would face a brick wall with no end or top.

Friday morning was gray and overcast. It was the middle of October and the wet-season rains were threatening. I had recently sold my motorcycle, so I rose early and caught a city bus downtown, were I caught the Muran'ga shuttle. It went through Thika, past Saba Saba, and on to the Kaharati junction. I soon found a *matatu* (pickup taxi) going toward Kigumo which would drop me off at the Chief's camp. From the Chief's camp, I descended into the Saba Saba River valley, crossed the river and climbed to the Mugumoini Training Center. I arrived as I had intended at about 8:30 A.M., which I hoped would be a time of quiet contentment just after breakfast. I had guessed right. Almost everyone was sitting around the *jiko* (charcoal burner) warming themselves in the chill of the early morning dew.

We greeted each other, I sat down and was offered *chai* and a piece of bread. We passed the time of day briefly and I began talking about the purpose of my visit. I had decided to couch this conversation in metaphor as much as possible. I began by telling them that I did not know what had happened, but someone had told me that there had been several phone calls from people in Mugumoini reporting a good deal of smoke and something very hot, something like the beginning of a fire. The situation was very dangerous because so many people could be burned. People acknowledged that there was cause for concern. Since I knew nothing about what had happened, I wanted to hear from those who were directly involved. I wanted to be able to clear the air and cool down a situation that everyone agreed was too hot for comfort.

I knew that the two women involved were from different tribes—Jennifer was Akamba and Lucy was Meru—and the resentment between them had resulted from disagreements between their children and between themselves about how the children should be handled. I wondered if there were different tribal expectations about children and how they should be raised. There was no disagreement about whether or not a child should be caned (physically punished with a stick), but there were differences of opinion about when a child should be caned and who should be designated to do it.

It was an important issue for them. While Lucy had been a member of the Training Center staff for the last year, Jennifer had just moved to the Training Center with her husband and family and there were ten other staff members who were new to the setting. Evans, Lucy's husband, had called Nairobi first, and Joshua, Jennifer's husband, was the director of the Training Center. Both men knew that more objectivity was needed than they could provide. The staff knew the situation needed a disinterested third party and were grateful for my coming.

I did not indicate that anyone should leave; the matter was every family's concern. I assumed that everyone who was concerned would stay and anyone who needed to leave would do so. I asked for one of the two women to begin by telling the story as she remembered it. I asked everyone else to remain silent and let the narrative stand on its own. Jennifer began with her story. When she was finished, I thanked her and asked Lucy to tell her story. When Lucy was finished, I thanked her. I told the group that I was not going to ask anyone else for his or her point of view, as other points of view would only begin a process of dividing the staff and drawing up sides. I offered my personal witness: "I cannot remember one disagreement with my wife in which one of us was to blame and the other was blameless. Always in our disagreements, we were both completely responsible for the disagreement. I believe that this is also true for Lucy and Jennifer."

I asked pointedly, "What will have to happen in order to heal this situation?" There was a prolonged silence which led me to believe that my question had been too direct. I began another direction by asking, "When you begin to feel the heat—the friction

> *The situation was very dangerous because so many people could be burned.*

> "Let the fire which was smoldering become cool."

between the children—what can you do to cool the situation down?"

The second question led to an energetic workshop; the whole staff was intent on beginning to establish parental consensus about how the children needed to be handled, individually and corporately. As the talk continued, Jennifer volunteered that she was angry and that as a human being she would not apologize for being angry. However, she would apologize for the hurt that she had caused to Lucy and to the staff families. Lucy also offered an apology to Jennifer and the staff families. We were all beginning to experience power returning to the group; I could feel the group's trust in its wisdom and strength.

I continued to use the metaphor of heat. "How can you recognize this heat the next time it starts to rise and create an opportunity to talk to each other about what you are feeling so you will understand what you need to do to accommodate each other?" Lucy said she could see that this could be worked out another way in the future. The rest of the staff families could come to some agreements on how the children should be handled. The discussion had given the whole staff permission to take responsibility for staff family disagreements by airing them in the open and letting them cool off before they became too hot to handle.

They saw that they could begin to talk together when it became necessary for an adult to speak to a child at risk in or around the common facilities, the cooking/dishwashing area, the garden, the dining room, the kitchen pantry, or the private room of someone other than a family member.

We had been talking for nearly two and one-half hours and the charcoal in the *jiko* had completely died out. I put my hand on the *jiko* and observed that our conversation had followed the same course—it was hot when we sat down together and over the course of time and conversation it had burnt itself out and was now cool. "I have no experience being a Witch Doctor, but I am going to try something. I am going to cast a spell of healing on the Training Center with these ashes." I rose, gathered a handful of ashes and circled the staff who were still gathered around the *jiko*, saying, "Let the fire which was smoldering become cool. Let all situations which threaten to heat up be cooled by the ashes from this fire."

I announced that I was through and needed to leave. With intense affection, I said my goodbyes to the staff. I was leaving Kenya to return to the US.

David Zahrt

Development Fighter

I can consider my coming to the ICA in 1984 as a coincidence. At that time I did not have a clear image about the development process and its tools. Many people shared in formulating my development learnings. Robert was one of those people. I think this man was born to be a Development Fighter: he had the morals of the fighter, the wisdom of the veteran and was very humble in his dealing with ICA staff and the local people.

Robert came at a critical time. The relationship with the community was not on the right track and the funding situation was very poor. He started to rebuild the relationship with the local people, especially with the village leaders. I was struck with his way of dealing with the people, especially with the village leaders, because it reflects his splendid experience in local community work.

I remember one situation when Robert invited me to participate in a meeting with community leaders to discuss the ICA contribution plan in supporting some activities in east bank villages. It was one day in 1987. The meeting was very friendly and warm. In this meeting Robert agreed to fund many villages' projects, but sometimes this kind of treatment creates a kind of greed with some village leaders. So one of the leaders wanted to put pressure on Robert to increase the proportion of ICA funding for some project in his village.

Suddenly Robert's attitude changed, his face became very red from anger and he refused strongly to accept the leader's pressure. The leaders became very surprised at the change of Robert's attitude, but finally they apologized to him.

After this meeting, I expressed to Robert my wondering about his attitude change. Robert laughed and told me that he was acting because working in development needs many skills to control the critical situation, especially if the developer is an expert person.

Sometimes working in development demands the ability to modify and act with the people, especially when you are dealing with attitude change. I became very convinced that the developer must be compromising in some situations and decisive in others. Robert was one of those because he was a Development Fighter.

Abdel Rahman Moundy

Meeting with village leaders

You Can't Do That

Some people did not think families would loan the money on such short notice.

One of the major issues that was on the mind of everyone in the community during the Lorne de Lacadie planning consultation was lack of fast access to fire protection, because the nearest fire station was in Jacquet River, approximately seventeen miles away. During the winter months, frequent snowstorms, seven feet of snow and unplowed roads meant that fire trucks simply could not make it to Lorne. During the consultation, we had stuck our necks out and committed to having a fire truck in Lorne by the Friday following the last day of the consultation.

The week following the consultation was the week for early accomplishments and fast miracles and everyone was busy working in teams on various projects. The team working on fire protection had found a used fire truck for sale in St. Quentin, some 150 miles away. On Friday—the day we had said a new fire truck would be in the village—the Fire Protection Team was trying to figure out how to raise the money to purchase St. Quentin's fire truck.

I was working with the Economic Team and was listening in on the conversation regarding the truck. Someone asked if the team thought that families could and would loan $500 per family to purchase the truck while the community raised the money to repay the loans. Some people did not think families would loan the money on such short notice. I responded by saying "I don't have $500, but I could loan $200. Who else do you think has $200?" I was asked to join the Fire Protection Team.

We came up with a list of twenty families to ask and in the next three hours we raised $7,000 in loans—mostly cash and a few checks. Two men from the community drove to St. Quentin and after a short demonstration by its enterprising owners, purchased the fire truck. They drove the truck back to Lorne and paraded the new fire truck through the village at 11 P.M., one hour before the midnight Friday deadline. Shortly after this early victory, a Firemen's Association, a Ladies' Auxiliary and a Junior Firemen's Association were formed and the firemen were sent to Moncton for training. The money to pay back the loans was raised through donations from each adult in the community and various fund-raising activities, which also helped pay for training, suits and fire fighting equipment.

As the men got better acquainted with their new fire truck, it became apparent that the pump needed major repair work. We appealed to the Department of Municipal Affairs for help. Because we had taken the initiative, raised the money and purchased a fire truck, the officials in the Department told us that if we could build a Fire Hall before the frost, they would give the community a new fire truck.

Because Lorne had a parish priest who was a carpenter and had built several houses in the village, the community decided that the Fire Hall could be built by local men with the priest's help. Construction began in July.

By mid-September the foundation was built and the frame was up, but we realized that if we did not get more people working, we were not going to meet the deadline. So we had a meeting with the various teams and asked who could build rafters and work on the Fire Hall. Several women said they could build rafters, and furthermore, could do some shingling on the roof as well. The parish priest and the men said, "Women can't do that." The ten women who had volunteered said, "Of course we can, and yes, we will."

The women made the rafters and helped with the roofing. The Fire Hall was completed on time by the end of October. We got the promised new fire truck and even had the old one repaired. The Fire Hall served Lorne and the surrounding villages. Apart from the help of the Department of Municipal Affairs and a Canada Works Project, the money to pay for the Fire Hall was raised by funding events like dances, cabarets, bazaars, etc. put on by the fire fighters and the Women's Auxiliary.

An event about five years later testifies to the importance of the Lorne Fire Hall. Two of the Lorne fire fighters were coming home from work at the Belledune Smelter one day. On their way through Doyleville, the next village over from Lorne and about seven miles from the Fire Hall, they noticed smoke coming from one of the houses. They rushed on to the Lorne Fire Hall, called other fire fighters and changed into fire fighting gear. They raced back to the house in Doyleville and began attacking the fire.

The woman whose house was burning said "I didn't call you, I called the Jacquet River Fire Hall." The Jacquet River fire truck did arrive later, but by then the Lorne fire fighters had put the fire out.

Sheighlah Hickey

"I didn't call you, I called the Jacquet River Fire Hall."

The Voyage of the Tatami Maru

Don, an Australian from Sydney, was a tall, bony frame cutting across the glaring white coral of the Marshall Islands during the 1970s. He had a great slow-coming smile that transformed his entire face and ended with a twinkle in his eyes. The fingers on his large, strong hands were often cut or nicked from his work, and dark, fascinating rings surrounded the nails. I liked standing next to him during our daily worship service. When we passed the peace to one another, his hands said more in a reassuring way than words could. They reminded me of what I had forgotten: "The peace of God is yours this day."

Marshallese coastal freighter

Don knew everything one could possibly know about two things on the atoll—scrap metal (mostly rusty) and dogs. The dogs were caramel colored, with long noses and substantial tails, that all looked the same, due to close inbreeding. Wherever he went, two or three dogs followed Don as if they were an integral part of his team at the Multi-Purpose Repair Center. He listened to classical music and carried on conversations with the dogs while he worked. When he petted the dogs, his touch literally drove them crazy. They wagged their tails until they threw themselves off balance. All one could see were dog legs up in the air and tails going sixty miles an hour in all directions.

Majuro must have been paradise for a man like Don, who got his kicks out of fixing things. It seemed that every possible moving thing on the atoll was in a constant state of disrepair. He was always working on five or six different things at a time. If it was not a broken-down truck, it was an outboard motor, or a big refrigerated storage unit, or a defunct generator from a copra freighter. When some little thing—small enough to hold between two fingers—broke, the consequences were complicated, costly and time consuming. There was no neighborhood Ace Hardware down the block. Replacement parts, if available, came only every other day from Guam or Hawaii, both eight to ten hours away by Continental jet airplane. Majuro was an impractical place for things to break, but over and over again, impossible situations catalyzed Don's unbelievable creativity and resourcefulness.

One of our most vivid memories involved a small freighter, the *Tatami Maru*. It was stranded in the bay at Kwajelein Atoll. Its Marshallese owner hired Don and flew him to Kwajelein to appraise the freighter's condition and, if possible, to fix it. Don boarded the plane to Kwajelein with a handful of tools and a very serious, determined look on his face. We did not hear from him for several days. Then one morning, among the scratchy spurtings of the CB radio, we heard:

"Kitco Majuro, calling Kitco Majuro." More spurting, crackling interference. "This is Don, calling Kitco Majuro. Do you read me? Come in please!"

"This is Kitco Majuro. Go ahead Don. We read you loud and clear. How's it coming with the *Tatami Maru*?" I yelled, straining for Don to hear.

"The engine room of the *Tatami Maru* is three feet deep in water." (Sputter, sputter, whistle, crack.) "She is listing to the far right." More interference, crackling and whistling followed, and then, in his most sober, deeply dramatic voice: "The crew has abandoned ship, but, Elijah and I remain." Elijah was the ship's engineer. It was not unusual for Marshallese to be given Biblical names.

The CB radio sputtered even louder then fell silent. Nothing. We had lost contact with Don. You can imagine all the dangerous things that went through our minds during the next several weeks as we awaited word from Don and the *Tatami Maru*. We imagined the worst sorts of tragedies. We imagined headlines reading "Engineer and mechanic with screwdriver in hand go down with their ship," or, "*Tatami Maru* Capsizes—Crew Feared Lost at Sea." Disasters surfaced in our imaginations that were too grim to repeat out loud.

Then, one afternoon, a young Marshallese man came running into the Kitco offices shouting that the *Tatami Maru* had been sighted as it entered Majuro's lagoon. People were shocked. Confusion and excitement reigned. "The *Tatami Maru*?"

"What? She is headed this way?"

"How can that be?"

Sure enough. In a short time the *Tatami Maru* had docked. Elijah and Don disembarked, walking tall and straight down the gangplank, beaming with the smiles of quiet, unassuming heroes. They had done it. As incredible as it was, they had fixed the *Tatami Maru*. Before an enthralled audience, Don relayed all the bloody details as only an authentic Australian storyteller could. He explained how he and Elijah rigged up a forge on the back of the ship. Using coconut hulls, they built up the fire and sustained its temperature long enough to forge a replacement part from scraps of metal and an automobile hub cap. Then, "on a wing and a prayer," they daringly sailed 275 miles on the open sea to bring her home.

Don's and Elijah's ingenuity resurrected a nearly sunken coastal freighter. Some believed the two were at the center of a modern day miracle. Miracle or not, the arrival of the old ship was a sign that gave many Marshallese and those of us who were close to them, a reason to lift our heads with hope. Today, the Republic of the Marshall Islands is a nation because its people rediscovered courage and self-determination in an isolated corner of the Pacific Ocean. This new nation exists in part because men and women used their less than perfect lives to turn matter into spirit.

There is a kinship, even a genuine affection, one feels toward such human beings when you have shared profound purpose, bleak despair and glorious fulfillment. Human connections forged while sharing such intense experiences are not easily broken by time, changes of interest, distance, or even death. Don died in 1995.

Leah Early

> Some believed the two were at the center of a modern day miracle.

Sir James

> "Don't say anything. I can explain why I am dressed like this for the meeting!"

It was a daunting task to work with the image that we had to raise all the money needed to do our development work in India. Hundreds of village development projects were underway by the early 1980s and thousands and thousands of dollars had to be raised each year to keep them going. From 1982 to 1985, my husband and I joined this monumental effort by the Development Team in Mumbai (Bombay). During these years, Sir James Lindsay was the only source of relief in an unending cycle of phoning, visiting, proposal writing and accountability.

Sir James visited Mumbai about twice a year in his capacity as President of ICA International. He had lived in India years before and had been the CEO of a large Indian company for many years. He was a distinguished gentleman and had been knighted for his public service while working in India. He had many friends and connections in high places, including many Indian industrialists. He was so well known and so well loved, he could get us into any company we wanted to visit. When we knew Sir James was making plans to spend a week in India, we spent upwards of a month lining up all his appointments. We scheduled every person he was to see and planned every move he would make, usually at least six or seven appointments a day. It was a very tight schedule.

While he was in Mumbai, Sir James was always hosted by one of the many companies where he had friends. He stayed at their guest houses with his own suite of rooms, a small kitchen, beautiful grounds and a swimming pool. Breakfast was brought to him each morning of his stay on a silver platter. India's company guest houses are lovely places and Sir James always received royal treatment.

It had been difficult to get an appointment with the Tata industrial house, the biggest industrial empire in India, until we mentioned Sir James. An early morning appointment was quickly arranged with Mr. Ratan Tata. On the day of the appointment, we got up early and called Sir James to make sure that he was ready. But there was no answer. We phoned at least a dozen times. No answer. We got worried. Had something horrible happened? Frightened out of our wits, we drove over to the guest house and nervously knocked on the door. We kept worrying to ourselves, "He's forgotten about the appointment and is sleeping!"

We knocked many times, but there was still no response. As we were wondering what to do next, Sir James appeared, dressed in his swimming briefs. Before we could open our mouths, he said, "Don't say anything. I can explain why I am dressed like this for the meeting!" That morning when he had left for a swim, he had inadvertently pulled the door shut without taking the key with him. He had been locked out. He had no access to a phone and had spent most of the morning wondering what to do next.

It was too early to call the guest house company for duplicate keys and too late to reschedule our appointment. As we scratched our heads for a solution, Cyprian pulled out the Swiss army knife he always carried with him. It had a tiny saw blade. Using that mini-saw, he cut around the door knob. When the hole was big enough, he put his hand through and opened the door. Sir James finally got to his bedroom and dressed in his own inimitable way—brown shirt, jacket and tie—and in all his wonder-filled glory, came out beaming. We met our appointment. Sir James spent the rest of the day with us and I am sure made thousands of dollars for the villages of India. He was the most disarming man I have ever met.

Before we returned Sir James to the guest house later that day, the whole door had been replaced by his hosts. A different kind of lock had been installed: it locked from the outside and required a key.

Kay P. Nixon, with Cyprian D'Souza

In The World Of Spirit

Tune: If I Were A Rich Man

In the world of spirit, radically contingent,
    trustful expectation, intense shock.
Life's impacted by the mystery, and it's all a
    cloud of awe!
In the world of spirit, revelation of enigma,
    wheel of fortune, no excuse.
One essential task, create the world, sudden
    reeling, mystery's won the day.

Oneness of all creation, wholly engulfed in
    marching with all of history,
Binding the wounds of time, everything's
    worthwhile.
The other world you see through all and
    move mountains, and there's none to show
    the way,
All in love with life and all poured out.

…the Swiss army knife he always carried with him …had a tiny saw blade.

The Handkerchief

When the Maliwada Human Development Project started, one part of their vision was to get electricity to the village. Some villagers got together one night and made the decision to get electricity in the village by Diwali, a big celebration near the end of the year. They appointed a group of people to go into Aurangabad to talk to the district collector's officers in order to see if they would extend the electrical lines to the village.

After the visit, the delegation returned to the village with the report that it was possible, but would require a deposit equivalent to about US$150 in Indian *rupees*—a sizable sum for a rural village. Since no one in the village had that kind of money, everybody left the meeting dejected. Whereupon, Chokababa, the old leader of the Harijan community, took matters into his own hands.

That very night, he went around to the houses in the Harijan community, the poorest section of the village. He literally went from house to house all night long, collecting money from the people. The next morning he came knocking at the door of the staff house. He came in, holding an old handkerchief which he laid down on a table. Inside was a great mass of rumpled one *rupee* and five *rupee* notes.

When the money had been counted, it was clear that a victory was in sight. The staff called the other people of the village together and showed them what had been collected from the Harijan community. Leaders then went from door to door and collected enough additional money to cover the deposit. The village delegation was sent back into town and returned with the needed certificate. Maliwada was electrified by Diwali.

Vinod Parekh

Chokababa holding up an "Iron Man" poster

Chapter Five
Beyond Expectations

Welcome to the great new home
the Mystery has prepared for us.
Do not be afraid of its size;
every corner is filled with grace,
every turn with adventure, and
every vista with promise.

The Baking Sun

We did not dance like we were at a college dance.

I remember the heat during the program we called Summer '66. Day after day the sun glared down on the city from a blue-white sky. There was no breeze. It rained a couple of times, flooding the basement of the old Administration Building on the Fifth City Campus. The respite was brief.

At 5:30 A.M. the sun was already a force to be reckoned with as it boiled in the bathroom windows on the fourth floor. We listened to lectures morning and afternoon accompanied by the sound of fans. We studied in the evening accompanied by the sound of fans. The heat intensified each day during the month of July and it never stopped.

In spite of that heat, we sang vigorous songs about the city, accompanying ourselves by clapping. Before I sang those songs, I had thought that life in the city was something to be avoided. I had never sung about an ugly, baked-sidewalk city. But the songs were like marches and the rhythm drew me in and pulled me along. Clapping on the off-beat was a novel experience; it was compelling and hypnotic. One song I first heard that summer was an old gospel song that has haunted me ever since: "Jesus Met the Woman at the Well"—"and he told her, everythi-ing, she'd ever dah-un." I've sung it for church and it seemed that it genuinely moved people in an unusual way.

For me, Summer '66 was that meeting at the well, transforming the energy of my life into an energetic new direction. I remember dancing in the alleys and streets after the Saturday night festivals. We did not dance like we were at a college dance. Everyone danced in a communal melee, just moving and shaking and letting it go. The blood boiled over and it was a blast!

Finally, there was the poetry, like the line from D.H. Lawrence: "Give, and it shall be given to you is still the truth about life." I've used that line at the office more than once, as well as: "Even if it's only in the whiteness of a washed pocket handkerchief."

Although it was more than thirty years ago, I have never lived through another month of such intense, transforming heat as Summer '66.

Glenda Long

River Of Consciousness

In 1986, I spent two weeks, including a long Easter holiday weekend, in Zambia, working with the Cooperative College. The visit gave me an opportunity to fulfill my dream of seeing the splendor of Victoria Falls with my own eyes. I had also heard about a raft trip down the Zambezi River, an adventure some old Zambia veterans had told me was *the* thing to do. I decided to check out the raft trip. I wanted to make the most of my visit and doubted that I would ever make it back. Victoria Falls was awesome, but the trip became even more memorable because of what happened below the fall's "smoke and thunder."

As soon as I arrived, I found a poster in the hotel lobby: "SOBEK—The Cutting Edge of Adventure." It showed two people hanging on for dear life to a rubber raft in a violent rapids. My interest was piqued, but the clerk at the reception desk was not encouraging: "Forget it. Bookings for the entire Easter weekend have been sold out for months." Still, I thought I would show up the next morning in hopes of a cancellation. When I arrived at the Sobek gathering place, I was in luck. I paid my money and listened carefully.

The Sobek people were not casual about the adventure which lay before us. Before passing out releases for us to sign, they carefully explained that the river was wild and dangerous, especially with the water as high as it was at that moment, and that while Sobek provided the opportunity to challenge the river in a controlled and organized manner, it could not eliminate all the risks involved. They elaborated on this theme directly to the oldest people in our group, a couple in their mid-fifties, which did not seem terribly old to me. Only then, after this thorough explanation, were we given the signature forms releasing the Sobek company of any liability. With the signed releases in hand, our leaders directed us to the Land Rovers and the unknown of the Zambezi.

Twenty minutes later we came to our departure point. Here we received a detailed safety lecture on how to react in case of trouble—especially if a raft flipped over in the rapids. The key was not to panic: though the current might take us under, our life jackets would absolutely bring us back up, where we need only remember to breathe. The Zambezi, we were told, was one of the "most forgiving rivers" in the world. It was wild, but it was also warm and deep. It did not have rocks and boulders ready to crush one's skull like other white water rivers. It was a reassuring talk and heightened our excitement as we worked our way down the five hundred foot wall of the gorge to the water's edge and our waiting rafts. Within seconds of pushing into the current, I was rudely awakened to the incredible power of the Zambezi. We crashed into a huge wave which left me gagging on river water and spitting for air. "Damn," I thought, "I'm gonna have to really hold on or I'm going into the @*# drink!"

Our party consisted of four rafts with five to six people in each. The rafts shot through the rapids one at a time. When one made it through, it waited and its crew watched as the others followed. After over an

> *The Zambezi, we were told, was one of the "most forgiving rivers" in the world. It was wild, but it was also warm and deep.*

> So we waited and waited, while our imaginations conjured up terrible images of what had gone wrong.

hour of this routine, through four or five gorges, we stopped to portage around a treacherous set of rapids and to have lunch. While we ate, we were told that we had a couple more hours of even heavier white water. The Sobek people were not exaggerating. In the first rapids after lunch, the six of us in my raft were "tube crashing"—throwing our collective weight to the high side of the raft to maintain balance and to avoid a flip—for all that our precious pink skins were worth.

Once again, our raft led the way, then stopped to watch the others make their run. The fourth raft, however, did not make it. It flipped as it rounded the only rock island of our trip.

Our crew swung into action. One crew member jumped ashore and scrambled up a rock for a better view. The others grabbed life lines in case a "swimmer" had been caught in the current and swept downstream. Two minutes later a swimmer rounded the bend. The life line from the raft in front of us failed to reach the exhausted swimmer. The crew member on my raft, a young woman from California made of absolute steel, threw her life line out sixty feet into the current. Her throw was perfect. The weary swimmer grabbed the line and was pulled ashore. It was the older lady, in an state of hysteria and shock. We tried to calm her and help her as she threw up what seemed like gallons of water. We watched for the fourth raft and the rest of the people to come around the bend.

We had been told to hold on to the raft if it flipped. A maneuver could right it again and anyone separated from the raft could be collected. We knew, of course, that this would take some time, but after considerable waiting without any sign of the fourth raft, we feared that it had gotten into some kind of extraordinary trouble. Our Sobek crew was so worried that two people working the oars of one of the rafts made a gallant attempt to cross the river in hopes of offering assistance. But after twenty minutes of strenuous work, it was obvious that they could not fight their way across the strong current. So we waited and waited, while our imaginations conjured up terrible images of what had gone wrong. While the terrified woman mumbled incoherently about her helplessness in the rapids, the rest of us—by now a very sober group—kept our eyes peeled on the bend hoping to see the last raft.

Finally, the unfortunate raft shot out from behind the blind spot and made its way to join our anxious party. As they pulled up along side of us, a burly Scotsman leaped ashore, loudly declaring, "That's it! I'm walking home!" Before trying to figure out what he meant, a quick count confirmed that everyone was present. Then we began to piece together the story.

When the fourth raft had flipped, everyone was immediately swept into a whirlpool with a tremendous sucking force. But just as the safety lecture promised, the life jackets had brought everyone to the surface, but not before panic set in among a few. Most people made it to the shore after a few moments—with the exception of our swimmer and the Scotsman. The latter made it to the rock island, but it had been very difficult to reach in the recovered raft. After a fruitless search for the lost swimmer, they could only pray that she had been picked up downstream. They turned their attention to the Scotsman and after numerous false starts and failed attempts, finally reached him on the rock island. The lost woman's husband was extremely distraught and everyone was very relieved to learn that we had his wife with us.

The Sobek crew then began to try to get the Scotsman back into the raft to continue the journey. There was no other choice but to do so. Both sides of the Zambezi river gorge were sheer cliffs and we were miles from anywhere, in the middle of untamed bush. The one and only way out was to proceed down the river, yet the big Scotsman insisted that he was not going again in the raft. While the rest of us watched impatiently, the Sobek people finally got him to grasp the real situation, and he climbed sheepishly aboard.

When we pushed out into the current, the swimmer went bonkers again. Her panic was going to be dangerous to us all because her thrashing around destabilized the raft. We quickly pulled ashore to switch people around. As fate would have it, the Scotsman was a friend of the swimmer and her husband. After his decision to raft on down the river, he climbed to the back of the raft to try to calm his friend's hysteria. The woman's husband was up front with me and began to act quite strangely. "Maureen," he yelled back to his wife, "shut up! Put two fingers down your throat and throw-up. You'll feel better." Then he began a bizarre, gung-ho act: "Oh, boy, ain't this fun. Let's get going again," which, out of necessity, we did.

Our Sobek crew member was now doing her damnedest to: 1) calm crazy Maureen in the back, 2) yell commands to those of us up front to shift our weight to keep our raft from flipping, and 3) steer us through the least turbulent sections of the river. Incredibly, Maureen's obnoxious husband treated it all like a lark and refused to obey, even when we came within an eyelash of flipping.

I had long since dismissed any notions that being thrown into the river might be fun and was working overtime to keep us upright. A flip would have been hideously traumatic for those who had already spent a difficult time in the water. After we nearly flipped, the Sobek lady told the husband that he simply must obey instructions and throw his weight in the right direction. In a sort of giddy, crazed defiance, he told her, "Take it easy," as if to say, "You've been on this river lots of times, but this is my first time, so, of course, I'll make mistakes." Meanwhile, his wife was still bumping around in the back, pleading with us to pull ashore every time we approached another rapids. I supposed that the husband's feigned lightheartedness was his peculiar manifestation of terror and shock. Another man and I decided to physically pull Maureen's shell-shocked husband left and right as needed to keep the raft afloat. It was a long afternoon.

When we finally reached the designated point to leave the river, we still had a long climb to get out of

> *I supposed that the husband's feigned lightheartedness was his peculiar manifestation of terror and shock.*

the gorge and up to the Land Rovers. I made it in about thirty minutes; it took the Sobek crew an hour and a half to walk Maureen, her husband and the Scotsman to the top. By the time they reached us, the three seemed to be back to normal and were buddy-buddy with the Sobek folks.

While we waited for these exhausted adventurers, people reviewed the events of the day. I was so tired I could only listen and reflect. The others chatted, concluding that the "older couple" should never have come. Some of the younger folks smugly agreed that the Zambezi was not really that good for white water rafting anyway: "…not as good as the Colorado River through the Grand Canyon." A young French couple arrogantly said that they were actually bored for most of the day. With that, I had to walk away.

It was too easy to make such pronouncements, I thought, at the end of the day. Maureen, her husband and their Scottish friend were all in good shape. Their real vulnerability had not been obvious at the beginning. Their challenge did not have anything to do with physical condition, but rather with the inner resources to see them through a difficult situation. I found myself reflecting that people join a "cutting edge of adventure" because they want to test their own resources, to see how they will respond to an extraordinary challenge. It is a shame to go to such extraordinary lengths in search of adventure, and then to miss it completely.

Terry Bergdall

> …people join a "cutting edge of adventure" because they want to test their own resources, to see how they will respond to an extraordinary challenge.

Speaking Farmer

On our first Sunday in a new three-church parish in rural Kansas that we would name "The Three Strongholds of Faith," one of the congregations provided a welcoming potluck. The food line began in the Sunday School classroom, snaked down the steps and into the basement fellowship hall. Ed, a man in his early forties like me, was standing in line nearby. He said, "Pastor Bill, I'm a teacher and I have the summer off. Do you know anywhere in the world where I could be useful for about thirty days?" I tried to contain my excitement, but blurted out that I knew of about three hundred places. I promised to get back with him in a couple of days.

On the following Monday morning I called the ICA office in Chicago. A "TRAG," a little riding carryall vehicle for farmers, had been donated to the ICA and needed an escort to a village development project in India. These neat little three-wheeled farm trucks were made by a United Methodist Men's group in Iowa which donated them to mission projects. I returned to Ed with a mission and he agreed to make the trip. We put Ed on the AMTRAK at Dodge City. In Chicago he picked up the TRAG for the trip to New York City. The taxi to the airport cost him $40, an enormous sum for a person who had never been out of western Kansas. Ed and the TRAG got on a plane for the other side of the world. My Kansas friend was becoming a global citizen.

The plan was for someone to meet Ed in Mumbai (Bombay). After a period of anxious waiting in the

Mumbai airport, someone showed up to take Ed to the ICA office, where he had a chance to eat and rest. Ed got his second wind and was put onto a rural train for the eight hour ride into the interior of Maharashtra state. Anyone who recalls a first trip on an Indian train will sympathize with the total immersion approach to travel in India.

Ed found his way to Maliwada village, delivered the TRAG and quickly settled into a rhythm of daily work with staff and villagers. That weekend, the American staff left the village and retreated to a nearby town for rest and relaxation, which, Ed was to learn, meant "to take a shower." The situation put Ed's Kansas farmer mind to work: why was there no shower in the village?

Ed went to work. There was a water cistern on top of the staff house. He followed the pipes down to the ground and into an old, abandoned well. With a rope and some assistance, he was lowered into the well where he found an unused electric pump. To everyone's surprise, when the pump was connected, the motor worked and water soon filled the rooftop cistern. But the cistern leaked like a sieve and had to be drained, patched and refilled. When Ed located the old pipes previously installed for a shower, there was one last missing link: there was no showerhead.

That weekend, Ed went into town with the rest of the staff. Though he never admitted to taking a city shower, when he returned to Maliwada he had a shower head! He spent the rest of the month continuing his work with the Maliwada village farmers and showering with sun-heated well water.

When Ed returned to Kansas after his excursion, he was filled with his experience. It had been the trip of a lifetime. With a wry smile, he seemed very proud of his achievement.

"Ed," I asked, "how did you get along in the village?"

"Oh," he exclaimed, "that was easy. I walked the dusty streets until I saw a villager doing something that I understood. One sharpened a one-way plow, another repaired equipment. I would go over, squat down and hand them a pair of pliers, chewing gum, or a roll of bailing wire. Pretty soon we'd be working together."

"But Ed," I queried, "how did you communicate? How did you understand each other? One of you spoke Marathi and the other English."

"No trouble at all," Ed replied. "Working together like we did, we both spoke 'Farmer.'"

Bill and Beverly Salmon

"I would go over, squat down and hand them a pair of pliers, chewing gum, or a roll of bailing wire."

A Man I Can't Forget

I will tell you one of my interesting stories that I will remember forever. In 1992, when I was working as Agricultural Program Coordinator, my responsibilities were managing a ten *feddan** land reclamation project and also implementing agricultural extension activities for local farmers in Beni Suef villages. In this year, a foreign volunteer named Jim came to work with the ICA staff to improve peoples' skills. He was about fifty years old. He was born in Britain, but was living in Texas, USA. He was a businessman and had a good education and experience background. He liked to travel and had visited about 101 countries around the world.

Mr. Jim started working with me to improve the project management. First of all, he held a meeting to create an implementation plan. He demonstrated high abilities to design an effective and good plan by using computer skills. He designed a reporting system for the project. He helped to create and update an effective communication network with different agricultural actors. He had a good personal character which was very modest, patient and intelligent when handling different issues. He worked hand-in-hand with farm workers for achieving daily farm operations such as plowing, irrigation, and pest control.

Usually at the end of the day after hard work, we sat down together and discussed different issues related to culture, psychology and peoples' behavior around the world. We had fruitful discussions and also went together to visit different places in Beni Suef city and other areas such as the American and British cultural centers in Cairo. He gave me a chance to know useful places which provide people with advanced knowledge and skills to face the requirements of globalization in an easy way.

Although he spent only three months with us, I learned a lot from him. He taught me project planning, reporting, and communication. I learned hard work, how to be patient, and how to organize and implement my performance in a successful way. I learned that life comes and goes but good values and principles keep forever. I also felt that Jim was a very close friend to me because he was a very kind, wise man. I invited him to visit my home town, Al Mahalla El Kobra, which is located in the Middle Delta zone in lower Egypt, about three hundred kilometers north of Beni Suef. He spent some days with my family, visited many places in the area and gained other friends. He respected our culture strongly and we had common interesting issues. I think Jim is the type of person whose happiness comes from helping others and from seeing a smile come over their faces.

Abdel Hamid Al Ashwah

Abdel Hamid visits a family in the village.

* one *feddan* is .4 hectare, approximately one acre

East Meets West

It was the second day of an event which we called the "World's Fair" in Kwangyung Il Ri, a village on the island of Jeju-do, off the coast of South Korea. To encourage a global village development movement, the ICA was hosting villagers and their urban partners from twenty-four projects around the world.

In a moment of relaxation in the midst of intensive activity, I stationed myself against a wall of volcanic stones to watch the scores of people who were gathering in the village square. From where I stood looking north, a broad dirt path bent around to my left in a gently sloping U-turn that led down to the main road through the village. The center formed by this U-shape had been carefully sculpted by villagers with shovels and the local stonemason into an amphitheater for the event's production stages. Colorful tents beckoned dignitaries and guests for music, presentations, speech making, eating and getting acquainted.

One guest, representing the Ivy City Human Development Project, was an African American woman from Washington, D.C. She was a stranger in a strange land filled with unfamiliar tastes and smells, and a stillness quite unlike the inner city neighborhood in which she lived. I watched her appear from behind the tent, trudge around the bend in the road, wheeze up the gentle slope, catch her breath, and turn toward me. Perhaps it was the hope of finding someone who spoke English that led to her exertion. A yearning for the familiar sometimes breeds courage to approach the unknown.

She broke into a smile and exclaimed, "I hope you speak English!" I affirmed that I did, and we began an exchange of observations and wonderment about the ongoing activities. The longer we talked, the more delightfully animated she became. She was a vision of greatness: graying hair, bright eyes and a large face atop a body barely five feet tall. Her diameter equaled her height and her entire body was involved in the conversation.

All the while I could easily see over her shoulder. Along the edge of the excavation behind her, five or six Korean women were obviously watching my conversationalist. They were considering her extraordinary backside, and in a way typical of Koreans, covered their mouths with their hands, giggling and elbowing each other. After a few minutes, one elderly grandmother stood, gathered her skirts about her, and came to stand directly behind the woman from America. The grandmother visually calculated the stranger's bulk with amazement. Finally, she could restrain herself no longer, reached out, and pinched the American woman's backside.

Think of it. An African American woman from the District of Columbia was talking to a white American man in Korea in 1977. Her instantaneous reaction was based on two hundred fifty years of slavery, on wariness of white people, and on hatred of injustice. I saw it flash through her eyes. She thought some white honky had violated her behind! She whirled around. West met East.

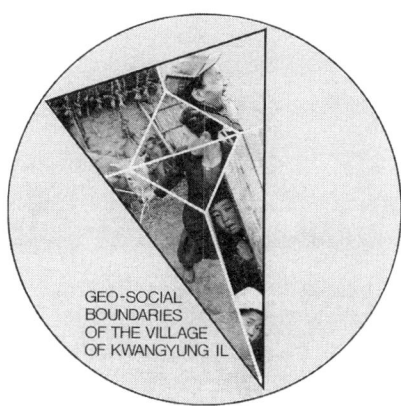

Symbolic map of the village boundaries

> *The gesture was accepted and the two unlikely partners walked down the gently sloping path…*

Slowly, she turned back to me. "You know," she observed thoughtfully, "this little grandma has never seen a woman as big or as black as I am." Her face aglow with love and understanding, she turned back to the grandmother and offered her elbow in friendship. East met West.

The gesture was accepted and the two unlikely partners walked down the gently sloping path, around the bend and disappeared from sight behind the colorful tents.

Bill Salmon

The Chickens Are Coming

In order to prepare for the "World's Fair" we held in Kwanyung Il in 1977, our staff had to help construct five major buildings, like a grain mill and chicken house, within two months. We worked along with the villagers to build the foundations, carrying wet sand up a steep incline from the river, and lugging heavy stones and cement on our backs. We kept reminding each other, "the chickens are coming in June" to keep the momentum going—building for international guests and Korean chickens.

It was a miracle to be ready. There were flags flying in the plaza from each nation represented, and when colleagues arrived from our sister projects around the world, I had a lump in my throat and tears in my eyes.

Judy Hamje

A Certain Quality

During our workdays in the village development projects in India, there was a certain quality of atmosphere and experience, something almost akin to light, that came to surround us. It was a different kind of experience and was very motivating. I especially remember my friendship with one young man on my team who was married and a few years older than most of the participants.

In principle, everybody who came to the Human Development Training Schools was supposed to speak English and Hindi and whatever their local language was. But actually, when we were conducting the first few Training Schools, there were many people who did not speak any English at all. My friend could not speak a word of English at the beginning and he could not speak a word of English at the end. Though he could probably converse in two or three local languages, I spoke only English. Yet in spite of this limitation, we got to know each other well and became very close.

After the school, he was assigned to work in Vaviharsh. I went up there to participate in the planning consultation for the Vaviharsh Human Development Project. My friend was there with Dharmalingam, our colleague from Malaysia. I was so happy to see him and he was so happy to see me in spite of the fact that neither of us could talk to the other! So we looked at each other, bowed to each other and hugged each other fondly. He indicated that he wanted to show me around the village.

We started to walk around the village. We walked a while in silence. Neither of us had any ideas about how to communicate with the other and I was beginning to feel as though I was walking around dumb. Do you know what he started to do? Rather than getting more and more frustrated, my friend started to hum one of the songs we had learned and sung at the Training School. I started humming the song with him. There we were, he from the rural East, me from the urban West, humming together as he showed me the village where he had come to live and work. It was a tremendous moment. Each of us was filled with our shared experience without any need for words and talk. This quality of relatedness, the quality of being together in the world, came out of the common experience of the workdays. The workdays gave people a sense—if not the skill—of how to make changes in the environment and how to make things happen.

James Wiegel

There we were, he from the rural East, me from the urban West, humming together…

Meeting Fr. Ilidio

He created the synchronicity that propelled our intention to accomplish something into reality.

After we were assigned to Madrid, we spent two weeks in Rome, Italy, visiting heads of Catholic religious orders with work in Spain. Armed with these men's blessings and their orders' contacts, we traveled on to Spain. John, a young Englishman whose mother was Spanish, had volunteered to help us get started and traveled with us constantly. We visited the religious orders' local leaders and learned about their work in Spain's villages and towns.

One of the religious orders that befriended us was the Sacred Heart Fathers. We visited them in many places throughout Spain and finally ended up at their residence in Lisboa (Lisbon), Portugal. While we were there, a Fr. Ilidio Fernandez happened to be visiting. He lived in Lamego in northern Portugal along the beautiful Duero River Valley, the lush wine-growing region of the country. When we told him about our work, he became very enthusiastic and begged us to visit him in Lamego. When we returned to Madrid, we wrote Fr. Ilidio and confirmed the date of our visit. We wrote that we wanted to talk with him about facilitating some Community Meetings in the local villages. After coming to see him and visiting the villages, we would then come back at a later date to lead the village meetings.

On the day of our trip, Barb, John and I hopped in our car and drove five hundred kilometers through western Spain and across the border into northern Portugal. Our route took us over very narrow, mostly cobblestone roads that wound through the mountains. We finally reached the town of Lamego and found Fr. Ilidio's residence right next to the cathedral. He immediately marched us into a large room containing more than fifty people from all the nearby villages and informed us that they were ready to do a Community Meeting!

We gulped. We had not learned yet how powerful Fr. Ilidio was in northern Portugal. The Catholic Church is the one common dominant influence in peoples' lives and priests are steeped in the understanding that the church is the foundation of the community. Northern Portugal was a region where some villages were so isolated that the local people had never seen cars! In such isolation, villagers lived in a culture where the friendly parish priest was expected to tell them what to believe and what to do and these fifty souls had been told to attend a Community Meeting.

We tried to explain to Fr. Ilidio that we were not prepared. We had only one copy of the Community Meeting materials in Spanish, not Portuguese. All our protests fell on deaf ears. He had already arranged things this way and that was that.

We swung into action. We discovered that Fr. Ilidio had a small photocopier and copied the Community Meeting booklet for everyone. Since Portuguese is so close to Spanish and the people were so imaginative, they understood enough so that John, translating our English into Spanish, was able to communicate effectively. Somehow, we got through it all and managed to excite everyone present. We were totally surprised by the very festive break in the middle of the meeting. The people had all brought food and wine which was laid out on a long table. It was a very heady time for all of us. Little did we realize at that moment that this was to be the beginning of many Community Meetings, an International Training Institute and a Human Development Zone.

We have often wondered what would have happened if we had not been in Lisboa the same day Fr. Ilidio was visiting. Without such a man, no group, especially an ecumenical one, could ever work in northern Portugal. Period! Fr. Ilidio—socially aware, oriented to helping people, and extremely popular—befriended us and became our great mentor. He created the synchronicity that propelled our intention to accomplish something into reality. By his insistence that we do that first Community Meeting, he set in motion events that made it possible for ICA staff to work in this area for the next ten years, starting many projects in all the villages and helping Portugal prepare to enter the European Common Market.

Bill and Barb Alerding

They Started Grinning

Some colleagues who had been in other projects said that the Kawangware Human Development Project was easier than most. In spite of their reassurances, I felt like I was walking into the village cold. It was an exciting, frightening experience.

The first thing we did was to leave our travelers checks, airline tickets, passports and wallets at the office so we would not have anything of value that could be stolen. Leaving my wallet any place was an act of faith; I had been patting that same wallet for forty years. Leaving it behind and going without identification or cash for a week was a shock.

Family homes in Kawangware

Once we moved into the village, we discovered that it was not just made up of Kenyans, but that it was a "refugee" village where people from many nations ended up living in their flight from injustice. We walked through this "refuge" to get a feel for the place before we led the village's vision workshop. What we saw was also a shock: mud, dust, children and dogs! Thirty or forty kids came along, touching us as we walked through the village. When we got to a certain part of the village, they all slipped away. Then ten or twenty others came up and followed us for awhile. It seemed as if there were invisible boundaries they were not supposed to cross. We discovered that Muslims lived in one whole section of the village with a mosque which was used regularly.

As we explored, people invited us to come into their homes to meet their families. Many houses were no more than mud huts, with mud floors and stick beds. They were dark and filled with smoke for want of ventilation. Dirt, filth, and flies were everywhere. In one hut, our host pointed to a lump on the bed, covered with flies: "That's granny." The lump moved once when the flies bit through the blanket. We saw children with flies covering sores on their faces without the energy to shoo them away. We were startled to meet people who remembered a time when English colonial law dictated that a white man could claim ownership of any Kenyan land that he could walk around in a day. Native Kenyans living on such expropriated land became the white man's servants. Yet here we were, invited into their homes, in spite of the fact that we were white strangers walking around their village. It was an amazing encounter with wonderful people.

A mud house

During our walks through the village we wanted to talk to many people and find out all we could. Only about 30% of the children were in school because there was either no room or they could not afford the tuition and the uniforms. Bureaucracy had penetrated East Africa. I remember Joe got upset and declared, "You can have school on a log!" We shopped at a little store. While we were visiting we decided to buy a spiral notebook for note taking. The shopkeeper would not sell us the spiral notebook, although there were two on the shelf. She had never sold a whole notebook and did not even have a price for one because Kawangware residents could afford to buy only a page or two at a time.

The church had been in Kawangware and many residents had learned to read and write in mission schools. One day we met three young men whose names were Peter, James and John. They told a story about the early missionaries that expressed how they felt about Europeans. "We were a proud people and farmed the land. The Europeans came and brought the Bible and Christianity. They taught us how to pray with our heads bowed and our eyes shut. When we raised our heads and opened our eyes, we had the Bible and the Europeans had the land."

The planning consultation began with the room filled to overflowing and several layers of onlookers at the door. The heads that peered in at the windows appeared to be stacked three levels high. During the vision workshop, the hopes that the people expressed were quite unexpected. They wanted a source of clean water. They wanted to be able to call a fire truck. They wanted to have a paved marketplace and street lights. They wanted some protection from bullies and drunks and access to a public telephone.

These hopes were all blocked by the prevailing belief that, "Nothing can happen in Kawangware."

This was their story. It was pervasive and debilitating. We wondered how to counter it.

In one of the groups, Charles asked the question, "How did you get independence from England?" Somebody said, "We worked together." Just like that, a light turned on in their heads. We saw it happen. Suddenly, people decided they could do something! After that question, the ideas started coming so fast we could not put them on the board fast enough.

We sang "Harambe" during the consult. It was a Kenyan song whose title meant, "Work Together," something like "heave ho" in English. The song's deep, historical meaning had come from workers throwing rails during the building of the railroad in East Africa. It had been a powerful symbol of working together and subsequently became the theme of the Kenyans during their struggle against British rule. I wish you could have heard them singing that song. It seemed to say, "Just watch what we can do when we decide to do it together."

We used a time-honored approach: the program followed a dinner that enticed people to participate. By the second night, word about the food had spread and brought out many of the village drunks. They were bumbling around and causing so much trouble that we could not get any work done. We struggled with what to do. We did not want to shut the door. The idea was to bring people in, not shut them out. We had to accept people as they were. We decided to have dinner an hour earlier than publicly announced, so that when the drunks arrived, everyone who was there to work would be sitting at the tables already working. We would not say no to anyone. The next evening, the drunks came, wandered around and then left, and the rest of the community got on with its work.

Only a small part of the village around the square had electricity and even that failed one night. We could not work, and an impromptu candlelight dance ensued. It was fantastic. People were beating on tables and drums and everybody was dancing, including women with babies on their backs! The dance was so spontaneous and everyone enjoyed it so much, we wondered if they often did that sort of thing. They told us that they had not had a dance like that in over twenty years, since the independence uprisings in the mid-fifties. They had been afraid to come out at night.

The ICA staff had arranged to bring two aboriginal colleagues from Australia to the consultation, to expand the Kenyans' world view. The arrival of these two aboriginal people was one of the most astounding experiences I had ever had. The Africans always size people up by their tribe. Someone who knows Kenyan culture can tell what tribe people are from by the way they cut their hair, or the way some have their ears scarred, or by something that they wear. When these black people from Australia walked in just as black as the Kenyans, but totally foreign, there was a hush. The Kenyans were deeply impacted by meeting people from another project. This little bit of a global awareness enlarged their world.

> The arrival of these two aboriginal people was one of the most astounding experiences I had ever had.

On the third morning of the consultation, the village song leader arrived. He had stayed away and kept his ear to the ground for a couple of days to find out who we were. By the third day he had decided that the consultation was something worthwhile and he wanted to participate. He came, sang songs to us and told us stories through an interpreter. It was absolutely astounding. Here was an old, neglected village leader who had been pushed aside during the Mau Mau uprising for Kenyan independence in the 1950s. He had spent seven years in a concentration camp during this period. Many of the villagers were Kikuyu, the tribe which was the source of the secret society called the Mau Mau. But whether this man was a rebel Kikuyu or a member of another ethnic group, we did not know. In any case, he recognized the importance of song leading and had decided to be part of the consult. He knew his own power and knew his village was being given a chance for a new life. When he put on his eyeglasses—over his ears with great big holes worked into them—to read a statement he had prepared for us, he symbolized the old and the new. He put those eyeglasses on right in front of the whole village and read, "You have given us a way to see and to revive us." In that moment, lives were changed.

Kawangware market

Before the week was over, some of the young men said they wanted to wear blue shirts. They knew that the blue shirts worn by project staff symbolized work and risk and expanding one's world. The next day they showed up in blue shirts. These people were proof that we were not fooling around with trivia. It was both frightening and amazing to see how many local people were willing to sign up immediately to care for their community with their lives.

At the plenary session on the last day of the consultation, we wanted to sing a song to celebrate Kawangware. A stanza of "A New Day" was changed and the phrase "Kawangware, a place of glory" was inserted. I was sitting across from two young men from the village. When they sang that song, their faces lit up all over.

But the success of the week was not assured. We had analyzed Kawangware's situation and learned about all the things that people wanted to happen. Yet at the concluding celebration, there was still concern over whether there was sufficient momentum for change. People were sitting around, some were sullen, some all dressed up. Joe had done some homework and told everyone that Kawangware was a name for the Guinea Fowl, which was a symbol of the bird of paradise. People became intrigued and made up a song with those images in it. As everyone sang the new song, the young men started grinning for the first time. Up until that time their whole story had been that nothing good could ever happen in Kawangware. With their smiles we knew that the project was going to be successful.

Richard D. Whanger

What Am I Doing Here?

In the fall of 1982 we were in Nigeria networking village development projects, collecting their stories and experiences and finding ways to get their representatives to the International Exposition of Rural Development (IERD) in India in 1984. We were confronted with many hostile elements: the government gave us only three-month visitors' visas, the heat was intense, the dust was oppressive, malaria was endemic, and the public transportation system was slow and frightening at best.

Though I could barely imagine myself raising money for village development, we decided to seek a donated car to enable our travels to projects around the country. Then my team partner contracted malaria. But as we had important appointments in downtown Lagos, I went alone. I sat in the office of one entrepreneur for a very long time while he ignored our appointment. Finally, I approached the receptionist, excused myself, and went to the second appointment. The "boss" was skeptical, but not unfriendly. He asked many questions which I answered as best I could. I knew in my heart that I should have been a Nigerian and a man to present a need that this Nigerian man could hear.

After the exhausting appointment, the lines were long and it was late before I finally boarded the bus. My feet ached from walking the hot dusty streets. As I sat on the narrow, crowded board seat, praying that I could get home before dark, I agonized. "God, what am I doing here? Is this where I belong?"

Other passengers were absorbed in their own thoughts and as eager as I to get home. They did not hear the voice or see the rosy light or feel the cool breeze that told me God was present. "Yes, Lynn, you are where I need you. You belong here."

The next week, on my follow-up visit to my second appointment, the skeptical boss called me his "Little Nun" and gave ICA Nigeria a fine little Volkswagen, the company car which they were retiring.

MaryLynn Bell

> *Other passengers were absorbed in their own thoughts and as eager as I to get home. They did not hear the voice…*

Wallboard For 4th Street

I was so stunned, I said, "Can I call you back?

In the spring of 1982, after the New York office moved from 119th Street on the Upper West Side of New York City to a tiny set of apartments in Hoboken, New Jersey—where the equipment had to be carried up three flights of stairs—we began looking for a more adequate facility back in the City. An old Catholic school building on 4th Street between Avenue A and Avenue B looked promising. The building was about one hundred years old and in need of complete renovation, at least if anyone wanted to use it. It had been vacant for years and the church offered to let us have it for one dollar a year. We decided to take the church's offer.

We knew we would need wallboard to renovate the building. One day, George, Tim and I were hanging out at the office in Hoboken, wondering where we could get enough wallboard to renovate the old school on 4th Street in Manhattan. I went to the phone book and looked up wallboard companies. George urged me to phone one of the companies and ask for the president. I dialed and asked for the president, and was connected on the first try. I described our wonderful renovation plans for the old school on the Lower East Side of New York and asked if he would donate wallboard for the project. He said the company would consider the request and asked me to write him a letter with the amount of wallboard we needed.

As I wrote the letter, we sat around the table wondering how many sheets we would need to convert a four-story school building into a residential training center and office space. Without any idea at all, I said, "How about two hundred to two hundred fifty sheets." George said, "We'll probably need at least one thousand sheets." I wrote the letter asking for one thousand sheets, thinking the whole time, "This is really crazy, they'll never give us one thousand sheets of wallboard."

About a month later, I was sitting in the office when I got a call from a warehouse on Long Island. A man said, "Your wallboard is here. Where and when would you like it delivered?"

I was so stunned I said, "Can I call you back? We'll have to figure out where and when to have it delivered." I hung up and thought, "This can't be true. They can't have given us all that wallboard." I was in such a state of shock I called them right back just to hear it again. They said, "Yes, we have two flatbed semi-trailers full of wallboard."

This was a lot of wallboard! We picked a date to have it unloaded on 4th Street on a Saturday.

We planned a workday and called everyone we thought might be remotely interested in helping us unload the wallboard. A few really sturdy guys were hired to do some of the muscle work.

Normally a city street had to be blocked from traffic to allow heavy unloading with a crane. This meant getting a permit, building a covering over the sidewalk to protect people, and paying someone to watch the street blockade. We did not want to pay the city to block the street and issue the permit or to pay someone to build the covering over the sidewalk. So Tim volunteered for street duty. He wore an official looking outfit—a baseball jacket and a borrowed hard hat. He found a couple of sawhorses which he put at either end of the block, stuck a few dollars in his pocket, and positioned himself as the guard at the busiest end of the street.

We spent the whole day unloading wallboard into the 100-year old school building. The school was so old and frail that George had to plan exactly where each load of wallboard would go so it would not unbalance the building and collapse the floors.

At first, the owner of the crane company wanted to be the boss of the unloading. He was sure that the most efficient way of unloading was to have all the wallboard for each floor brought in through one window on that floor. When he finally got tired of the project and left, we talked to the crane operator who gladly lifted the wallboard to each window so that we could distribute the weight without breaking peoples' backs.

The unloading crew was great! At the end of the day, the fellows who were driving the truck said, "We have never had a truck unloaded this fast in our whole life." We brought in food and celebrated in one of the classrooms after cleaning up in the splash sink in the boys' restroom.

Over the next two years, at least 240 people were involved in renovating the old school on 4th Street. We gave two hundred to three hundred sheets to community groups and still had plenty of wallboard for the old school. People created wonderful living spaces and it felt like a training center—in a school. The office in the attic had a wonderful view of Manhattan.

I'm not sure exactly when the renovation was declared done. Renovation was a lot of work and there were many other things to do besides renovate the building. The school definitely looked different as a result of many weekends of work by more people than I can name.

Those particularly crazy regional colleagues gave each other the nerve to say "yes" to doing outrageously wonderful things.

Beret Griffith

"We have never had a truck unloaded this fast in our whole life."

The Power Of Workdays

Workdays were always powerful events integral to the Training Schools that we conducted. One of the most memorable was a workday we held during a Training School in Bangalore, where we dug a ditch and cleaned up the area between a road and a school.

The second was during a Training School in Taipei. We had quite a number of Filipinos in the school, some of whom were from religious orders. Many had never soiled their hands in "dirty work." A heavy rain had given us a unique opportunity for a workday by sweeping debris from the town dump onto the bridge that connected the town with the dump. The town had asked us if we would clean the garbage off the bridge. Although some of our students put masks over their faces and gloves on their hands, they were right in there, digging and hauling all of that garbage back to the dump site. They willingly admitted that they had never done such a thing—and probably would not do it again—but they had risen to the occasion and it had been a great experience in their lives.

Heidi Holmes

> *The town had asked us if we would clean the garbage off the bridge.*

I Know Why
Tune: You're Just in Love

I see wonder coming everywhere.
This strange presence seems to fill the air.
New communities emerge that care.
I wonder why? I wonder why?
Old worlds passing quickly out of sight.
New is dawning with its shocking light.
Old despair is finally in the past
Our destiny recast.
I now know why!

The whole world is arisin'.
It is no time for cryin'.
The old way's death is but new birth.
Beyond all expectations,
The new aeon's awaitin'
Awake now! See the common earth.
Put the globe on your shoulders.
You will find you'll be bolder
And you'll live with the final One.
You will see life's deep surprise
Burst before your very eyes.
For you'll see the Kingdom's come!

Life's Resale Shop

When I arrived in Conacaste, Guatemala in 1978, the bishop visited our project and told me the people would not understand it if a priest who was working there did not say mass. That meant I started saying Mass each Sunday, whether my listeners understood my Spanish or not! I carefully wrote out my homily and memorized every word, including the grammatical mistakes. Then I delivered the homily with sincerity, but without any idea of whether I was getting through to my congregation or not. This continued as my weekly practice until the project opened its resale shop.

The Tienda Economica—our "economy store"—was stocked with donated discards from wealthy patrons in the city, which became instant treasures for local residents. I wrote down a whole page of words trying to describe how all of life is about recycling one treasure into another. When I talked about our little resale shop, I spoke about a pair of shoes that pinched one lady's toes and exactly fit another. I spoke about the picture book discarded by one child, now delighting a new family of children. As I stumbled on, I saw a light turn on in the face of Donato Flores who nodded to his wife, "¿Se, como no?"

One day, as I was sitting in my hut, without windows, I heard a little girl crying out "¡Esperame, esparame!" I transliterated the question, "Who is she asking to 'spare her'?"

Then the insight hit. I realized she was using the command form of the verb *esperar*, "Wait for me, wait for me!" and had no idea about the grammar, only about what worked.

From then on, I stopped laboring over grammar and started saying whatever I could think of that communicated. I asked more for help, "¿Como se dice?" and cared less for correctness. People laughed and caught on and said what I wanted to say for me, in words we both understood. People were only too willing to straighten me out because they knew exactly what I wanted to say. I could make all the mistakes in the world and they could make all the corrections. I brought my paltry phrases to the resale shop of their minds and they recycled all the used words into effective communication. While the sacrament was my gift to them, their gift to me was help with my Spanish. We all knew that I was the beneficiary of their generosity and that their response to my individual weakness had became our community strength.

Don Richards

Conacaste, Guatemala

Midst Of A Revolution

In 1983, the project in Conacaste, Guatemala was expecting a visit from the U.S. ambassador and his entourage. The previous ambassador had been shot and killed and guerrillas were still active elsewhere in Guatemala. We knew that serious precautions would be taken.

As we waited, a man leaped into the office with a submachine gun pointed at my face. The advance team was searching to make sure that all the rooms were free of any danger. The next thing we knew, an imposing convoy came up the winding road. One Suburban van was in the front, followed by the ambassador's car, then a third van followed behind. There were three black vehicles in all.

We greeted the Ambassador and his wife, then drove out to the drip irrigation demonstration plot that was the major activity of interest. Walt and I were in the advance van. As we drove down the road, I noticed several men in a van whose doors remained open. The van walls were covered with bulletproof steel plate and there was a box of hand grenades on the back seat.

We arrived at the drip irrigation plot. The driver left the engine running while four men armed with submachine guns flung open their doors and ran to the four corners of the field where they stationed themselves as lookouts. The ambassador arrived next and walked into the field surrounded by four guards. All the men carried machine pistols and submachine guns. I felt mixed emotions. I was amused and awed: I had never been so close to such weapons before. I was also concerned that we were living in more danger than I had ever imagined. This was simply what it meant to live in the midst of a revolution.

Jack Gilles

The drip irrigation plot: "Don't drink the water."

"Then We Will Walk."

After the American Ambassador's visit, we became the "in" project among ambassadors and cabinet ministers. Soon, I was invited to an event whose security went far beyond anything we had previously experienced. I was introduced to many people who got excited about our drip irrigation project and wanted to see it—all because the American Ambassador had come out to see us. We were suddenly very busy hosts.

The Argentine Ambassador was one of our guests in Conacaste. He looked around and asked if he was going to be shown the drip irrigation system. We said, "yes." When we started toward the car, the Ambassador turned to me and asked if his American counterpart had driven or walked? I said, "He drove."

The Argentinian said, "Then we will walk."

Donnamarie West

Growing A Larger World

I was one of five businessmen who had come to the Philippines to participate in the Human Development Project in the village of Sudtonggan. We spent most of our time in the city of Cebu, visiting Filipino business people to see what could be done to accelerate economic development in the village. The business people in Cebu were very much aware of conditions in the villages. A wealthy businessman said to me, "The villagers need to participate more in the economic life of this country and share in the benefits. If they don't, there will be violent revolution." They did not need visiting Americans to convince them of the need for rural people to improve their lot.

We sought the advice of the business people we visited, on how to develop industries and other work for the village, how to secure equipment to drill in the rock field and how to get a truck to move the rocks. We did get support from them, but what really touched them was the fact that five Americans had come to the Philippines because we cared about what was going on in a village near their hometown. The effect we had on business people was extraordinary.

The young men in the village, meanwhile, had decided to build a *buri* (a type of palm tree) factory to process palms for making furniture and other crafts. This was one of the income schemes that had come out of the planning consultation. Another was to intensify the building rock and rope-making industries. So many good ideas had been proposed at the consultation, that it had been difficult for the village people to decide where to place their energy. When we arrived six months after the planning consultation, we found them planning to do many things but concentrating on nothing. It was hard to sit down and push good ideas aside in order to concentrate on three or four. When we picked out the most promising ideas, one of them was a *buri* factory.

The young men already knew how to work with the *buri* palm because they had done it at somebody else's factory. They just wanted to work in their own factory. They were so pleased to be focused, they looked like they had been given permission to do something magnificent! It was wonderful to look at the excitement in their faces! They were great young men who wanted to grab onto something real and move it forward. There was no doubt in my mind that they would succeed.

Rabbit raising was also under consideration. The diet in the village consisted of rice and bananas and bananas and rice. We knew from personal experience that a rice and banana diet was pretty hard on people; we had been buying peanut butter left and right trying to maintain my wife's high protein, diabetic diet. A veterinarian from Iowa had come with his family to spend six months working in Sudtonggan. He came up with the idea of raising rabbits. When he talked with the villagers about his idea, it was amazing to hear all the information that came out of those people. They said knowledgeably, "Oh yes, and you need to raise geese, too."

They were so pleased to be focused, they looked like they had been given permission to do something magnificent!

> One of the men in Sudtonggan was so impressed by what was going on …he named his new baby daughter "Maliwada…"

The trained veterinarian asked, "Why do you need to raise geese?"

"Why, don't you know? The food that spills out of the rabbits' cages attracts rats. Geese eat the spilled food and chase the rats away." We were always amazed at how much the villagers knew.

The villagers were also eager to know more. The forty-five year old wife of the village mayor had wanted to learn English all her life and now she had a chance. Being able to speak English broadened one's world in unexpected ways. Each week we shared reports from projects in other parts of the world, including the Maliwada Human Development Project in India. One of the men in Sudtonggan was so impressed by what was going on in his own village and in the other projects he learned about in the global reports, he named his new baby daughter "Maliwada," the name of the sister project village in India. It was exciting to see the villagers' world grow larger and begin to work, through connection and revitalization.

Richard D. Whanger

The Wind That Made History

When we arrived in the desert village of El Bayad to prepare for a Human Development Project planning consultation, the local ICA staff and the consultation team spent time visiting throughout the village. About a week before the consultation, we met in the mayor's home with his elected village leaders, all of whom were men. For centuries it had been the custom of the men to make all the village's decisions. The women's place was in the home! Period! Yet we knew from our many visits that the women really wanted to participate in the planning.

At first, the mayor and his cohorts did not think it would be possible for the women to meet with the men. They thought only the men should participate. We simply told them that when we do a planning consultation, everyone in the village is invited—both men and women.

They put their heads together and decided that the women could participate, but not in the same tent as the men. We would have to put up two tents: one for the men and one for the women. We told them that we could not do a consultation that way. All the participants had to be in the same area in order for us to gather their information and ideas.

They put their heads together again and spoke in Arabic for a long time. They finally agreed that the men and women could be in the same tent, but that the women would have to sit in the back. Since we had gotten that far and understood that what we were proposing had never happened in the history of the village before, we decided to be satisfied with this decision of the village leaders.

We put up a large, very beautiful *shamiana*, a tent in the desert with "walls" of colorful Persian rugs sewn together to create a large meeting "room." In the front of the space, an eight foot long blackboard was nailed to a framework of wooden 2x4s sunk into the sand. We divided the village into five teams and had each one go through the village gathering information. Then, for three hours each day, the whole village gathered inside the tent to help get all their information up on the blackboard. After these sessions, when everyone had agreed on the summary chart, the village women spontaneously lifted their heads and let out a high-pitched wailing sound, shaped by their fluttering tongues into a constant warble as it rose from the back of their throats. While this ululation seemed extremely eerie to our Western ears at first, we soon learned that it was an expression of great rejoicing that Egyptian women customarily do on high festive occasions.

The third day of the consultation, a strong gale swept across the desert and slammed into the front of the tent, toppling the huge blackboard and pulling the 2x4s out of the sand. It was too difficult to put the blackboard back in the same place because of the strong wind, so we decided to place it at the back of the tent where the women were sitting! For the rest of the consultation, the women were in front. The men, in order to see what was going on, began to edge forward and by the last day, the men and women were all working together. They were so focused on getting their four-year development plan done that they paid no attention to the miracle which was taking place all around them! For the first time ever, the men and women worked together to decide the future of their village. We felt then that history was being made right there for the people of El Bayad.

Bill and Barbara Alerding

Consultation participants inside the "shamiana"

A Big Event

When a project is just beginning, it is hard to see its deep meaning because everything is so new—too new for people to totally grasp. But there was something striking about the preschool staff. They were all local women whom project staff had trained to be teachers. You could see that they knew they were involved in a significant task. The preschool was the biggest accomplishment the first year of the project in Delta Pace, Mississippi.

Project office in Delta Pace

When I came to Delta Pace near the end of that first year, the people were very excited about their vision and what was going on in their community. One of the most energetic residents was an older man whose name was Mr. Hall. He could not stand still whenever he told the story of the project. He often said, "I was an old man, seventy years old, just sitting down, waiting to die. Then the project came to Delta Pace and I got involved. And now I walk down into the village every morning."

Mr. Hall just could not contain himself, he was so excited to tell us about what he was doing. He talked about his travels and the towns he had visited. It finally dawned on me that he was talking about visits he had made to all the little towns along State Highway No. 3 into the adjacent county.

The ICA staff knew Mr. Hall was a great community spokesman and they asked him to tell state officials about the project in Pace at a big event down in Jackson. When the leader of the meeting invited Mr. Hall to come forward, he called Mr. Hall an honored guest. Mr. Hall said, "Twenty years ago they were trying to hang a rope around my neck, now I'm an honored guest!" He was a changed man. I believe that everything had changed in the first year of the project in Delta Pace. The residents had seen the significance of what they were doing and I believe they experienced deeply meaningful lives as a consequence.

Richard D. Whanger

What Happened In Edgard?

Edgard is the parish (county) seat of the civil Parish of St. John the Baptist. I was assigned as pastor in Edgard at the beginning of July 1977. The Town Meeting we held in Edgard that September was one of the first activities for the civil parish we had in the church hall.

The leadership team facilitated a first class event from 10 A.M. to 4 P.M. with fifty-five participants. It was well recruited: we had everybody from the parish sheriff to poor African American plantation workers, and everyone in between. There was an incredible celebration of the whole day's work: vision, contradictions, proposals, strategies, and tactics. The spirit throughout was extremely high and participation was unbelievable. People went home with twelve specific, concrete proposals in their back pockets.

I showed the proposals to a community worker from Edgard who worked for Total Community Action in New Orleans who said, "Pie in the sky. You'll never accomplish any of those proposals." He was from Edgard, but had given up on the town. He knew that although it was a predominantly black community (95% African American), the basic structures were all white. He had given up hope of any kind of transformation taking place in that community.

There was no follow-up meeting of any kind because the people at the town meeting came from every level of society: educated/uneducated, rich/poor, young/old, white/black—you name it.

Five years later, two ICA colleagues spent a week with me, working on a workshop they were preparing for African Americans from all over the country. I invited them to Edgard. They could not believe they could be so royally treated in a Roman Catholic rectory. Each had a private suite and we had an extremely good cook. They asked, "What can we do for you?"

I said, "Wait a minute. I'd like a follow-up on that Town Meeting." Within twenty-four hours I gathered twenty-two of the fifty-five participants from the 1977 meeting. We did a reflective conversation that refreshed our memories of the Town Meeting. When we looked at the twelve proposals, to our amazement, every single one of the twelve had been implemented!

There was only one in which the implementation had not been completed. That proposal was for a new senior high school building. The proposal had gotten through the bidding, but the bids came in a million dollars over budget. The budget was for $3 million dollars and the bids came in at $4.3 million. West St. John, the Baptist parish, was rural, black and poor. The East Bank part of the parish was white, suburban and rich—and dominated the school board. When the bid came in over budget, the proposal was put on the back burner. They were happy to let it go. As a result of our review meeting, we got the PTA together, they put pressure on the school board members from the West Bank, and in a year the new senior high school had been built!

Every single proposal had been implemented in five years and without follow-up meetings!

"Pie in the sky. You'll never accomplish any of those proposals."

> *For the first time, members of a diverse group shared a common vision that helped them shift from "no possibility" to "possibility."*

I asked myself, "What happened? Why was it so effective?" The Town Meeting catalyzed the community by beginning with relationships. Never before had such a varied group gathered to discuss what was best for the whole community. For the first time, members of a diverse group shared a common vision that helped them shift from "no possibility" to "possibility." Then the leaders helped the participants "pull their vision through the contradictions," i.e., to see what needed to be done in light of the underlying obstacles blocking their vision. Participants were then able to create twelve specific, concrete proposals. In a discussion about opportunities, the participants explored all the openings for action. Finally, participants listed strategies and tactics for all the proposals. The participants left ready to move into action, which they did in the years that followed, without realizing that they were implementing the twelve proposals from the Town Meeting.

I have seen the Town Meeting's "vision, contradiction, proposal, strategy, tactics" approach produce results in two congregations as well: in the mid-1980s, in my parish in Edgard; and in the late '80s, in my last assignment, Our Lady of Lourdes, in New Orleans. The five-step approach empowered the congregation's members to take responsibility for being the church in the community, just like it helped Edgard's citizens take responsibility for being leaders in the civil Parish of St. John the Baptist in 1977.

Winus Roeten

A Light Is Now Breaking
Tune: Washington Post March

A light is now breaking, showing the secret,
that meaning is everywhere in life,
And I am the bearer of the light.
A peace is now present, hopes are banished,
and cares are all gone and nothing's to hate,
and self is the only war to fight.

What powerful light, it blinds, it dazzles me.
I'm spun in a wildly crashing whirl
aware that I'm sent for all the world.
And finding the terror, peace, I'm silent.
As never before, I encounter the calm
of knowing that's held before my eyes.

A wild kind of joy bursts forth,
a singing that's free, a dancing on sea.
My life's transformed, bliss unknown before;
I'll never live more than each moment in hist'ry.

A Word About Singing

At the last minute, in the summer of 1978, I was asked to be a small group leader for the Kinney Community Consultation. For the first time in my life, I was to lead a group using ICA methods without backup from an ICA person in the room. I worked very late Friday evening at my government architectural office so I could be gone the next week.

I had only Saturday to travel from my home in Winnipeg, Manitoba to Kinney, Minnesota, in Minnesota's Iron Range. The shortest route from Winnipeg to Kinney was a total of ten hours. It took me along the lonely back roads of northern Minnesota; one road was nothing but ungraded, loosely packed sand. In my 1976 full-size American Plymouth, it was a slow trip. The desolation of Koochiching State Forest, Nett Lake Indian Reservation, Superior National Forest, and the backwoods of rural Minnesota was something the extent of which urban Canadians have rarely experienced, even in Canada.

I arrived in Kinney just in time to see the week's tight schedule laid out for all the group leaders. The planning consultation started on the Monday morning, with a community vision workshop, and ended on Friday. Each day's work included reporting and discussion among all the groups each morning and brainstorming in small subgroups each afternoon. It was the practice of the ICA to begin all of these group sessions with the singing of songs, usually written by the community for the community.

I felt tired and inexperienced, even though I thought I was confident with the ICA methods. To make matters worse, I was assigned to a strange group. One man was tiny, barely five feet tall. But what he lacked in size, he made up for with a persistent booming voice. One woman was a marked contrast. She was about as tall as I am, 5' 10", but I guessed about four times my weight. Most of the time she was silent. We were assigned to meet in a small tent and in my most tired moments, I imagined that the ICA staff had purposely picked this motley crew just to test my mettle as a group leader.

On Thursday morning, there was the usual plenary for all participants. It was the day for brainstorming "tactics," the concrete actions that would help transform the community.

Thursday afternoon was extra hot and dusty in Minnesota's summer heat. After lunch, I met again with my group in our hot little tent. Coming up with practical follow-up actions is often the most difficult time for a group leader. Dealing with the issues in Kinney was also no easy task and I felt my group was making particularly slow progress.

Hot, tired, bloated from lunch, and impatient, with my back to the group and a felt marker poised in my hand ready to write the first person's thoughts on the flip chart paper, I started right in. Behind me, a small voice said, "We did not sing a song." I turned around and looked at the short, vocal man. His face was beaded all over with sweat and his blank look told

> *Behind me, a small voice said, "We did not sing a song."*

me he was not the one who had spoken. While I was wondering if I imagined the voice, it came again, only louder and commanding, "We did not sing a song. We have to sing a song, before we start." It was the large, silent lady.

There are brief moments in life whose impact lasts forever. That Thursday afternoon, all of us sang like never before. In that instant in a sweaty tent in rural Minnesota, I learned a lesson about honoring individuals and trusting methods that care for the human spirit that has stayed with me ever since.

Gathorne Burns

> *There are brief moments in life whose impact lasts forever.*

All Need To Play

A simple square platform of beautiful black marble set in a grassy park at Raj Ghat in New Delhi, marks the spot where Mahatma Gandhi was cremated following his assassination in 1948. Pathways radiate out from the monument to the edges of the park, symbolizing the global impact of this man whose presence affected the whole world. The memorial shares the man's power to stir the human soul.

As our group was returning from the memorial to our buses, a pack of young beggar boys—five to ten year olds—surrounded us. They were all crippled one way or another and their faces looked wrinkled and old. Their cries for *rupees* were pitiful. I instinctively wanted to help, but I felt certain that I did not dare to give money to any one child. I was afraid that if one got a few coins, the rest of the little mob would turn on the lucky one and steal it away. The group and I were paralyzed.

One of my traveling companions stepped forward, clapped his hands and motioned the little boys to come to him. He somehow made them understand, "Do you know how to greet people?" They executed the Indian greeting, *namaste*, palms up, pressed together. "Do you know how Americans greet each other?" They stuck out their hands and each shook his hand in turn. "I'll bet you don't know how Africans greet one another." He preceded to show each one how to execute a high five. "Why don't you try it with one another? Why don't you try it with that group? Introduce yourself. Tell them your name and how old you are." The boys seemed delighted with how much they understood.

Our paralysis vanished as we were drawn into this impromptu game. In their excitement, the young beggars had become laughing, shouting, active children having a good time. They were the same crippled little creatures, but everything was different. When we left, they were all smiles as they thanked us and gave each of us a good-bye high five.

Georgianna McBurney

Seeing The World Transformed

Joseph had sent us on the Global Odssey with the assignment, "See if you can find 'the other world' in your experience." When we returned to Chicago, he conducted an intensive debriefing of our travels. We told him story after story, but it was not until I spoke of the experience with the children at Gandhi's memorial that Joseph finally said, "Yes, that's 'the other world'—when you see a situation transformed."

India colored all of us. Thirty years later, many pictures of India are still in my mind. At the time of the death of my husband George, in 1996, I wrote to my children about "participating joyfully in a world of sorrow." India taught me about joy. Joy is deciding to see the world transformed.

Georgianna McBurney

…Joseph finally said, "Yes, that's 'the other world' —when you see a situation transformed."

The Sharbat Riot

The village wanted pure water very badly. In fact, in Bayad, Egypt, pure water was the main thing. Almost no one believed that it would be possible to get pure water running into the village. One fellow who worked for the local government unit insisted, "I know. I know where to drill."

So Gene and a whole crowd of villagers went out with the great, heavy, well-drilling rig that they had concocted. They slammed this big iron monster into the ground and straight into bedrock. This was not quite the place.

Filling water jars at a tap

They decided to explore further. The village's excitement was piqued and the children tagged along for the sport. They dug and dug into the sand near the river until their pit was about a meter and a half deep and a meter square. One of the boys reached down into the pit and when he pulled up a handful of wet sand, he yelled excitedly, "*Kadarah! Kadarah!*" *Kadarah* is the Arabic word for green, but it can also mean fertile, and this excited young well driller meant, "We've reached it, we've gotten to water-bearing sand."

That is where they drilled the well. It was a huge job to drill the first well, to lay the first pipe and to get the first pure running water flowing out of a tap inside the village. But they did what they said; they got a single water tap just barely inside the village. It was a magnificent achievement and everyone knew it was a day for a celebration.

In an Egyptian village, the favorite thing for turning a gathering into a celebration is concentrated rose water syrup—what people all over the former British Empire call cordial. When people hit on the idea of making rose petal cordial (*sharbat* in Arabic) with their pure running water, they all came out to share cordial with their neighbors. In a village like Bayad, it is one thing to be told there are so many hundreds of people living in the village and another to see them together all at once. We had never seen so many of the villagers out at the same time, let alone for a grand celebration. We called it the "*sharbat* riot."

The rose hip cordial and rose petal cordial that people made that day with the fresh Bayad water was delicious. There were tables and glasses everywhere. People were so happy, they were exchanging glasses and pouring each other more and more cordial. It was thrilling to see people exploding with such delight in a new water system.

Wayne Nelson

You Can Do It!

At the ICA meeting in Bilboa, Spain, we decided to do a great education conference for Latin America in Caracas, Venezuela because Dr. Luis Machado, first elected Minister for the Development of Intelligence, lived there. He brought in many experts in new methods of learning and created a whole system of projects to improve intelligence for people of all ages across Venezuela. For a variety of reasons, it soon became clear that a conference in Caracas was not to be. So when I returned from a meeting in Venezuela, Barb and I decided to do the conference in Guatemala.

I had recently retired from teaching at the Colegio Americano in Guatemala City and wanted to do something to update Central America on the latest developments in methods of learning. I gave a long talk about the latest brain research to the Board of Directors of Guatemala's most prestigious management association. They were surprised to learn about such research. When I realized that the business community in Guatemala was unaware of these developments, it dawned on me that probably no one in Central America knew about them. It seemed likely that news of developments in brain research and learning had impacted North America, Europe, South America and Asia, but completely by-passed Central America. With this understanding, Barb and I were becoming highly motivated to do an education conference in Guatemala.

We spent a whole year setting up and recruiting this conference. We turned the garage on the front of our house into the Registration Office. Then Berta Sarmina, a Mexican-American woman living in New York City, decided to volunteer for a year and came to Guatemala to help us. We worked with Dr. Dee Dickenson of Seattle and decided, with her help, to call the conference "New Horizons in Learning." The four-day conference was scheduled for October, 1987 at the Hotel Sheraton in Guatemala City. Eight international presenters were expected and four hundred participants were registered. The participants included teachers, school administrators, psychologists, lawyers, health care professionals, and business persons—a cross section of the society. We felt that if new insights about learning were going to impact the educational system, the whole community needed to be knowledgeable and supportive.

Each of the presenters was given a three-hour workshop which would be simultaneously translated by a professional interpreter. We spent many anxious hours at the airport, praying that each presenter arrived safely on time. Making sure that all the presenters actually came on the right plane had turned us into nervous wrecks and we heaved great sighs of relief every time a presenter walked through the gate and was actually there, ready to work at the conference.

Dr. Luis Machado from Venezuela and Dr. Reuven Feuerstein from Israel were the last two presenters scheduled on the final day of the conference and were to arrive the day before on the same plane from Miami. When I went to the airport to pick them up, I was greatly relieved when they, too, had actually

Making sure that all the presenters actually came on the right plane had turned us into nervous wrecks…

> *It was an electric moment and the spirit happening of the conference!*

arrived. We drove to the hotel and arrived at the conference center while the last session of the day, conducted by Dr. David Perkins of Harvard, was still going on.

Both Dr. Machado and Dr. Feuerstein wanted to look in on the session to see how it was going. I took them into the main hall where four hundred participants were listening to Dr. Perkin's presentation. At that very moment, a problem with the earphones occurred and Dr. Perkins paused while the equipment was being repaired. Some of the people looked around and noticed Dr. Machado and Dr. Feuerstein standing at the rear of the hall. These were the two presenters that most of the audience had come to hear and they immediately recognized them from their photos in the conference brochure.

Spontaneously, several people rose to their feet and started clapping for the two men. Others looked up to see the reason for the applause, and when they recognized who was in the room, they also rose and started clapping. In a few seconds all four hundred participants were on their feet cheering loudly. Dr. Machado's and Dr. Feuerstein's eyes showed their amazement; they felt a bit self-conscious as the applause went on and on. There was great excitement in the Conference now and a warm reception such as neither man had ever experienced in many years of presenting at conferences around the world. It was an electric moment and the spirit happening of the conference!

The next morning, Dr. Feuerstein's workshop was well-received and then it was time for Dr. Machado. He was giving a speech entitled, "You Can Do It!" He spoke in Spanish and an interpreter translated his remarks into English for the few who did not understand Spanish. The interpreter was so taken with the speech, she refused to let the backup interpreter spell her for fear that the powerful emotional impact of his words would be lost in the transition. Dr. Machado's remarks had a tremendous impact on the audience; when he finished, all four hundred people rose to their feet, cheering loudly for what seemed like twenty minutes. It was a very emotional moment which provided absolution for our year's labor.

Bill and Barbara Alerding

Celebrating A Completed Life

Two weeks after the fact, we heard in Mumbai (Bombay) that our colleague Ellen had been admitted to the Intensive Care Ward in the hospital in Sevagram, Gandhi's village. Charles and I set out immediately from Mumbai to see what was happening. We took a flight to Nagpur and then a bus out to the village. By the time we arrived, Ellen had passed away.

Ellen was a psychologist who had come to India in 1983 to live in this Indian village as a staff member of the Sevagram Human Development Project. She had come down with severe diarrhea and had been admitted to the local hospital, one of the larger hospitals in the area, where local doctors received their training. We went to the hospital and talked with the medical director. Ellen had received good care and had been improving, we were told, but toxins from the infection had reached her heart and cardiac arrest had followed.

It was a profoundly sad, greatly challenging moment. We needed to notify her family in the United States. It was very difficult to get calls through to the States in the early 1980s. We usually waited for days in local mail and telephone compounds to get a connection. But with the efforts of our colleague Cyprian, who had company contacts and knew how to instruct telephone operators to respond to emergencies, we made two rounds of phone calls to Chicago and her family in just a few hours.

Family members agreed that her body would be cremated in the village. Our colleagues were a very concerned and caring group of many cultural and religious backgrounds, and we began discussions about how we would celebrate this completed life. Some said we must use the Christian form of worship. Others said we must honor the culture that Ellen had come to serve. It was passionate, intense decision-making that took most of the night. In the process, we hammered out a service that had elements from both cultures, along with the symbols of Ellen's life.

We soon learned that a gentleman from China, who had been staying at the Gandhi Ashram in the village, had passed away that same night. We were approached by people from the Ashram who suggested that we share a joint service, rather than have two separate services in different corners of the field used for cremation fires. We agreed, with the provision that we could keep intact the part of the service that we had planned.

The next morning, the women of the village took us to the hospital to prepare Ellen's body. The people of Sevagram were Buddhists and I was very squeamish about going through their rituals of washing and dressing her body. But the village women caressed her with such warmth and tenderness, I realized that this was part of saying goodbye in a rich and meaningful way. She was covered with flowers and carried on a stretcher at shoulder height down the lane. We joined the women of the village in a procession behind her. The wooden wheels of the ox cart carrying wood for the funeral pyres squeaked behind us.

It was passionate, intense decision-making that took most of the night.

> As the fires burned, the villagers began the most beautiful chanting I had ever heard.

The procession from the Gandhi Ashram came from the other direction and met us in the middle of the beautiful, gently rolling field with trees on the far edges. The wood was arranged, the bodies were laid on their pyres and the people encircled them both. The two services were carried out as planned.

But then came a wondrous surprise. As the fires burned, the villagers began the most beautiful chanting I had ever heard. At first slowly and softly, then with increasing intensity, they chanted with a soaring rhythm that I felt could literally carry these two departed souls to heaven. In the midst of the chanting, one of the nurses who had taken care of Ellen stood with us, in tears. "Why did the Lord take her? Why not me?" he asked in his grief. Ellen had obviously made her mark in the village in a very profound way. Dianne said quietly, "Who would ever want a service in a funeral home after something like this?"

Hiraman went out the next morning and gathered the ashes into an urn to take back to Ellen's family. I tried to figure out what I would say at Customs when I presented a sealed urn from a funeral home in Mumbai. When I explained to the U.S. Customs official what I was carrying, he just gulped and waved me on without a word. I was finally able to tell family and colleagues in Chicago of the glorious and universal celebration of Ellen's life in the village of Sevagram.

Heidi Holmes

No Problem

MANCHESTER, NEW HAMPSHIRE, USA, 1976. My husband, Larry, laughed as he chatted with someone calling from Chicago. I stood eavesdropping in the office doorway, guessing at my next assignment. "We're on our way to Kuh Du E Ri in Korea!" he announced as he tossed the receiver back onto the phone in a delighted frame of mind. At long last we were on our way overseas to serve the villages of a developing country, our dream since joining the ICA six years before. Larry envisioned walking the fields of the "Hermit Kingdom" —a name from several centuries ago when Korea was less connected with the world. He had been there as a young man during his army days. I just knew we would awake to crowing roosters and anticipated a reawakening of my love of nature. Our whole family, including our young children, prepared for the trip to Seoul.

SEOUL, KOREA, 1976. A handsome, square-faced young Korean minister named Sung Chul, holding a placard with our name on it, met us at the airport. We were soon unceremoniously crammed into a lime-green taxi and whisked off to do battle with the sluggish traffic we came to dread and endure. We learned that staff were urgently needed in the city and that job ideas had been flowing on our behalf long before we arrived. Only moments into this conversation, it dawned on us that we were not headed for a village. We arrived at our new home in the city within minutes. The taxi turned north and then west a block into a narrow dirt alley the likes of which we had never seen before.

With all our worldly possessions stuffed into two suitcases each, we climbed up the cement steps in the back of a typical square red-brick Korean home where we would live for nearly a year. Gray file cabinets were crammed in the back of the main room and a homemade wooden table covered with navy blue plastic almost filled the space that was left. This was the new Seoul office. Our family was to live in the room off the office to the right.

Our family room contained a pile of pink and red padded bedding, neatly folded in a corner. It clashed dramatically with the gold linoleum on the floor. Sung Chul, in high spirits, showed us how to turn on the kerosene heater. He showed us the water spigot which drizzled a cold stream, and a hot plate that was a first cousin of the one I used in a high school science lab. Finally, he took us back downstairs for a tour of our toilet, a shed equipped with a concrete slab with a hole in the middle. The lady of the house faithfully washed this simple toilet every morning all year round. When winter arrived and the temperature dropped, we practiced some amazing acrobatic feats, skating on that icy slab.

How totally willing we were! If we were disappointed about not living in the village, we dropped it. "Whatever is needed" was our watchword. We had an awful sinking feeling an hour later when Sung Chul stood up to bid us farewell. He had a bus to catch back to the village. We spoke not one word of Korean. How were we to eat? Where were we to shop? How would I do laundry? Sung Chul gave us some unrecognizable currency before he dashed off.

Still in shock, but hungry, our jet-lagged little family took our first excursion out onto the streets. Not far away we discovered an open market. We selected a few things we recognized from the fruit and veggie lady and held our money out in the palms of our hands. She sorted through the change with a big smile. More questions began to nudge at me. Where did we bathe? What about real heat when winter arrived? Never mind; for the moment we had arrived safely. It was a glorious sunny fall day, fresh-scented with all the aromas of the East. We had begun a great new journey in the Hermit Kingdom that was to last for the next thirteen years.

HONG KONG, 1991. Thirteen years later, on another sunny September day, I got up from my business-class seat and emerged from the jet plane at a very humid Kai Tak Airport in Hong Kong. Larry had taken a position with a large American multinational corporation based there. I was met at the airport by a smiling Chinese man holding a placard with my name on it and ceremoniously helped into a waiting limousine. A doorman held the entryway open for me at the elegant Marriott Hotel. I was not allowed to so much as touch my luggage, which these gentlemen each attended to on my behalf. In my room, a note was waiting on the table. A secretary was very concerned that I should have no difficulty in adjusting. She phoned later with an outline for my first three days of

Still in shock, but hungry, our jet-lagged little family took our first excursion out onto the streets.

orientation. An American woman had been hired to show me how to manage finding whatever I needed in Hong Kong. A real estate agent would then show me flats that we might like to consider and an interior decorator was available to help me decorate my flat. They were "most concerned" that I not have any difficulty adjusting to my new home in a foreign land.

I chuckled to myself and smiled. Probably I could handle it.

Dianne Greenwald

> *They were "most concerned" that I not have any difficulty adjusting to my new home in a foreign land.*

The Preschool Miracle

The planning consultation that formally launched the Marshalls Human Development Project was held in the fall of 1974. It was not surprising that a preschool program was one of the first proposals to come out of the consultation—children are highly valued in Marshallese society. Project staff felt confident about launching the preschool: we had the Fifth City Preschool curriculum from earlier work in Chicago and Kathleen had been a member of the Fifth City Preschool staff for several years. But we did not have the children and we did not know how to find them.

Queenie Ria decided to solve the problem of finding the children. She had been the treasurer at KITCO (Kwajelein Importing and Trading Company), a business on the island of Majuro which we had helped to turn around financially during the early 1970s. Several Marshallese leaders had asked, "If KITCO can be turned around, what can be done for all of us?" Queenie and her husband had been involved in the plannng consultation that resulted. The community's long-range vision and plan included a preschool.

Queenie Ria was a joyful doer and said, "You get the curriculum together and I'll get the teachers and kids." A parent group, led by Queenie, recruited five teachers, gathered the children, and collected the fees.

We had originally intended to offer a morning session for fifty children. But on the day the preschool opened, so many more children showed up than we could accommodate in the one session, we had to amend our initial plans.

Queenie said, "No problem. You have the five teachers; they'll work in the afternoon. I'll just get fifty more kids." With Queenie's gusto and assurance, the afternoon session was filled with fifty-two children. Between the two sessions, three ICA staff members and five Marshallese community teachers taught more than one hundred children five days a week.

From where I worked in the KITCO offices—on the second floor of the huge warehouse—I could watch the preschool program unfold. The ground floor of the north wing of the warehouse was designated for the preschool, with its own separate outside door, apart from the business entrance to the warehouse. A sign was placed nearby which read, "Marshall Islands Preschooling Institute." The teachers, parents, and volunteers painted a mural on the side of the concrete block warehouse wall. Parents pitched in and created a playground just under the large mural, away from the trucks and the busy street.

Shortly after the preschool opened, I flew to Ebeye, a small island about 250-300 miles from the Majuro Atoll, on business. A woman whom I had never met before stopped me on the path and asked, "What is this about a preschool in Majuro? I understand they have a hundred children in that preschool."

"Yes, and those children are learning things," I said enthusiastically.

The woman shook her head. "I don't know about this. How can that be? Marshallese children this little do not learn."

I assumed that the woman had heard news of the preschool on Majuro by way of "the coconut wireless," the mystifying communication system understood only by the Marshallese. It was an effective way of spreading news, rumors and stories throughout the islands and atolls. Her doubts stemmed from three pieces of incredible data which were simply hard for the average Marshallese person to believe: 1) more than one hundred five year olds were attending a preschool; 2) effective teaching was being done and the children were learning; and, 3) Marshallese parents were willing to pay for each child's participation. All this was true, but the facts were incongruous with her previous experiences with education.

"I don't go into the preschool," I explained, "but I hear the children singing because the preschool is located in a temporarily walled-off area of the KITCO warehouse. The music and the voices spill over and through walls and floors, out the doors and into the light Pacific breezes." As if to add a touch of realism, I added with a smile, "Why, the KITCO warehousemen know how to sing all the preschool songs!"

"And I understand the parents pay to have their children go to school?"

"That's right, they pay $5 a month for tuition for their children."

The sign by the Preschool entrance

We named the main implementation efforts that came out of the planning consultation "miracles." They were the major focuses of activity that finally resulted in a program, a structure, or a new community pattern. The Majuro Preschool was one of the miracles. Perhaps the naming happened innocently. Perhaps calling the implementation efforts "miracles" happened as a casual reflection something like: "Why, when we actually get that accomplished (for example, a Marshall Islands Frozen Fish Processing Plant, a Multi-Purpose Repair Center, rehabilitation of the 'downtown shopping area' on Majuro, Saturday Clean-Up Days, an Outer Island Health Delivery System, or a Majuro Preschool—whatever people hoped for), that would be a miracle!" Miracles were useful things common people dreamed about, but supposed impossible. They were made possible by local work involving many minds and many hands. The very fact that Queenie Ria's recruitment, the teachers' hard work, the parents' support, and our own actions came together to produce a preschool was, in fact, miraculous! On reflection, a miracle was not anything special. A miracle was something we did every day, but we called it a miracle because the work and the results of the work created a sign of hope for the people of the Marshall Islands.

Teaching Marshallese children nutrition

As the various miracles or programs became visible, present, real, and functioning, possibilities grew. A weakened and downtrodden people, for the most part forgotten by the world, strained to become self-reliant, self-confident, and fully participating citizens of the globe. The impossible became possible. At first, the realization glowed as a lighted match flickers in a gentle wind on a moonless night. Unspoken hope happened quickly and disappeared just as quickly. The next time it emerged, hope was a stuttering, stammering, softly-whispered: "Per—haps, we . . . might, may–be." The spirit of self-determination caught on tenuously, then grew and became stronger. We hoped that it would ignite peoples' imaginations.

During a documentation period years later, Amata Kabua, then President of the new nation called the Republic of the Marshall Islands, was interviewed regarding the results of the work of "The Blue-Shirts" (the name ICA staff members were given by the Marshallese). He quickly admitted that though the planning consultations were invaluable, not all the targeted programs worked. Some did and some did not. "However," he said, "that was not what was important. What was important was that the ICA was instrumental in changing the imaginations of the Marshallese people." When I heard this, I wept. The years of caring investment and expended lives had created the miracle for which we had hoped.

Leah Early

Creating A Nation

ICA staff had worked in the Marshall Islands since the early seventies and in 1976, Majuro became the first Human Development Project where we held a formal planning consultation. In 1983, a year or two after the big tidal wave wiped out many businesses and houses on the island, Sandra and I went there to see what could be done to reorganize the wholesale food business and transfer the management completely to local people.

The first evening we were invited to dinner at the home of Oscar De Brum, the Chief Secretary of the Marshall Islands, who had been instrumental in inviting the ICA to come to Majuro twelve years before. His solar-powered house is located on a narrow part of the atoll with a view of the ocean on both sides. We sat on his porch watching the beautiful sunset and talking about all the activity that was going on in the islands. On the way in from the airport, we had been surprised to see significant new construction. Many new houses and a new power plant were going up. Just then his son stopped by and we were introduced. We asked Oscar what his son did. He said a long-awaited appropriation had come from Congress for development of the Marshall Island's economy and that his son had just finished working on the $600,000 project to clear buried munitions from the outlying islands.

The munitions clearing project illustrates the long-term complexity of development strategies. During World War II, thousands of bombs were dropped and thousands of shells were fired at the islands by the Japanese, British, and American forces as they fought from island to island. Many bombs and shells remained, buried unexploded in the soil, where they had been a deadly threat to life and limb for decades.

Preschool children in Majuro

The natural resource with the greatest possibility for development in the islands was the harvesting of coconuts. The copra from the coconuts was processed for use in soap and cosmetics in a plant that the project had set up when the ICA first came to Majuro. But the plant had never gotten up to full capacity because the older trees were dying and new trees were not being planted to replace them—people did not want to dig in the soil because of all the shells that were just below the surface. Oscar's son and a team had been trained in how to recover the shells and disarm them. When the team first drilled into the shells to disarm them, they found that every shell had dry powder and was therefore essentially live ammunition. Fortunately, no one was injured in the recovery project and hundreds of tons of munitions were safely removed. New trees were being planted throughout the islands and a viable copra industry had taken off.

The development process had come full circle. During the mid-seventies, the ICA's fund-raising staff had made many trips to Washington and had held many conversations with Senators and Representatives to secure funds for development work in the Marshall Islands. The $600,000 spent ridding the Marshall Islands of its deadly legacy of buried World War II munitions in 1983 was one half of the $1,200,000 appropriation that they had been working so hard to get from the U. S. Government. The strategy had taken a decade to fulfill.

World War II legacy

Oscar spoke of the new housing, the new power plant being built by the Japanese, and the new telephone system that would make it possible to talk on the phone at a conversational level rather than having to shout loud enough to be heard in Hawaii. We reminisced about the shoestring economic ventures we had tried over the years that fell in the category called "difficult learning experiences": the vegetable farm on Laura Island, the coconut lumber sawmill, banana chip and perfume making, shark and tuna fishing, and trying to keep food on the shelves of the wholesale food business. We recalled the magnificent quarter mile of sidewalk that had been laid along the dusty street in downtown Majuro, the fine preschool and the training schools. Oscar said, "None of the things we have now and in the future would have ever come into being if the ICA had not come to Majuro."

The next day we went to Oscar's office to learn more about the development in the islands. I noticed a bound blue book on the corner of his desk. He saw me look at it and said, "This is the *Ten-Year Plan for the Marshall Islands*. It replaces this!" He opened his right desk drawer and pulled out a copy of the gold ICA consult document. He continued, "When the ICA came to Majuro, the Marshall Islands were considered to be behind every other island nation in the South Pacific. Now, we are the only island nation to have anything like a ten-year plan and we are far, far ahead of any other island nation in the South Pacific in every measurement of development."

As we left Oscar's office, we met the Japanese economic delegation in the outer office. Oscar said representatives were there to negotiate tuna fishing rights for Japan in the Marshall Islands. In the past, Japanese fishing companies had just sailed up and taken whatever they wanted, whenever they wanted. It was a new day.

David Rebstock

The Blue Shirts

Joe and I happened to be in Washington, DC in 1992. We bought a copy of *The Washington Post* and noticed an article about the opening of a new embassy. The Republic of the Marshall Islands was opening its embassy in Washington, DC that very day.

I said to Joe, "Why don't we call and see if we can get an invitation?" We called the Embassy and I spoke with none other than the President, Amata Kabua, and was immediately invited over to the event!

Participating in the opening of this fine nation's Embassy brought us full circle, twenty years after we had begun working in the Marshall Islands. It was thrilling to walk in and see Amata Kabua again. When we arrived, President Kabua said, "Oh, the Blue Shirts." That was something! We had been known by the blue shirts we wore.

Patrick Moriarty

Believe
Tune: The Sloop John B

Chorus:
Believe that the time has come.
This world's going to live as one
And people are ready now
To create a new way.
New Spirit alive
New dream on the rise
One world together
Create the new day.

Everybody can see
A new way that it can be,
But so many things
just seem to get in the way.
The chains that bind us are strong.
The road to liberty long
Toward one world together
New earth, a new day.

Listen and you will hear
The future is coming clear
And everybody alive
has something to say.
We share a bit of the load,
Walking down the same road,
Working together,
New earth, a new day.

Yesterday And Today

> In our wildest dreams, we could not have imagined that the harvest would be gathered across national and continental boundaries.

I grew up on the border between Texas and Mexico where opulence and poverty interweave uncomfortably. There was always a project to initiate, a campaign to join, and more work to do. When I was a teenager I began asking the question, "What would really make a difference?" I was overwhelmed by the challenges that greeted me daily—people living in cardboard shacks, children without shoes, unclean water and no sewage systems. I left to find answers, first to college, then to a development project in the tiny village of Sol de Septiembre, Chile.

Sol de Septiembre was economically poor but filled with riches—clear air, deep water wells, lush vegetables, and energetic people. The village was full of people who were eager to fulfill their dreams about what life could be in their home place. Adults, teenagers and children joined us in creating a development plan for the village. Teenagers came daily to contribute their time and energy to putting the plan into action. Adults in the village participated on weekends and evenings as their time allowed. Together we cleared irrigation ditches, hosted agricultural think-tanks, initiated greenhouse projects, experimented with a shared equipment pool, initiated a preschool and an after-school program, and inaugurated a bakery.

Raul was one of the energetic teenagers who came to planning sessions and study sessions, helped plant trees, and organized workdays. His mother greeted us on the dusty roads as she walked to the store in the village. She was proud of her son's work that was creating new options for others in their community, even though it meant that he did not have as much time for work in his own family's fields.

Angelica, her sisters Joaquina and Isabel, and her brother Esteban, were among the others who joined in the work. As teenagers, Angelica and Joaquina helped to organize the preschool, and as elementary school students, Isabel and Esteban were active participants in the Niños del Sol after-school program. They helped to paint the welcome sign at the entrance to the village. "Bienvenidos a Sol de Septiembre ¡Cultivando Hacia el Futuro!" (Welcome to Sol de Septiembre Cultivating Toward the Future!)

When we were painting that sign, we thought that the future we were talking about was the future of that little village in Chile. We thought we were planting seeds and cultivating resources like vision, hope and cooperative skills to make Sol de Septiembre a better place. In our wildest dreams, we could not have imagined that the harvest would be gathered across national and continental boundaries. I had no idea that the work I was doing with these teenagers in Chile was preparing us for the work we would do together in my home place in Texas twenty years later.

Raul and Angelica eventually married and worked together to extend village development work in Peru. Joaquina married a Guatemalan who had also been involved in the development of his village as a teenager. Together they expanded village development work throughout Guatemala. Isabel became the head of the village development association in Sol de Septiembre, and Esteban has continued to raise the crops that are the backbone of his village's economy. Years later, Raul and Angelica brought their development experience to work in neighborhoods in the United States.

It was a delight for me to return to my hometown to jointly teach a training course in neighborhood development with Raul! We taught the course in Spanish and English. Raul stayed in my parent's house, as I had stayed in his mother's house in Chile. My mom and dad were part of our team and helped to photocopy and collate our course materials. As I watched Raul make a presentation to a group of sixty development workers in the presence of my own mother and father, it dawned on me: this is how development can happen—across borders, across languages, and across time. When people risk new situations, when everyone pitches in, when people plan, plant seeds, and cultivate their work over many years, sometimes they are allowed to enjoy such a surprising harvest.

Keith Packard

The Preschool Manual

I received a call from LDS Charities, an international development agency that works in fifty-four nations. Their representative had just returned from a conference in Guatemala, where he had come across a preschool training manual published by the ICA. The development agency had seen that the manual was based on sound learning theory, and asked us to consult with them on developing an approach to early learning that could be effectively used in more than one country. We agreed to share our experience.

Joaquina brought her experience in Chile to the work of training village preschool teachers in Guatemala and played a major role in developing that manual. Later, Joaquina hosted representatives from LDS Charities in Guatemala on a visit to village-based preschools to talk with teachers. Her sister, Angelica, joined Paula and me for the consultation. Angelica joined us in doing training for preschool staff of Migrant Head Start programs in Utah.

While we were in Chile, we thought that we were working to develop one village. We'll never know all that came from that effort, but I see the potential of one village to reach out to the world.

Keith Packard

We'll never know all that came from that effort, but I see the potential of one village to reach out to the world.

The Baptism

They were spellbound; neither made a sound or squirmed.

When our daughter, Esther, was born in Pittsburgh, her father and I had hoped to have her baptized in Chicago. When we were assigned to Italy, all plans went up for grabs. We had assumed that Esther would travel with us, but that plan fell apart and we went on ahead to take up our new assignment. So Esther made her first transatlantic flight to Rome all by herself when she was eleven months old. Her sister, Naomi, was born in Italy just five months later.

Naomi and I came home from the hospital the same Saturday that a team arrived to finalize arrangements for Italy's new human development project in Trastevere, then planned to be among the first eight projects worldwide. The two men on our Rome team were fairly small in stature. The site selection team from out-of-town were all large men by comparison. When Naomi and I arrived home from the hospital, the landlord told me all about the arrival of the "pezzi grossi" (big pieces) who were staying at our house for the week.

Sunday night we asked Joe if he would be willing to baptize our daughters while he was in Rome. He said that he would have to think about it. Over the course of the week, one by one, all the others came to us to say that Joe would probably not baptize the girls. They said that we should be prepared and not take it personally; Joe had a theological problem with infant baptism and had not baptized any infants in twenty years. He believed that people were trying to predetermine the faith and belief systems of those who were too young to object. We were told that Joe believed baptism was only valid when chosen by an adult. We supposed that was the end of the matter and did not bring it up again.

Then late Friday night, after the decisions to do the Trastevere project had been made and plans for our move there had been set, Joe turned to us and asked, "When are we going to do this baptism?" Obviously we had to do it the next morning because the international team was flying out in the afternoon. We scurried around half the night, preparing for the event and a big breakfast celebration.

Joe baptized the girls the next morning at our daily worship service. When the time came, he took them both in his arms, holding Naomi (two weeks old) in one arm and Esther (sixteen months old), seated on his hip, with the other. For nearly twenty minutes, he talked directly to them. They were spellbound; neither made a sound or squirmed.

He explained the theological journey that he had been on in his understanding of baptism. He had thought for years that people should only be baptized as adults, when it was their own choice. He had thought that in the act of baptism a particular kind of commitment was being made to the Church and that it was not fair for parents to impose such a decision on their children. He then explained that he had come to a new understanding, that this was a rite within the Church that marked the beginning of the life journey, and it was the Church's way of declaring that beginning to the whole society. He explained what he was going to do with the water and that it symbolized the purity of Being. It was that without which the journey could not be made at all. He told them that this was a ritual about showing up in this world whole and perfect, just as they were. He said that this was a truth about life now and that it always would be. He cautioned the girls that throughout their entire lives, there would be those who would attempt to dissuade them. There would be adults, teachers, and even friends who would at different times try to convince them that they were not accepted. He warned them that they would need to especially watch out for their parents; that every time their parents said no or tried to convince them not to do something, it would be a subtle way of trying to convince them that they were not received just as they were. He explained that parents usually saw it as a part of their job to convince children that they were less than perfect, but that it was Naomi's and Esther's job to understand that nothing could ever change the fact of their acceptance, just as they were, from the beginning of time.

Twenty years later, I was reminded of these events and the words spoken at the baptism while planning for Naomi's and Colin's wedding. In agreeing to do the service, Rev. Emery Purcell had said that he would require at least three meetings with the couple to discuss their intentions for their family. At the first meeting he mentioned that he might choose to share in his homily some of what they had told him during their discussions. He also mentioned that he felt he should credit one of his mentors, a professor of his at Southern Methodist University, Joseph Mathews. At that point Naomi exclaimed, "Oh, you mean the guy who baptized me?" She then told this story as she remembered it having been told so often in our family.

In their second meeting, Rev. Purcell mentioned the possibility that Naomi's and Colin's son Austin might be baptized as a part of their wedding. He mentioned that he would like to use a very special eleventh century Coptic cross that had been given him by an exiled Ethiopian priest who had become a deep spiritual friend. Rev. Purcell's friend had received the cross as a trust from the priest of his village church in Ethiopia the first time he had returned home after taking his final vows. At that point Naomi asked, "You aren't talking about Father Michael are you?" The pastor was stunned—he had indeed been talking about Father Michael Taffessee. Naomi explained that Fr. Michael had been a family friend for many years and would be attending the wedding.

Throughout these revelations of historical and global connection, Colin had been surprised and repeatedly delighted. It seemed that if one touched the spider web of the church at any point, one could sense the vibrations coming back from other points all around the world. Colin was aware of being drawn into a community that spans the globe.

Austin was baptized in the midst of Naomi's and Colin's wedding: before their vows, after their promises to the congregation and the congregation's

> *"Oh, you mean the guy who baptized me?"*

promises to them. After the baptism, Rev. Purcell carried Austin down the aisle, through the congregation, introducing him and telling parts of this story. It was a theologically brilliant commencement to filling all of life with "pezzi grossi."

Margaret Helen Aiseayew

It was a theologically brilliant commencement to filling all of life with "pezzi grossi."

Lifeprints

When all is said and done,
what will we be remembered for?
   The gray or lost hairs?
   The internal struggles?
   The checks we write?
   The accidents along the way?
No, if we are remembered at all,
   It will be for the "lifeprints"
   We leave upon the earth.
     The lives we touch,
     The things we grow,
     The gifts given, our life blood's influence.
This should be the striving of any human—
   To leave a lifeprint
   Such that others
     May see the caring,
     Smell the blood,
       and taste the calling.

Jon Elizondo

The ICA: An Evolving Story

The stories in this book were written by people affiliated with a unique service organization called The Institute of Cultural Affairs (ICA). They reflect important moments in the ICA's early history as an intentional community and as a volunteer movement for releasing the power of local people.

The ICA has roots in several important social movements of the twentieth century—civil rights in the United States, peace and justice in the developing world, citizen empowerment and local initiative in communities worldwide, and the post-World War II renewal of the Christian church.

The ICA has been continuously reinventing itself from its earliest roots in the Christian Faith and Life Community at the University of Texas at Austin in the 1950s. From the 1960s through the 1980s, it found expression as a leadership training movement for laity and clergy called the Ecumenical Institute, a division of the Church Federation of Greater Chicago. The Dean of the Ecumenical Institute was Dr. Joseph Wesley Mathews, known to many as "Joe" or "Joseph."

At the core of the life work of the Ecumenical Institute were the values of volunteerism and service. The work extended to seven continents and included the talent and energy of people of multiple spiritual traditions working together.

Originally the research division of the Ecumenical Institute, the ICA is now an international network of autonomous, national, nonprofit organizations supporting social innovation through participation and community building.

This book is a collection of stories about this evolving movement's journey. Some stories take place in North America, but most are set in far-flung places around the world, principally in small, rural villages, the location of the "Human Development Projects" and "Human Development Training Schools" mentioned in many of the stories. This work emphasized the training of local leaders and development of indigenous staff to be agents and architects of their own development. It culminated in the ten-day International Exposition of Rural Development in India in 1984.

A pivotal aspect of this development work and key to this collection of adventures in service is the power of story. The ICA has understood that the stories people tell themselves about life become the reality they experience. Storytelling has always been central to the life and work of the ICA, whether in community projects, organizational change efforts or intentional communities. This collection of stories continues in that tradition.

Indexes

Note:
Story titles are listed with double quotation marks.

Titles and Topics

"1000 Single Beds" 85

A

"A Big Event" 142
"A Certain Quality" 127
"A Man I Can't Forget" 124
"A Meeting In Worcester" 51
"A New and Fearful Task" 45
"A New Day Dawning" 53
"A Rock Through The Window" 61
"A Small Miracle in Salzburg" 46
"A Taiwan Thanksgiving" 92
"A Word About Singing" 145
"Absolutely Other" 11
"All Need To Play" 146
"Almost Caught" 76
Amata Kabua 156, 159
"An Egyptian Hello" 21
"And Then It Hit Me" 47
"Anger Transformed" 40
Authors: see page 169
"Awesome Encounter" 63

B

"Baboons Direct the Buses" 28
"Bald-Headed Tom Sawyer" 52
Battle of the Bulge 51
"Being A Mother" 39
Bethany Hospital, Chicago 8, 62
Bethany Seminary, Chicago 36
Bicentennial celebration 56
Blackfeet Reservation 15
Bombay. *See* Cities: Mumbai
"Both Sides" 8

C

Canadian International Development Agency 80
"Casting Out Demons" 106
"Celebrating A Completed Life" 151
Christian Faith and Life Community 36, 165
Church Federation of Greater Chicago 165
Cities: see page 169
Communities: see page 170
Community Development Associations
  Kendur, India 96
  Til Abo Marouz, Egypt 72
Community Meetings 53, 56, 128, 143
"Consensus" 6
"Considerations of the Whale" 32
Countries: see page 170
"Creating A Nation" 157
Cultural Studies I 8, 61
Cyclone Tracy 29

D

Daniel Moi 76, 99
Desaparecidos 74
"Development Fighter" 109
"Drunk Shrimp" 24

E

"East Meets West" 125
Ecumenical Institute 6, 12, 37, 60, 61, 165
"Eleven Flights of Stairs" 77
"Encounter with *Desaparecidos*" 74

F

Fifth City Preschool 37, 39, 154
"Finding The Center" 96
Forrest River, Australia 32

G

Global Odyssey 11, 147
Global Women's Forum 97
"Growing A Larger World" 139
"Growing Up" 9

H

"He Slowed Down A Train" 104
Hokkaido, Japan 90
Home for Dying Destitutes 12, 15
Hong Kong map 34
Human Development Training Schools 45, 95, 97, 127, 136

I

ICA background 165
ICA International 114
ICA Japan 81
ICA Nigeria 133
ICA Zambia 81
"ICA: An Evolving Story" 165
"I'll Bet You A Dollar" 22
"I'm The Greatest!" 39
Imaginal Education 39, 98
International Exposition of Rural Development 133, 165
International Training Institutes 47, 48, 128
Inyan Wa Ka Gapi. *See* Communities: Cannon Ball, North Dakota
Iowa United Methodist Men 122

J

Jeju-do, South Korea 125
"Just Cry" 91

K

Kansas 122
Kemper Building 85, 88
Kerala (State), India 38
KITCO (Kwajelein Importing and Trading Company) 154
Kwajelein Atoll, Marshall Islands 112

L

Lagos, Nigeria 30
Leadership Effectiveness in the New Society 69
"Learning To Read" 62
"Letter From Caño Negro" 40
"Lifeprints" 164
"Life's Resale Shop" 137
Living Effectively in the New Society 8
"Lured By The Mystery" 38

M

Machakos District, Kenya 45, 73, 104
Maharashtra (State), India 16, 43, 96, 123
Mahatma Gandhi 146, 151
Marathi 17, 43, 96, 123
Marshall Islands Preschooling Institute 155
Martin Luther King 62
Maryknoll Brothers 38
Masai 99
Mayor Richard Daley 61, 88
"Meant To Happen" 34
"Meeting Fr. Ilidio" 128
"Metamorphosis" 16
"Midnight Danger" 70
"Midst Of A Revolution" 138
"Miracle in Gunfoundry" 48
Missionaries of Charity 14
Missionary Brothers of Charity 10
"Moth To A Flame" 36
Mother Teresa 10, 12, 14, 15
"Mother's Advice" 25
Mt. Kilimanjaro 63
Mugumoini Training Center 106
"My Life Took a Turn" 72

N

Nava Gram Prayas 43
"No Problem" 152
Nungi, Oombulgurri 32

O

Oklahoma (State), USA 56
"Oklahoma 100" 56
Order: Ecumenical 165
Oscar De Brum 89, 157
Other World 147

P

Panchayat 38, 96
"Panic" 20
Photographs: see page 171

"Pigs In The Bedroom" 27
"Precious Memory" 15

R

"Raising The I-Beam" 100
"Right On His Derrière" 89
"River Of Consciousness" 119
"Rupert's Vision" 80

S

Salzburg Seminar 46
"Saving Face" 90
"Seeing The World Transformed" 147
Sesame Street 60
"Shantumbu" 25
"Shocking" 30
"Sir James" 114
"Smell The Jungle" 19
Songs
    'A Light Is Now Breaking' 144
    'All Life Is Open' 7
    'At The Center Tranquil' 51
    'Believe' 159
    'I Know Why' 136
    'In The World Of Spirit' 115
    'On A Clear Day' 87

'The Cost Of My Care' 42
'When You Are Aware' 20
"Souvenirs" 99
"Speaking Farmer" 122
Sumatra, Indonesia 52

T

Technology of Participation® 46, 47
"Terror At 36,000 Feet" 69
"The Altar Guild" 49
"The Baking Sun" 118
"The Baptism" 162
"The Blue Shirts" 159
"The Chickens Are Coming" 126
The City of Joy 10
"The City That Works" 88
"The Company Store" 50
"The Cyclone" 29
"The Earthen Dam" 95
"The Falling Lizard" 27
"The Flames Leapt Up" 62
"The Handkerchief" 116
"The Power Of Workdays" 136
"The Preschool Manual" 161
"The Preschool Miracle" 154
"The Sharbat Riot" 148
"The Unforgettable Egg" 73

"The View From The Train" 105
"The Voyage of the *Tatami Maru*" 112
"The Wind That Made History" 140
"Then We Will Walk." 138
"They Started Grinning" 129
"Those Who Wait On The Lord" 15

U

"Ukrainian Meatloaf" 84
"Unforgettable Characters" 23

V

"Village Economics" 94
Villages. *See* Communities Index
"Visiting Mother Theresa" 14

W

"Wallboard For 4th Street" 134
"Water Tank Miracle" 78
"What Am I Doing Here?" 133
"What Happened In Edgard?" 143

"Where Is Our Luggage?" 101
"Who Would Have Guessed" 60
"Will The Terrorists Return?" 77
Women 8, 49, 78, 89, 97, 99, 106, 110, 140
"Women Of The World" 97
Women's Advancement Module 99
Workdays 48, 52, 95, 127, 134, 136
World War II 51, 89, 90, 91
World's Fair 125, 126

Y

Yoruba 30
"Yesterday And Today" 160
"You Can Do It!" 149
"You Can't Do That" 110
"You Stand On Your Head" 71
"You've Got To Be Crazy" 43

Z

Zambezi River, Zambia 119

Authors

Abdel Moneim, Nagwa 23
Aiseayew, Margaret Helen 162
Al Ashwah, Abdel Hamid 124
Alerding, Bill and Barbara 25, 73, 90, 128, 140, 149
Archibald, Ruth 62
Ballard, Louise N. 27
Balm, Mali 48
Bell, James 53
Bell, MaryLynn 15, 133
Bergdall, Terry 63, 119
Burns, Gathorne 145
Carter, Ruth 60
Clutz, Ronald 51
Coffman, David 28, 71, 104
Coffman, Patricia 76
Coolidge, Jeff 19
Crandall-Frink, Leila 28
Davila, Rafael R. 38
Druckenmiller, Doug 24
Druckenmiller, Pat 92
D'Souza, Cyprian 114
Early, Leah 112, 154
Elizondo, Ellery 74
Elizondo, Jon 164
Epps, John 56
Gadway, Kay Hayes 36
Gilles, Jack 43, 138
Gilles, Judy 21
Greenwald, Dianne 152
Griffin, Muriel 39
Griffith, Beret 134
Grover, Laura 15
Hamje, Judith 77, 126
Hamje, Ken 94
Harper, Gordon 6
Hickey, Sheighlah 110
Hill, Elizabeth 8
Holcombe, George 40
Holmes, Heidi 136, 151
Khalil, Dina Raouf 46
Krauss, Kit 29
Lanphear, Nancy 25, 45
Latham, Jan 100
Long, Glenda 118
McBurney, Georgianna 11, 14, 146, 147
McCleskey, David 96
Moriarty, Patrick 34, 89, 159
Morrill, Justin 9
Moundy, Abdel Rahman 109
Nelson, Wayne 30, 80, 148
Nixon, Geoff G. 88
Nixon, Kay P. 114
Packard, Keith 101, 160, 161
Parekh, Vinod 39, 116
Pierce, Carol 91
Portman, Penny 99
Rebstock, David 52, 157
Richards, Don 137
Roeten, Winus 143
Salmon, Bill 122, 125
Salmon, Beverly 122
Shafik, Azza 72
Singleton, Louise 16
Slicker, Joe 105
Stanfield, Jeanette 20, 97
Staples, Bill 70
Walker, Darrell 69
Walters, Rick 47
Wegner, Tim 22
West, Donnamarie 138
West, George 61, 77
Whanger, Richard D. 50, 62, 129, 139, 142
Wiegel, James 84, 95, 127
Worden, Rod 49
Zahrt, David 32, 78, 85, 106
Ziegenhorn, Donna 40

Cities

Aurangabad, India 96
Austin, Texas 36
Bangalore, India 136
Beni Suef, Egypt 21, 72, 124
Bilbao, Spain 149
Cairo, Egypt 21
Calcutta, India 11, 14, 15
Caracas, Venezuela 149
Cebu, Philippines 102, 139
Chicago, Illinois 6, 8, 9, 11, 36, 39, 56, 60, 61, 62, 69, 84, 85, 88, 118, 147, 152, 162
Dar-es-Salaam, Tanzania 63
Darwin, Australia 29
El Paso, Texas 160
Guatemala City, Guatemala 77, 149
Hong Kong, China 27, 34, 91, 152
Jackson, Mississippi 142
Lisboa, Portugal 128
London, England 100
Lusaka, Zambia 25
Madrid, Spain 128
Majuro, Marshall Islands 112, 157
Manchester, New Hampshire 152

Communities

Manila, Philippines 47
Mendoza, Argentina 74
Mombasa, Kenya 71, 104
Mumbai, India
  48, 70, 114, 122, 151
Nairobi, Kenya
  71, 73, 76, 99, 104, 105, 106
New Delhi, India 69, 146
New Orleans, Louisiana 143
New York, New York 134
Patna, India 98
Perth, Australia 40
Pune, India 97
Rome, Italy 162
Santiago, Chile 74
Seoul, South Korea 152
Taijung, Taiwan 24
Taipei, Taiwan 136
Teheran, Iran 69
Tokyo, Japan 91
Washington, DC 125, 159
Winnipeg, Manitoba 145
Worcester, Massachusetts 51

Al Mahalla El Kobra, Egypt 124
Bubun, Indonesia 52
Cannon Ball, North Dakota 53
Caño Negro, Venezuela 40, 49
Chikhale, India 25
Conacaste, Guatemala 27, 137, 138
Delta Pace, Mississippi 56, 62, 142
Edgard, Louisiana 143
El Bayad, Egypt 21, 22, 72, 140, 148
El Hamraya, Egypt 23
El Warsha, Egypt 23
Fifth City, Chicago 39, 60, 61, 62, 88, 118
Hai Ou, Taiwan 92
Ijede, Nigeria 30
Isle of Dogs, London 100
Ivy City, Washington, DC 125
Kamweleni, Kenya 73, 104
Kapini, Zambia 80
Kawangware, Nairobi 62, 76, 129
Kelapa Dua, Indonesia 52
Kinney, Minnesota 145

Kuh Du E Ri, South Korea 152
Kwangyung Il, South Korea 125, 126
Lamego, Portugal 128
Langub, Philippines 73, 77
Lorne, New Brunswick 110
Maliwada, India 94, 95, 116
Maragua Ridge, Kenya 78
Mugumoini, Kenya 78, 106
Nam Wai, Hong Kong 27, 34
Narayan-Chincholi, India 44
Oombulgurri, Australia 32
Oyubari, Japan 90
Pandur, India 16
Paragur, India 70
Sevagram, India 151
Shantumbu, Zambia 25
Sikror, India 38
Sol de Septiembre, Chile 74, 160
Sudtonggan, Philippines 19, 62, 101, 139
Uptown, Chicago 85
Vaviharsh, India 127
Widen, West Virginia 50

Countries

American Samoa 9
Australia 9, 29, 32, 40
Austria 46
Bolivia 38
Canada 80, 110
Chile 74, 161
China 27, 34, 90, 91
Egypt 21, 22, 23, 46, 72, 109, 124, 140, 148
Guatemala 27, 77, 137, 138, 149, 160, 161
India 11, 14, 15, 16, 20, 25, 38, 43, 48, 70, 95, 96, 97, 114, 122, 127, 146, 151
Indonesia 52, 101
Japan 10, 39, 90, 91
Kenya 28, 45, 71, 73, 76, 78, 99, 104, 105, 106, 129
Malaysia 9
Nigeria 30, 133
Philippines 11, 19, 73, 77, 101, 139
Republic of the Marshall Islands 89, 112, 154, 157, 159
Singapore 9
South Korea 10, 125, 126
Sri Lanka 10
Taiwan 24, 92
Tanzania 63

Photographs

United Kingdom 100
United States 6, 8, 9, 36, 39, 50, 53, 56, 60, 84, 85, 88, 118, 134, 142, 143, 145, 160, 162
Venezuela 40, 49, 149
Zambia 25, 80, 119

Argentinian Customs (Elizondo) 75
Calcutta, Home for Dying Destitutes (Archives/Global Odyssey) 14
Calcutta rickshaw (Singleton) 11
Cannon Ball office (Bell) 54
Chilean switchbacks (Elizondo) 74
Conacaste drip irrigation (Walt Epley) 138
Conacaste street (Epley) 137
Daramuthi and Louise (Singleton) 18
Delta Pace project office (Archives) 142
Egypt, Abdel Hamid visits a family (Jim Glendinning) 124
Egypt,: meeting with village leaders (Archives) 109
El Bayad consultation, *shamiana* (Archives) 140
El Bayad crowd (Archives) 148
El Bayad, filling water jars (Wilson) 148
El Bayad pumphouse (Archives) 22
El Bayad tap (Archives) 72

El Bayad woman selling vegetables (Beth Kangas) 23
Evelyn Johnston Mathews Edwards, Lonavala, India 1990 (Don Elliott) v
Fifth City preschoolers and Iron Man Statue (Archives) 39
Fifth City preschoolers on the lawn (Archives) 37
Fifth City preschoolers, Ruth Carter (Archives) 60
India scrapbook (Singleton) 16
Joe addresses planning consultation (Wilson) 21
Joseph and James Mathews listening (Archives) 6
Kawangware homes (Portman) 129
Kawangware market (Portman) 132
Kawangware mud house (Portman) 130
Kenya, *jiko* (Portman) 106
Kenya, souvenir gourd (Portman) 99
Kenya, village women with Bernadette (Portman) 99
Kitchen duty (Archives) 84

Kwangyung Il, symbolic map (Archives) 125
Maharashtra, celebrating 232 villages (Archives) 44
Maharashtra, Chokababa with Iron Man (Wilson) 116
Majuro preschool children (Wilson) 157
Majuro Preschool sign (Wilson) 155
Marshall Islands, freighter (Archives) 112
Marshall Islands, World War II debris (Archives) 158
Marshallese children (Wilson) 156
Oombulgurri (Burbidge) 33
Oombulgurri, Camera Pool (Archives) 32
Oyubari plenary (Alerding) 90
Pandur village temple (Singleton) 17
Welcome to Widen (Archives) 50
Widen mural (Archives) 50
"Women of the World" (Archives/Stanfield) 98